Do not trace
, notes replaced

Religious Ferment in Russia

Religious Ferment In Russia

*Protestant Opposition to
Soviet Religious Policy*

Michael Bourdeaux

MACMILLAN · *London · Melbourne · Toronto*
ST MARTIN'S PRESS · *New York*
1968

© Michael Bourdeaux 1968

Published by
MACMILLAN & CO LTD
Little Essex Street London W C 2
and also at Bombay Calcutta and Madras
Macmillan South Africa (Publishers) Pty Ltd Johannesburg
The Macmillan Company of Australia Pty Ltd Melbourne
The Macmillan Company of Canada Ltd Toronto
St Martin's Press Inc New York

Library of Congress catalog card no. 68–15656

Printed in Great Britain by
R. & R. CLARK, LTD.
Edinburgh

To my parents and many friends in Cornwall

Contents

Abbreviations and Russian terms

AUCECB   All-Union Council of Evangelical Christians and Baptists.
CCECB   Council of Churches of the Evangelical Christians and Baptists.
CPSU   Communist Party of the Soviet Union.
dvadsatka   'Council of Twenty' (group governing individual local Orthodox churches).
ECB   Evangelical Christians and Baptists.
GPU   Secret police.
KGB   Secret police.
MVD   Ministry of Internal Affairs, i.e. Secret police.
NKVD   Secret police.
RSFSR   Russian Republic.
soviet   Policy-making and administrative council under the Communist Party.
SSR   Soviet Socialist Republic.

Preface

1968

In recent years there has been increasing evidence of stirrings in Soviet society to gain freedom from restrictive state control. Sometimes these have been instigated by an individual; more often they seem to have had a broad democratic base within a certain sector of society. The best known example of this is the urge for greater ideological latitude among younger writers during the early 1960's which, since the trial of the writers Sinyavsky and Daniel in February 1966, has become a ferment. The primary purpose of this study is to demonstrate that a movement demanding similar freedoms has arisen within the Christian Church. Compared with developments in the literary world it is an almost unknown subject: yet when a final reckoning can be made on the growth of the democratic tradition in the USSR the religious 'front' may be found to have its place.

A second aim of this book is to illustrate what is being said about Christianity in the Soviet Union by people who live there (both believers and atheists). It is, first and foremost, a collation of documents which speak for themselves so strongly that commentary is necessary principally to link rather than to interpret them. Ecumenical contacts with the Eastern European Churches have been growing for some time, but, generally speaking, churchmen in the West have lacked background information on the lives of those churches with which they are entering into closer relations. It was not considered either desirable or necessary to write a history of the Baptist movement in Russia — not desirable because it would have destroyed the unity of this book which concentrates on a particular reform movement that evolved in 1961 as a result of a change in Soviet anti-religious policy; not necessary because, by a happy circumstance, the publishers of the present work also brought out *Religion in the Soviet Union* by Walter Kolarz, Chapter IX of which contains a first-class history of the Russian Baptist movement. His work ends in the year this begins and is therefore essential background reading for this book. In taking up at the point at which he ended, I pay a conscious and humble tribute to a fine man and a magnificent scholar. By confining myself rigidly to one narrow aspect of religious life in Russia today, I have tried to provide information in depth which may be of some small service to the Ecumenical Movement in promoting a growing understanding between East and West.

A third aim is to honour Evangelical Christianity in the Soviet Union in its centenary year. The first Russian convert to the Baptist faith was N. I. Voronin (1840–1905), who was baptized in the river Kura, near Tbilisi, on 1 September 1867. It is particularly appropriate to examine the progress of the movement fifty years after the 1917 Revolution, and this study reveals grounds for both disquiet and hope. It is a matter for regret that my researches on the period under review have not uncovered more positive reactions from the official leadership of the Evangelical Christian and Baptist Church and that the documents present more cogently the point of view of the reformers (because they wrote them). Official replies in the pages of *Bratsky Vestnik* are bound to be muted by comparison, and one hopes that soon a sympathizer with the official leadership will write up its case with full frankness. Until this happens, one must remain content with the knowledge of the achievements of the official Baptist Church before the reform movement began.

Some of the material used here has appeared only in Russian émigré journals or is as yet unpublished. A careful study of the documents, however, has convinced me of their genuineness, and the authenticity of no single one has, as far as I know, ever been challenged by the Soviet authorities. Where, in the very nature of the case, it is impossible to track down the full story from official public sources it would be unscholarly to omit any evidence relevant to the subject.

Since it became known that I was engaged on the present work, I have been sent material by a number of people. There are too many for me to list them all, so I will mention none by name, but express my thanks here to the many friends who have helped me. At all stages of the work Peter Reddaway has been my friend and adviser, and his encouragement has been of more value than I can easily express. I am grateful, also, to Miss Xenia Howard-Johnston for her help in preparing the manuscript.

My thanks are due to the following for permission to reproduce documentary material: U.S. Government Printing Office, B.B.C. Central Research Unit, *Le Messager Orthodoxe*, *Nashi Dni*, *Newsweek*, *Novosti*, *Posev*, *Religion in Communist Dominated Areas*, *St. Vladimir's Seminary Quarterly*, *The Baptist World*, *The Reporter*, *The Times*, *The Watchman Examiner*.

Where Russian originals of the documents used were available, I have made my own translations. However, despite strenuous efforts I have not been able to obtain these originals in every instance. The major passages of which I am not able to guarantee the verbal accuracy are on: pp. 20, 28, 32–37, 42–46, 53–63, 64–65, 78–83, 83–93 and the major part of 191–229. Translations from Ukrainian are by Olga Hrubý.

Unfortunately, the only book on the reform Baptists so far published, *Na iskhode nochi* ('The Passing of Night') (Alma-Ata, 1966) by A. Sulatskov, has not become available in the West, but two remarkable and similar descriptions of the movement have just reached me as this book goes to press. L. N. Mitrokhin has written *Baptizm* (Moscow, *Politizdat*, 1966) (see pp. 79–89 and 248–250). Mitrokhin and A. I. Klibanov collaborate in a more detailed essay, 'Schism in the Baptist Church today', in *Voprosy Nauchnovo Ateizma*, vol. 3 (Moscow, *Mysl*, 1967, pp. 84–110). The latter is the first Soviet attempt I have seen to set out objectively what the reform movement is about. Many lengthy extracts from its documents are given, confirming and expanding what is printed here. My passage on the 1960 *Letter of Instructions* is verbally substantiated. As the reformers are now simply known as 'young Baptists' in some areas (p. 105), my use of the word 'ferment' in the title is more than ever justified.

Chislehurst, April 1967

MICHAEL BOURDEAUX

1 Introduction

The persistence and growth of sectarian groups is one of the most interesting features of the Soviet scene today. A book was recently published by F. Fedorenko[1] which, as a Soviet reviewer rightly says, treats 'more than 400 religious sects'.[2] Even since the writing of that book another new sect has appeared upon the scene, a group known as the *Pokutniki* ('Penitents' in Ukrainian) who seem to be descended from the suppressed Uniates (Eastern Rite Catholics).[3] The difficulty of organizing church life on a national scale has contributed to the appearance of local sub-variations of some denominations and where a sect has been declared completely illegal (as in the case of the Uniates) this tendency has become even more apparent. It would not be too strong to talk of the 'hydra' principle here — cut off one head and many others grow in its place.

There also seems to be an element of social protest against communism to be discerned in this growth of sectarianism. Referring to new members of the Baptist Church in the 1920's, a Soviet author has stated:

> For many of them, joining the sect was a form of social protest against the new system.[4]

It should, however, be emphasized at the outset, and it is one of the purposes of this book to demonstrate, that membership of a sect does not of itself in any way imply opposition to the Soviet state. We shall quote a number of atheist texts which suggest that sectarians can be among the most respected and hard-working members of the community.[5] Although the total strength of the Evangelical Christian and Baptist Church in the USSR is small compared with the Russian Orthodox Church, this movement has an influence which has now become so important that it demands the specialized treatment which this book assigns it.

Since 1961 the Russian Baptists have attracted a degree of attention in the Soviet press which seems out of all proportion to their numbers. Yet we do not know what their numbers are, and experts in the West are able to do no more than repeat a few rudimentary official statistics. There have been oft-repeated variations on a figure of something over half a million,[6] yet this refers to full adult membership — those who have undergone baptism by immersion. Before a person can be so accepted into the congregation he must satisfy certain stringent conditions, in the Soviet Union as elsewhere. We do not know how many adherents of the movement there are beyond this. It is obvious that in any country many people attend Baptist worship, often with considerable regularity, who are not baptized members of the church. In a society where official membership of a Christian body makes it difficult to receive higher education and to be employed in a good job, this number may well be proportionately greater than in other countries. In 1954 the official publication of the Russian Baptists, *Bratsky Vestnik* ('Fraternal Chronicle') made a statement which is crucial to our knowledge of the size of the Baptist Church:

> We have as many as 5,400 congregations, each of which consists of not less than twenty members, and 512,000 believers who have been baptized for their faith. But if one takes the members of believers' families and other people close to our brotherhood, then the total number of such can be reckoned at three million.[7]

Since 1954 there has been much evidence of successful Baptist evangelism (which we shall be describing in later chapters), and the resulting increase in numbers may well be considerable. We tend to hear more about the progress of the movement in the cities, yet we know that there has been expansion in the countryside, too.[8]

Despite all this the latest statistics show a drastic reduction of Baptist strength. Fedorenko gave the number of communities as 'about 2,000'[9] in 1965, while a Baptist World Alliance delegation in 1966 reported a total of 4,500.[10] Fedorenko gives the total number of members as being 'more than 200,000',[11] which suggests a dramatic drop on the 1954 figure. His estimate received unexpected confirmation from Alexander Karev, general secretary of the Russian Baptist Church, at the October 1966 congress. He recorded the total strength of the movement as now being no more than 500,000, while those who are full baptized members comprise no more than half this total.[12] In other words, the strength of the Russian Baptist Church has officially declined by over three million in twelve years.

Almost certainly these figures reflect the disbanding of some congregations since 1960 and we have the exact statistics for the reduction of communities in Latvia.[13] Other congregations may have seceded from the official church and the figures do not exclude the possibility that as many as three million people may have gone into schism from it.

This brings us face to face with the central theme of this book — the emergence of a group of Baptists who are in opposition to the Moscow leadership of the movement. It seems probable that where a schism took place a registered community of some sort often persisted,[14] so the question of statistics is immensely complicated, and we are not yet in possession of enough data to give any final assessment of the present strength either of the official or of the reform Baptists. An important consideration which leads on from this is what we mean by a 'registered community'.

REGISTRATION

Although it is not our purpose in this book to make a full enquiry into the history of Soviet legislation on religion,[15] we shall be referring to the laws from time to time in the text and clarifying certain related questions.[16] The requirement of registration of religious communities, however, is of such fundamental importance in our study that we must present some evidence about it at the outset.

If a religious community is to function legally in the USSR it must apply to the local secular authorities for registration. This

provision was introduced into Soviet law in 1929[17] and has never
been repealed. It is a matter between the local congregation and
the state, with the central church authorities having no say in
the matter whatsoever.[18]   Yuri Alexandrov, a Moscow lawyer,
has recently written an article in an authoritative periodical of
the Central Committee of the Communist Party of the USSR
which sets out to give clear guidance on the subject:

Concrete juridical relations between local *soviets* (councils) and
religious communities come into being the moment a religious society
or group is registered with the authorities. The law grants all believing citizens in the USSR who have reached the age of eighteen the
right to meet in order to fulfil their religious requirements together.
Depending on the number of believers, these religious communities
are of two kinds: religious societies and religious groups. If there are
not less than twenty believers, this constitutes a society; if less, a group.

Believers forming a community submit an application for its
registration to the executive committee of the district or to the muni-
cipal *soviet* of Working People's Deputies. But these authorities cannot make the final substantival decision. They can only state their
findings and submit the believers' application to the executive committee of the regional, provincial (or city, in Moscow and Leningrad)
soviet of Working People's Deputies, the Council of Ministers of an
autonomous republic, or, in union republics which have no provincial
divisions, to the Council of Ministers of the relevant republic.

These state authorities in their turn present the application of the
religious community to the Council for Religious Affairs, attached to
the Council of Ministers of the USSR, which makes the final decision
on the believers' application.

Registration should not be thought of as a mere formality, necessary only for counting the religious communities of the country. It
is an obligation stipulated by Soviet legislation on religious cults.
Registration sets up concrete juridical relations between the religious
community and the local *soviet*. These relations are composed, on the
one hand, of the rights and obligations of the religious community
and, on the other hand, of the rights and obligations of the registering
authority; the latter include the duty of surveying the group's activities and guarding their rights. What are the possible reasons for refusing to register a religious community? There can only be one: if the
members of the religious community do not recognize Soviet legisla-

tion on cults and their religious doctrine and rituals incite believers to break state laws and the country's established order.[19]

Firstly, it will be seen from this exposition that the actual mechanism governing registration is a bureaucratic and potentially slow one. The question will be raised in this book by the authors of some of the documents of whether the law on registration as it stands does not in itself infringe the requirement of the separation of church and state which was written into the 1918 Constitution.[20]

Secondly, Alexandrov's definition of the reason for which registration may be refused brings up the issue of whether there is any democratic possibility, according to the current Soviet interpretation, of believers entering into discussions among themselves or with the state about present-day legislation on religion.

Provided, however, that a religious community does observe the existing laws and does not attempt to change them, Alexandrov states that there can be no further bar to registration. And yet in practice the outcome would not appear to be automatic or so simple. An unpublished document from a Christian source which we shall later quote in full[21] states:

Registration of Evangelical Christian and Baptist churches was accepted for only two years (1947-48). During this time only a small proportion of churches were registered . . .

Further evidence for this contention is contained in an appeal to Mr. Khrushchev from the Baptist congregation in Vladivostok, dated October 1961:

Here the principle of the freedom of conscience and religion has been severely violated. There is not a single registered community in the region. We are all forced to assemble without registration, although we have asked for it continuously and insistently. There is not a single community where workers of the police have not appeared with threats to prohibit church services.[22]

Local church leaders have been criticized in the Soviet press for attempting to register their communities,[23] so it is hardly surprising, if there is some truth in all these statements, to find

B

that the number of unregistered communities is high. An authoritative Christian source states that two thirds of the total number of Evangelical Christian and Baptist communities have remained unregistered.[24]

This is one of the main reasons why our discussion on statistics above remained so tentative. We have no definite information either on the total number of unregistered communities or on the numerical strength of individual unregistered congregations. The very act of registering entails the yielding of statistical data to the state authorities,[25] so the failure to register (for whatever reason) implies that such statistics will not be known. Thus, in the very nature of the case, the numerical strength of a movement originating with the unregistered communities cannot be established by the state and we have very restricted information upon which to base our own estimates.[26]

THE ALL-UNION COUNCIL OF EVANGELICAL CHRISTIANS AND BAPTISTS

This cumbersome name dates from 1944, when a conference was held in Moscow to unite the two main Protestant streams which had existed on Soviet soil since the Revolution. Shortly afterwards the Russian title was modified by the exclusion of 'and' between 'Christians' and 'Baptists'; a hyphen was substituted in order to emphasize the unity which the two merging bodies claimed to have attained.[27] We shall refer to this body by the initials 'AUCECB', while the terms 'Baptist' and 'ECB' refer to any person or group, whether affiliated to the AUCECB or not. In 1945 the new united church was joined by a number of Pentecostal groups.[28]

From the outset, the merging of these bodies seems to have been beneficial to the state as well as to the church. It certainly made a measure of state control over the whole organization easier to effect, and there was no secret about such supervision. From the government's side this control was implemented through the Council for the Affairs of Religious Cults, which dealt with all sectarian groups, and was parallel to the Council for Russian Orthodox Church Affairs. These two bodies continued to exist until 1966, when they were merged into one Council for Religious Affairs.[29]

Referring to the Council for the Affairs of Religious Cults, M. A. Orlov, the chairman of the unification conference, stated:

This Council has its local representatives attached to the provincial *soviets*. These representatives decide the problems of our congregations and take an extremely attentive attitude towards our needs.[30]

This is as clear an indication as we are likely to find that from the earliest days of the AUCECB the legal requirement of separation of church and state was not strictly observed in practice. We are not told exactly what decisions could be taken by the local Party organizations on behalf of the congregations, but it is clear that a measure of control existed.

Officials of the AUCECB quickly began to play a part in reducing anti-Soviet opposition among various Protestant groups, particularly in Western border areas which had only just come under Soviet domination. As a result, some congregations agreed to organize their communities 'in accordance with the laws of the Soviet Union'.[31]

Further, the leadership of the AUCECB was mainly in the hands of ethnic Russians, among whom Evangelical Christians predominated numerically over Baptists.[32] This seems to have accorded well with Soviet policy towards the national minorities at the time.

It is hardly surprising, then, that there were potential seeds of discontent within theAUCECB fr om the very first.[33] An element of confusion was added to the situation by the daunting administrative task facing the AUCECB if it wished to keep in touch with Protestant groups over the $8\frac{1}{2}$ million square miles of Soviet territory. In the years after the formation of the AUCECB the population pattern of the Soviet Union was extremely fluid. Some national groups, wholly or in part, had been deported to opposite ends of the Soviet Union, and a number of these, like the Estonians and Volga Germans, contained a strong Protestant

element. A few of these managed to retain their Lutheran faith
in its pure form,[34] while others probably did not. Beyond one
or two isolated congregations, no official Lutheran organizational
structure was allowed to exist outside the Baltic States.

When prisoners were released from the concentration camps
(1953–57) they often had to settle near the place of their former
confinement. <u>Given the lack of hierarchical structure in many
strands of Protestantism and the belief in the 'priesthood of all
believers', new self-sufficient congregations were formed in many
remote parts of the land and they were often groups with mixed
religious traditions.</u> Even if they had sought registration as soon
as they were formed, it is highly unlikely that they would at
once have come to feel any loyalty for the remote, Moscow-
centred AUCECB.

Thus from the very first the AUCECB was an unstable organization. The majority of the Pentecostals left it within a year
after their inclusion,[35] and *Bratsky Vestnik* stated that when
prisoners returned from the concentration camps (that this is the
meaning is hardly concealed) they at once called in question the
basic inclusivism of the AUCECB:

In 1953–54 several old colleagues returned to the communities. For
a long time they had not been participants in the complicated and
laborious work of unifying the three separate streams which were
closely similar in faith. Maintaining their former negative views on
the collaboration of Evangelical Christians, Baptists and Pentecostals,
they began attempting to organize their own groupings, such as the
so-called 'Pure Baptists' or the 'Evangelical Christians-Perfectionists',
and the like.[36]

An informative account of the schisms which plagued the
AUCECB from its inception has recently been published in
Nauka i Religia, ('Science and Religion'), the chief Soviet atheist
journal:

With the formal unification of several rather heterogeneous ECB
groups, a new stage in the bitter internal conflict began. This conflict
has itself led several groups . . . to break away from the AUCECB

over the last few years. Their predecessors were those who would not enter the 1945 unification, especially the more fanatical elements of the Pentecostals who followed Voronaev and aimed at preserving their ecstatic (and partially barbaric) form of worship.

Certain Evangelical and Baptist communities took up the same position. For example, the Evangelical Free Christians, whose appearance dates from the 30's and 40's of this century, represented that section of Evangelicals which refused to be amalgamated with the Baptists. On the whole these were people who did not recognize the laws and accepted way of life of the Soviet state. Under camouflage of the Bible they carried on open anti-Soviet propaganda, calling their followers not to serve in the Soviet Army and to desert; they tried to drag people away from social and political life. A significant proportion of the sect's members do not work and receive material support from foreign religious organizations, including the European Evangelical Movement.

Another similar organization was the Ukrainian ECB Community, composed of Evangelical and Baptist sects in the Western Ukraine, formed to terminate doctrinal disagreements amongst Ukrainian nationalist elements and to draw them all into one organization, having as its aim 'the evangelization of the Ukraine'. The leadership of this union was provided in the past by the U.S.A., England, Fascist Germany and capitalist Poland. There is evidence about the substance of their preaching in the journals and newspapers of the sect which stated that 'only Americans will foster the enlightenment, well-being and culture of the workers'. In order to foment national discord amongst believers, the sect announced that it was breaking off all relations with the 'Moscow-dominated Baptists'. Even the 'Mission of Evangelical Christians' which united a section of the Evangelicals in the regions of the Western Ukraine took up this same position. A few other groups, such as the 'Ancient Christians', isolated communities of which are to be found in the Leningrad and neighbouring regions, also remained outside the AUCECB.

In particular, the congregations of Baptists which refused to unite with the Evangelicals and Pentecostals comprised a rather numerous group of 'Pure' and 'Free' Baptists who maintained that in their religious activity they were 'free' from submission to any religious hierarchy and to the Soviet authorities. Some of them had existed even before the formation of the AUCECB, while others came into existence as the result of schism after this event. These congregations at first formed the basic nucleus of the Prokofiev group in the ECB Church.[37]

The last two of these potentially schismatic groups were of sufficient importance to be referred to in other sources. *Izvestia*, the government newspaper, carried an attack on the 'Perfectionists' in 1960,[38] while *Bratsky Vestnik* later described them in these terms:

These attempts at schism and disunity in our brotherhood originated principally in the Sumy region where the so-called teaching on perfectionism arose, spread by a certain Kornienko. However, by now this group has almost entirely disintegrated and exists as small pockets of less than ten people in only two or three places. Kornienko, the initiator of this teaching, has no influence whatsoever in our societies at the present moment.[39]

A more serious schism was threatened by the 'Pure Baptists'. Their unhappiness at centralized control was in part, according to AUCECB officials, a doctrinal issue, for they were against any form of hierarchical organization and demanded that every member of the congregation should be equally commissioned by the laying on of hands. *Bratsky Vestnik* described their activities thus:

In the Ukraine we had to meet the followers of so-called 'Pure Baptism'. They began to carry on their work in the congregations at Donetsk, Lugansk, Zaporozhie, Dnepropetrovsk, and several other regions. At first they succeeded in achieving some temporary successes, and several groups of 'Pure Baptists' were founded. Their main teaching was opposition to the unity already achieved. They taught that it was obligatory for all Evangelical Christian brothers and sisters to receive the laying on of hands, they condemned receiving brothers and sisters from the Pentecostals into our ranks, and criticized the leadership of our Union for the unity achieved, considering it to be impure.[40]

An atheist source, however, suggests that there were other motives present in the campaign of this movement against the AUCECB:

The so-called 'Pure Baptists' demand a more active and diversified religious propaganda and the attracting of a large number of new members into their sect.[41]

Having hinted at the real reason for the split in the Baptist congregation he is describing, the author of these words, A. Kafarov, goes on to say of the leader of the break-away group:

These intentions lined Stepan Saveliev's coat, too. He became tired of his unostentatious and modest role of private in the 'army of Christ'. He wanted power, or, to be even more specific, he wanted the money box of the congregation . . . However, Saveliev was not able to seize the minister's office by a direct attack and so he accomplished a deft strategic manoeuvre. He split the existing congregation, established a new one and became its minister.[42]

Saveliev was sent to prison for five years as a result of all this — ostensibly for having denounced a member of his congregation and driven him to suicide.

By 1963 the AUCECB leadership was able to claim that the influence of the 'Pure Baptists' had waned:

Today almost all the groups of 'Pure Baptists' in the Ukraine have dispersed, with the exception of four small groups in the Donetsk region. These groups have no influence whatsoever on our societies.[43]

As the article by Kafarov shows, this diminution of influence was certainly due in no small measure to the stern application of police power backed by show trials. It is very possible, too, that 'pure Baptists' did join the reform movement (the subject of this book) when it emerged in 1961. If so, however, they must have changed their views on Evangelical Christian and Baptist unity, for where the documents quoted here mention this, they do so in a positive way.[44]

Due to our present lack of knowledge, there are unresolved problems about the relationship between the 'pure Baptists' and the reformers.

The daily newspaper, *Pravda Ukrainy* ('Ukrainian Truth'), dates the schism dubiously from the mid-1950's, not from 1961.[45] Fedorenko is much more explicit:

These are the basic factors behind the schism which has occurred

in recent years between the ECB and a group of 'Pure Baptists', or
Prokofiev-ites (called after one of their leaders) ... A few years ago
the group of Pure Baptists called into being an Action Group for the
convening of an extraordinary congress of the ECB Church, with a
demand for changes in the statutes of the church, and the replacement
of its leadership.[46]

Before we begin our discussion of this reform movement, it
is necessary to give, in the briefest outline, an indication of the
general trends in Soviet policy towards religion from 1959 to 1964.

THE KHRUSHCHEV CAMPAIGN

During the later years of the Khrushchev regime the situation of
Christianity in the Soviet Union changed radically. We base
our discussion here upon the Russian Orthodox Church, in order
to prove that similar facts which we shall be reporting in the life
of the Evangelical Christian and Baptist Church were not confined to a single religious group only. If there were space, these
references could be multiplied for other churches as well.

The Society for the Dissemination of Political and Scientific
Knowledge (later simply the 'Knowledge' Society) is a central
body which has the control of anti-religious propaganda as one
of its main functions. In January 1960 it held a congress which
was attended by a number of prominent men, including the
political leaders Brezhnev, Kosygin, Mikoyan, Suslov, Ignatiev
and Polyansky.[47] Religion seems to have been a main topic for
discussion, for regional Party organizations were at once instructed strictly to enforce all the existing laws affecting religious organizations.[48] In his address to the 22nd Party Congress
in 1961 Khrushchev personally demanded that measures against
religion should receive greater attention,[49] and two years later
Leonid Ilichov, at that time Chairman of the Ideological Commission of the Central Committee, put this even more strongly
at a closed session.[50] Early the next year Ilichov called for a
stepping-up of the campaign in all sectors and listed his demands
under fourteen headings.[51]

Metropolitan Nikolai, who was principally responsible for the foreign policy of the Moscow Patriarchate in the 1950's, seemed to have come to an understanding, almost a 'live and let live' agreement, with G. G. Karpov, the head of the Council for Russian Orthodox Church Affairs. However, in a short time and coincidental with the Party's new policy, they and a number of others were replaced.[52] The basic organization of the Russian Orthodox Church was radically altered in 1961, when the control of local church affairs passed into the hands of the parish.[53] Priests were from this time considered to be employees of the *dvadtsatka* (church council of twenty members) and they had no longer any legal control over the administration of their own parishes.

The renewed campaign against religion was not confined to the press, but had the direst practical consequences for the church. Article 227 of the revised Penal Code of the Russian Republic which appeared at this time prescribes a penalty of up to five years' imprisonment or exile for these offences:

Organizing or leading a group whose activities are carried on under the guise of teaching religious doctrine and carrying out religious rites which entail harming the health of citizens or any other encroachment upon the person or upon the rights of individuals, either prompting citizens to refuse to participate in social activity or fulfil their civil obligations, and likewise enticing minors into this group.[54]

This ill-defined article gave blanket cover for numerous arrests and sentences. Many monks and at least three bishops were imprisoned,[55] but more often the Soviet authorities tried to avoid inflaming popular sentiments by confining those under attack to hospitals or mental institutions without ever bringing them to trial.[56] There was a massive closure of monasteries, churches and cathedrals at the same time, and often the Soviet press did not bother to mention even the most tenuous legal justification for this.[57] Indeed, it seems that local Party organizations vied with one another to effect the largest number of church closures. In 1961 the Soviet press reported that 500 churches had been closed in two provinces alone,[58] and it was later estimated that 10,000 churches in all had been closed during Khrushchev's

last four years in office.[59] In order to give a semblance of legality
to the closure of Orthodox seminaries they were artificially
emptied by the removal of students to do military service or by
the withdrawal of residence permits.[60] The official organ of the
Russian Church, *Zhurnal Moskovskoi Patriarkhii* ('Journal of the
Moscow Patriarchate'), could not of course record the exact
means by which the state expropriated seminary buildings, but a
comparison of what it said about the possibilities for theological
training in and after 1960 is revealing.[61] Eight seminaries had
existed in 1958,[62] but by 1965 the number had finally dwindled
to three.[63]

While good sources are available on this open side of the campaign, there is another aspect to it which is almost impossible to
document: the existence of secret or verbal instructions given
by central secular authority either to the church's administrative
centres or to the local Party organs. For some time there has
been reliable evidence that such dictates existed,[64] but until
recently it was impossible to establish what they were.

Now we have a document which goes a long way towards
establishing the type of instructions which were handed out in
this way. It is a circular letter addressed to local representatives
of the Council for Russian Orthodox Church Affairs from the
central administration of that body. Although the document
contains neither source nor date, when Metropolitan Nikodim,
head of the Foreign Relations Department of the Russian Orthodox Church, was shown it in London on 20 February 1967, he
confirmed that, although he had not seen these particular instructions, it was just the type of memorandum which was in circulation around 1961.[65] The text reads in part:

1. Social 'commissions for assistance' in supervising the implementation of legislation on cults have been established and are attached to
   the Urban District Committees . . .

                 .   .   .   .   .

3. The commissions are made up of well-informed, politically
   educated people, capable of supervising and observing the religious
   communities . . . Deputies of the local *soviets*, representatives of
   local cultural and educational institutions, propagandists . . . and

other local activists are elected to these commissions . . . Their size is determined locally in order effectively to study and supervise the activities of religious communities in the area and to unmask and liquidate the illegal activities of unregistered religious groups. The commissions are headed by the deputy chairman or a secretary of the Urban Executive Committee.

4. It is the duty of these commissions:

   (a) systematically to study the religious situation on the spot to find out whether there are any registered religious communities there; to collect and analyse the data on the frequenting of religious services; to study the characteristics of people who carry out religious rites, such as christening, funeral services, weddings, confessions; to verify the degree of influence of the religious communities and their ministers on youth and children; to verify the regularity of the carrying out of religious rites and to suppress christenings without the consent of both parents.

   (b) Continuously to study the ideological activity of the church, its preaching and its adaptability; to study the various methods used by ministers to expand or contract their sphere of influence on some sections of the population, particularly children and youth; to discover which young people the ministers are trying to draw into religious work.

   . . . . . .

   (d) To analyse the make-up of the religious communities and parish councils, unmasking the most active of their members.

   . . . . . .

   (f) To offer assistance to the Soviet financial authorities in exposing ministers of religion who unlawfully execute religious rites at the private homes of believers and receive gifts for that without proper receipts, and conceal this income from the taxation offices.

   (g) To expose unregistered ministers of religion who appear illegally in towns and villages and perform religious rites, and report them to the local executive committees . . .
   One of the most important aims of the 'commissions for assistance' should be to discover means of limiting and weakening the activities of religious communities and their ministers (in the framework of the existing legislation) and offer concrete suggestions on this problem.

On the Conclusion of Agreements with the 'Council of Twenty'

The present 'councils of twenty' in all the religious communities are untrustworthy. They consist almost entirely of elderly, illiterate or fanatical people and we cannot entrust them with state property.

Suggest to them that they form new 'councils of twenty' consisting of literate people, capable of ruling a community (not fanatics), who would honestly carry out the Soviet laws and your suggestions and requests. Only when such a 'council of twenty' is formed, and if it satisfies you, should you sign an agreement with it.

There should be exactly twenty members in a 'council of twenty'. It should be formed of citizens who have applied to the religious community expressing their desire to serve on such a council, and 'willing to be materially responsible for the property passed over to the community'. They must also state their age, education, place of work and home address.

Annul all the agreements between the church communities and the local Soviet authorities previously concluded.

Let the 'council of twenty', after the agreement has been signed, elect its executive body ... It is desirable that you should take part in the selection of members of such an executive body and that the members selected should be those who carry out our line.

... A list of the members of the 'twenty' and of the members of the executive body of the parish and of its auditing commission must be submitted to the local representative of the Council for Russian Orthodox Church Affairs and to the regional executive committees.[66]

Valuable confirmation of this type of instruction, but referring to the sects, is contained in a complaint, printed in *Izvestia* late in 1960, that the local Party organizations were allowing Christian groups in their areas to go unregistered; steps must be taken, the article stated, to regularize the position.[67]

DRAMA AT THE AMERICAN EMBASSY IN MOSCOW

At the very beginning of 1963 an incident occurred in Moscow which serves to illustrate more fully several of the points which we have briefly made in this introductory chapter. Firstly it demonstrates what it means to belong to an unregistered religious community. Secondly, it proves that even after the emergence of an organized opposition to the AUCECB, other unregistered Evangelical groups continued not only to exist but to be very active. Thirdly, it illustrates in human terms how far religious persecution went during the Khrushchev period (though even more extreme examples will be quoted later). The initiative of this group also achieved the first real publicity on this campaign.

A Reuter report dated 3 January 1963 described the episode thus:

> A group of 32 Russians of an evangelical sect forced their way into the American Embassy compound today complaining of religious persecution and pleading to be sent abroad. They left nearly four hours later in a bus, some weeping bitterly, accompanied by Soviet Foreign Ministry officials.
>
> At first the group refused to enter the bus. A young man in a black fur hat and dark coat said: 'We do not want to go anywhere. They will shoot us.' An elderly man shouted: 'There is no place for us in the Soviet Union. We demand of those people who believe in Christ and in God — help us.'
>
> The group consisted of six men, twelve women and fourteen children. American Embassy sources said they had made a four-day train journey from the Siberian coalmining town of Chernogorsk, more than 1,800 miles from Moscow. Some of the children appeared to be ill after the journey . . .
>
> They brought with them a 'small stack' of petitions complaining of religious persecution and expressing a desire to leave the Soviet Union. These were left at the Embassy . . .
>
> The Russians described themselves as Evangelical Christians 'who regarded each other as equals and did not believe in a church hierarchy'. They said they had not been allowed to hold religious services.[68]

From the names given in the *Novosti* press release on the incident[69] and by J. C. Pollock in his book[70] inspired by it, there is a possibility that some of the Evangelicals at Chernogorsk were of Ukrainian and Volga German origin (Shevchenko, Miller). This religious community may have grown up in conformity with the resettlement of the population described earlier in this chapter, so it is not surprising that no exact definition of their religious adherence emerges from the available accounts. *Novosti* accuses them of being 'clandestine fanatics' and of practising 'savage rites',[71] while Moscow Radio said:

> When people protested against the actions of this fanatical sect, they tried to pretend that the Soviet government was attempting to deprive them of their freedom of religion, which is a lot of nonsense, you'll agree, because this fanaticism has absolutely nothing in common with religion.[72]

Neither *Novosti* nor Moscow Radio produced any evidence whatsoever to substantiate this last accusation. They asked the Americans to send them to Israel,[73] possibly thinking of it as a religious paradise, but this suggests a hazy knowledge of the outside world rather than fanaticism.

According to the evidence of a document which the group wrote:

> The court said that we are Pentecostals, but we are not members of any sect. We are called Christians of the Evangelical faith. As for the charge that we threatened to make sacrifices of our children, this is not just, for we are believers and could not even think of such a thing.[74]

They were, then, simply one of the thousands of unregistered Protestant groups scattered over Siberia. *The Times* confirms this obliquely:

> Tonight the Reverend Ilya Orlov, a Baptist pastor, said that his church 'might be able to help' the group, though it had not been in touch with the Moscow Baptist Church. He described the group as 'Evangelical Christians' who were reported to have merged with the Baptist Church in Russia during the war; several 'Evangelical Christians' refused to do so at the time and these might be some of them.[75]

The authorities might possibly have refused to consider an application for registration because the Chernogorsk Evangelicals had broken the law. One of their main complaints had been that their children were being forced to become atheists and this brought them to the drastic step of withdrawing their children from school.[76] In reprisal, some children were forcibly removed to boarding schools, a measure which is still taken to re-educate the children of religious parents.[77] Some children managed all the same to send letters home and their contents speak for themselves. Tanya Vashchenko, aged eight, wrote:

I cry at night. The boys beat me . . . God still keeps us. Valya and I cry because they don't let us go home. Mummy, come![78]

Her sister, Valya, aged twelve, shows she resisted even more forcibly:

Mama, we have another misfortune here. They called me to the meeting where they take new members into the Pioneers. I didn't go and they forced me to. Then I started to sing at the meeting and the headmaster sent me to the corner and said 'Take her dress off her,' but I said if you take it off then I won't eat. Well, all right, then they put the pioneer uniform on me and they say, 'I will take the oath for you as if you were doing it', so that I should become a member of the Komsomol (Young Communist League); then they took the banner and hung it over me and he gives the promise and I sing psalms and cry and then I sing psalms and pray all the more and every one made fun of me . . . and then they made out that I had given a promise.[79]

Such treatment of their children was not the only cause for discontent among the Chernogorsk Evangelicals. Several, including men named Vashchenko and Miller, had served prison sentences.[80]

All these factors contributed towards persuading the community to take the action it did in going to Moscow, but otherwise their case was not exceptional; it merely confirms what we know of the religious situation in other parts of the Soviet Union at the same period.

2 The Baptist Initiative

In this chapter we shall discuss the new regulations which were imposed upon the Russian Evangelical Christian and Baptist Church in 1960 and see how they had the effect of uniting various strands of discontent with the AUCECB into a determined and energetic opposition.

In 1960, at the beginning of the period of renewed pressure against the church, the AUCECB adopted the so-called *New Statutes* which are printed in full in Appendix I.[1] At the same time a *Letter of Instructions* was issued by the AUCECB to all senior presbyters. The full text of this has never become available, but there are now several sources which give us a good idea of what the letter contained. The basic reference is in *Bratsky Listok* ('Fraternal Leaflet') Nos. 2–3, (February–March) 1965. This is the illegal publication of the group of Baptists who pressed for a reform of the AUCECB, several numbers of which have become available in the West. The relevant extract is here published in full for the first time:

In your *New Statutes* and particularly in your *Letter of Instructions* you disobeyed the commandment of Christ by prescribing the following:

§4. At services a presbyter must not allow digressions which tend to become appeals . . .

§5. Zealous proselytization in our communities must definitely stop . . . and an effort must be made to reduce the baptism of young people between the age of 18 and 30 to a minimum.

Disobeying the commandment of Christ ('Suffer little children, and forbid them not, to come unto me': Mat. 19. 14) you prescribed that:

§6. Children . . . should not be allowed to attend services.

You have also issued many other similar instructions. With these 'documents' and 'statutes' you have denied salvation to the sinner; when salvation is denied, then it follows there is no need for a Saviour. Through this, then, you have rejected even the Saviour himself.

And all this has been done to pander to atheism and to the world![2]

Very useful confirmation of these instructions is contained in an article which appeared in an American magazine. The author, George Bailey, visited the Baptist church in Moscow in 1964, where he was shown the complete text. His quotation from it does not exactly correspond with the extract from *Bratsky Listok* above (he was, therefore, probably shown the original text, not the *Bratsky Listok* version). The later points he quotes are identical, but in addition he mentions the following which come before the point at which *Bratsky Listok* begins:

> The senior presbyter must remember that at present the main task of divine services is *not* the enlistment of new members; the duty of the senior presbyter is to check unhealthy missionary tendencies; . . . neither should he become too involved in preaching . .[3]

The promulgation of the *New Statutes* and the issue of these secret instructions had one effect which was of vital importance for the life of the Evangelical Christian and Baptist Churches in the Soviet Union: opposition to the AUCECB, which up to 1960 had been diffuse, became crystallized into a movement led by Alexei F. Prokofiev and Gennadi K. Kryuchkov.

It is important to establish a terminology for the reform movement, because Soviet sources are unclear on this. The state's original name for the group seems to have been *Prokofievtsy* ('Prokofiev-ites'). It is little more than a nickname, but it is nevertheless useful because it suggests that it was Prokofiev who was the group's prime mover in its early days. The *Initsiativniki* was another name by which they became commonly known, and this is a shortened form of the term, *Initsiativnaya gruppa* ('Initiative-' or 'Action-Group'). The 'initiative' referred to was specifically the attempt to convene an extraordinary congress of the AUCECB.[4] Although the secular press still referred to the *Initsiativniki* in 1966, they later called themselves the 'Organizing Committee', which term refers to the enlarged Action Group, and was used by the leaders from early 1962.[5] From September 1965 they used the name, 'Council of Churches of the Evangelical Christians and Baptists' (CCECB).[6] The use of this term marks the beginning of an open schism and the final abandonment of the attempt to reform the AUCECB.

C

We do not have much evidence about the personalities of Prokofiev and Kryuchkov. Their own documents deal mainly with constitutional and legal matters and therefore eschew manifestations of character and personal details about the authors. The virulent attacks against them in the Soviet press enable us to gauge the success of their evangelizing activities, but are too polemical for us to be able to make an objective analysis of character.

The new persecution of the church made the position of the Baptist movement so extreme that elements opposing the AUCECB for alleged compromise with the state were bound to be strengthened in their resolve. It is natural that the leader of one of the existing unofficial groups should have challenged the Baptist hierarchy, but the unity of the new movement and its tenacious development in the most adverse conditions over a period of six years suggest that Prokofiev and Kryuchkov were religious leaders of more than ordinary stature. Once they had shown the way others were not lacking who were prepared to step at once into any gaps created by arrests of the existing leaders.[7]

A pen-portrait of Prokofiev's activities appeared in the Soviet press early in 1963:

Who's this Prokofiev, then? You can't describe the life of this 'saint' without a feeling of indignation. Under the guise of religious activity this latter-day 'apostle' shows malice towards everything Soviet, interprets freedom of conscience according to his own whim and breaks our laws. In 1941, at a time of severe trial for our people, he engaged in anti-Soviet propaganda and was convicted as a traitor.

Ten years in prison taught this renegade hypocrite nothing. After his release Prokofiev continued to live like a parasite, organizing illegal Baptist sectarian groups and preaching libellous sermons against the Soviet way of life. He was convicted a second time, but the Soviet state found it possible to remit part of his sentence.

'However much you feed a wolf, it still looks towards the forest', says the proverb. Even this time punishment did not deter this opium-peddler. Prokofiev continued to develop his clandestine missionary activity, visiting various towns in the RSFSR, the Ukraine, Belorussia and Kazakhstan. He sent his sermons and letters containing evil aspersions against our system to all corners of the country, calling on Soviet citizens to renounce earthly blessings, to 'repent of their sins', and to give up work for prayer. 'Every human friendship is debauchery', expatiated the obscurantist.

This man has had an especially baneful influence on young people. He has been trying to kill their inclination toward earthly joys, to disseminate pessimism and scepticism among them, calling upon them not to go to the cinema, theatres and clubs and to refuse to do military service. At Kharkov and in the Donbass towns Prokofiev illegally performed the rites of 'water baptism' on young people. At Zhdanov this obscurantist 'washed' a group of girls and boys in icy water. One of these who received 'baptism', a young worker, Anatoli Shatsky, developed a severe mental illness.

This obscurantist even tried to influence the upbringing of children. Pyotr Miroshnichenko, a worker from Volnovakh, made a public appeal to have his daughter, Lyusya, a school-girl, protected from the influence of Prokofiev, who was disposing the girl towards him and inculcating belief in God in her by giving her presents. This sectarian gave Miroshnichenko's son a Bible and dragged him along to a school which he had organized for the study of that pernicious book.

This parasite and good-for-nothing didn't work for years, yet managed to live well. He used money earned by the hard work of deceived believers to go around in taxis and travel frequently by plane. Other good-for-nothings like himself were his supporters in his murky deeds. At Kharkov, for example, this opium-peddler received help from A. Lozovoi, who let his house be used for the duplicating of Prokofiev's missives. Lozovoi combined serving God with speculating in stolen goods. Prokofiev's right-hand man was a certain B. Zdorovets, against whom judicial proceedings have now been taken.[8]

This attack has its place in a long line of similar attempts to denigrate character which have regularly appeared in the Soviet press and which seem to be a part of the judicial system. At the time of the show trials during the purges of the 1930's Vyshinsky, the prosecutor, made every kind of attack against the accused (lust for money, sexual aberration, anti-Soviet activity of all sorts) in the hope that something would stick. The reader unfamiliar with Soviet affairs should perhaps be reminded that such accusations were often made without any grounds whatsoever, and these methods continue to be used right up to the present. They have been used frequently against Christians and several more examples will be quoted in later chapters.

Soviet policy at this time was to represent Prokofiev as a religious fanatic who would stop at nothing to draw people into the sphere of his influence. The true nature of his activities was not revealed, but when this became known it was at once obvious that <u>he was, from the Soviet point of view, a more dangerous force than this accusation dared reveal.</u> By 1966 the atheist movement was prepared to make a more reasonable assessment of what Prokofiev and Kryuchkov had been doing five years earlier:

A. F. Prokofiev, G. K. Kryuchkov and others, leaders of one of the fanatical Baptist groups, are trying to seduce believers to support them at the present time by appealing to the history of the Baptist Church and finding ideological support and encouragement in it. In their first *Letter to all Registered and Unregistered Congregations* A. F. Prokofiev and G. K. Kryuchkov wrote: 'In the Pergamum period[9] Satan and the world penetrated subtly into the church. Something similar happened with us in the 20's when Satan began gradually to subdue the leading brethren and to influence the church through them; slowly and cleverly Satan enticed them into his toils . . . In our days Satan dictates through the servants of the AUCECB, while the church accepts all sorts of statutes which openly contradict the commandments of God . . . <u>Because of the subservience of the AUCECB leadership to human directives, the church has deviated from the Lord's teaching and become cluttered with unworthy people; this is the reason for the schisms which have occurred in our congregations.</u>[10]

This is not the only major quotation in Soviet sources from the writings of the Action Group leaders at this time. A recently published book prints an extract from a manuscript by Prokofiev and Kryuchkov, entitled *Communication on the Work of the Action Group for the Convening of an Extraordinary All-Union Congress of the ECB in the USSR:*

'In our congregations many Laodicean Christians have appeared, people who have lost their zeal and who are indifferent to everything. They attend worship once a week to hear pious exhortations and beyond that they want to know nothing. It is nothing to them if the true children of God are debarred from office and removed from the church, to be replaced by those who will destroy the things of God . . . The church has permitted free promotion to leadership of ministers who are not God's or the church's; they . . . having acquired unlimited rights, have prescribed statutes and instructions for the church which contradict God's word.'[11]

We have even more precise information in an article by F. Garkavenko about the early stages of the movement:

The official date of the emergence of the Prokofiev group was, according to them, 13 August 1961,[12] which marked the beginning of the 'internal church movement demanding a congress, a renewal and a re-dedication of our Evangelical Baptist brotherhood'. On that day the so-called 'Action Group' released its first appeal signed by Prokofiev and Kryuchkov.

From 1960, with the general decrease in the number of believers, the conflict of groups of people who had not joined the Evangelical Christians and Baptists became fiercer. In these conditions A. Prokofiev cunningly exploited the fact that the AUCECB had responded to the wish of the majority of believers actively to participate in the building of communism. Most believers were urging the lifting of the ban on visiting theatres and cinemas; they wanted to listen to the radio and to watch television and to renounce forcible religious upbringing for children and young people.

Those who have gone into schism produce several underground publications.

What is the content of this literature?

Prokofiev's followers assign first place to religious legal problems, both internal church ones and those which relate exclusively to the authority of the state. They write a good deal about self-sacrifice in the name of Christ and the necessity of suffering for the faith. Those who suffer in Christ's name are extolled as people 'who have received baptism in the name of the Holy Spirit'. In one of his recent works A. Prokofiev made three demands upon believers: separation, sanctification and dedication, in the specific sense of self-sacrifice in Christ's name.[13]

Here Prokofiev's evangelizing activity is dismissed in a mere paragraph and with nothing like the violence of the attack on his character reproduced above which had appeared three and a half years earlier. It is useful to find official Soviet confirmation for the type of documents which are presented in this book, and the extract from the *Letter to All Registered and Unregistered Congregations* gives evidence that from the beginning one of the principal causes of concern among the reform movement was the nature of the relations between the AUCECB leaders and the secular authorities. This is a subject about which fuller evidence will be presented in the next chapter.

The claim that the reform movement arose as a reaction to a 'general fall in the number of believers'[14] has to be counter-balanced by the alternative evidence which we have that it was specifically connected with the *New Statutes* and the *Letter of Instructions*. Even without this knowledge, the timing would suggest that the movement was connected with the change in Soviet religious policy which had just preceded its emergence.

These impositions upon the ECB Church were having a profound and prejudicial effect upon its life. This extract from *Bratsky Listok* shows just how this worked out in practice. Addressing the AUCECB leaders, the reformers say:

Thousands of ministers in whom the Holy Spirit dwells were removed and not allowed to fulfil their office by you; as a rule, pulpits were offered only to those who were filled with the spirit of this world and who zealously carried out your instructions and the will of the church's enemies.

During the period of your leadership of the church after the war, in the Ukraine alone more than 800 ECB congregations were disbanded and the number of believers there dropped from 180,000 to 120,000, i.e. the ECB brotherhood decreased by one third.

In the three years during which the *Statutes* and *Letter of Instructions* have been in force fourteen Latvian congregations have been disbanded out of the 82 existing in 1960. The number of people baptized in Latvia and Estonia from 1960–62 was only 195, whilst the number of deaths in the same period amounted to 1099. Before your *Statutes* came into force 1,246 people were baptized in Latvia and Estonia in a similar period of time (1957–59). This is what your anti-evangelical action brought to the Latvian and Estonian brotherhood, and such are the results of your activity throughout our country.

Thus the friendship of the world has brought you into enmity against God (James 4. 4).[15]

This is the most specific evidence we have on the reduction in formal membership of the Baptist movement during the period under review, and it may well be representative of the general trends we noted in Chapter 1. Such a statement by no means implies, however, that the actual number of ECB believers was reduced, and undoubtedly many of those debarred from official membership joined unregistered congregations. Further evidence on this follows in the next chapter, where we shall assemble such facts as we know about the relative strength of the official and unofficial members of the ECB movement.[16]

A later document from the reformers describes the effect of the 1960 regulations in these terms:

The church's activities are limited and measures are being taken so that they should cease altogether. The contents of all sermons are strictly controlled by the atheist censorship. Evangelical sermons are forbidden. Preachers try in their sermons 'not to arouse the congregation' but rather to stifle the lofty spirit of belief. Presbyters and deacons (some of the latter are collaborators with the KGB) try their hardest to turn recent converts away from the church, especially the young. Here is a typical example: a young woman, who has recently been converted, came to a service. The minister of the church, seeing a new person there, went up to her and spoke in approximately these terms: 'How poor it looks that one so young as you should come here. Only old people do so. What have you come for? Have you any children? You'll soon be bringing your children and for that you can go to prison.' These false brothers have also committed treachery: they have been informing the enemies of the church about particularly zealous and active Christians. These false brothers and sisters monitor the behaviour and lives of believers and inform the authorities of their prevailing mood. Bibles imported by foreigners are sold to believers by AUCECB ministers for 40–50 roubles, and they live well on the proceeds. Many examples of immoral unchristian behaviour amongst AUCECB ministers (drunkenness, deceit, fornication) are well known, and even when exposed by believers they do not wish to repent, and make no effort to uproot the evil.[17]

It is important to emphasize that although Prokofiev's supporters often use direct language tinged with usages from the
comminations of the Old Testament prophets, they do not lose
their self-control. More than this, they take great pains to point
out that they are in no sense seeking to engage in anti-Soviet
activity, but are concerned purely in a movement for putting
their own house in order. In October 1961 their leaders sent the
following message to the Chairman of the 22nd Congress of the
Communist Party:

We send greeting to all the delegates of the 22nd Congress and wish
them success in their work for the good of all mankind. Having read
the draft of the CPSU programme (for building communism in our
country), we Christians also experience happiness that many of us who
are writing these lines will be able to live under communism, and we,
together with all Soviet citizens, are contributing our work and our
knowledge so that we may more rapidly achieve in our country an
abundance of food products, consumer goods, equipment and automatic devices, and a growth of moral qualities and culture. What a
wonderful sound have the sublime words of the Party programme,
'Man is a friend, comrade and brother to his fellow-man'. Finally the
age-old dream of mankind, 'From each according to his ability, to
each according to his needs', will be fulfilled.[18]

It is not known for certain where the Action Group met to
organize their early plan of campaign, but one Soviet source
suggests that it was near Moscow.[19] This is confirmed by the
fact that Kryuchkov was working at Tula at the time when the
reform movement began.[20] Much of its early activity consisted
of preparing an agenda for the proposed ECB congress and in
drafting a revision of the statutes. The record of this committee
work has now become available and the constitutional amendments suggested by Prokofiev and Kryuchkov are published in
full in Appendix I.[21] This extensive document puts in a clear
light the issues at stake between the Action Group, the AUCECB
and the state. It is not possible to offer any comparison between
the 1948 statutes and the 1960 revision, because the former have
never been published and are not available; the latter are here
printed for the first time.

The Action Group's basic demand is for a widespread relaxation of control and for a greater democratization in church life. An exhaustive analysis of the proposed changes would demand more knowledge of the internal situation than we have at present, but we offer a tentative summary of what seems to have been in the minds of the reformers and present it under three headings: the State and the AUCECB, senior presbyters and the local communities. The figures in brackets refer to the paragraphs in Appendix I, columns I and II.

1. *The State and the AUCECB*

Although freedom from state control is the basic question at issue, Prokofiev and Kryuchkov do not say so explicitly in the suggested revision of the statutes — probably because this control is not expressly written into the 1960 version. They merely remove, point by point, the clauses which might allow the state to intervene in church affairs. The reformers are therefore trying to insure that true separation of church and state shall prevail, and that the AUCECB, as a religious organization, shall not assume duties which belong to the state. The registration of religious communities is a state matter and therefore the AUCECB must not make it a criterion for membership (10, 13, 22(a), 22(d)). Similarly, attachment to a central body should not be compulsory (1). The Bible, not AUCECB regulations, is the ultimate authority on church order, and it is not the business of senior presbyters to see that state regulations are enforced (12). There is potential danger to be seen in the too meticulous written recording of statistics (14, 22(d), 27, 36(b)). There must be less control over the premises used for worship; the change in text here would make it possible to have 'house churches' and organize unregistered worship (29, 30). The line between state and AUCECB authority is not always clear. It is not stated in the original version on whose authority 'a central supervising organ has been created', which could make state interference possible. The suggested revision would make this body completely democratic (3).

Further demands for the easing of restrictions are made on the question of juvenile admission to membership of the church (25), administration of baptism in the winter (28), the frequency and nature of services (30, 31, 37(b), (c), (d)). In all these matters the Action Group apparently wishes to reduce the possibility of state control.

The whole structure of the AUCECB must be more democratic. Its members must be elected by an all-union congress 3, 18), which is to be elevated to asupreme position. The second of these clauses omits the unclear phrase, election by 'special conferences of responsible representatives', a serious opening for non-democratic control. There must be a more frequent airing of problems at plenary sessions of the AUCECB (6). There must be less AUCECB control of senior presbyters (11, 12, 14, 21, 22(c), 23, 24) and local communities (13, 14). AUCECB finances must be the responsibility of the whole church (19) and the AUCECB's stringent control of regional finances must be relaxed (24). The statutes of the church must be controlled by the congress, not the AUCECB (20), but the Bible must be the final arbiter in all matters of church order and discipline (12). The AUCECB should organize more theological training (15), distribute Christian literature to the communities (16) and invite more foreign visitors (17).

2. *Senior Presbyters*

The power of senior presbyters must be reduced (22(b)). They should have less control over the admission of new members and and the type of religious services and meetings held in their districts (22(a)), and they should have less say in appointing ministers (22(c)). Their role as financial intermediaries between the communities under them and higher authority (the senior presbyter of the republic and the AUCECB) should cease (24), but they must report on their work to regional conferences, as well as to the presbyters of the republic and to the AUCECB (though their reports to the latter need no longer be quarterly) (24). They should be elected, not appointed by the AUCECB (11, 23).

3. *Local Communities*

There should be more freedom for local communities to govern their own affairs and to practise 'the priesthood of all believers'. They should be able to accept anyone of suitable age (25, 26) as a member of their corporate fellowship, provided he has asked for it (27) and that the community has assured itself of his faith and administered water baptism to him (25, 26) at any convenient time (28). There should be no restrictions upon when services are held (30) and the breaking of bread must be held at least once a month, or more often if desired by the community (31). Worship may be more varied in its locale (29) and in its musical content (37), and there should be increased attention to children (33). The community should have greater control over its own affairs (32(b), 36) and should have the right to invite anyone to conduct services (33) and to preach (34). Restrictions on preaching by visitors from other communities should be removed (34).

This draft revision of the statutes suggests very strongly that doctrinal issues were not at stake between the Action Group and the AUCECB. It may be true that the original 'Free Baptists' inclined to the more 'evangelical' wing of Protestantism, but if so this was not a discussion which was carried over into the period when the Action Group became dominant. An eminent American Baptist visitor to the Soviet Union recently confirmed this when he wrote:

> The tensions in relation to the unaffiliated groups ... concern 'order' rather than 'doctrine'.[22]

At the end of 1961 the AUCECB held a consultation on the issues which had arisen and it certainly lasted long enough for them to have been discussed in some detail:

> From 29 November to 2 December 1961 a conference was held by the AUCECB and senior presbyters in connection with the activities of the so-called 'Action Group', which had arisen under the leadership of A. F. Prokofiev and G. K. Kryuchkov. In addition to the members of the AUCECB and the Auditing Commission, 19 senior presbyters were present at this meeting.[23]

The Action Group obviously decided as a result of this meeting that it was no longer possible to hope for a change of attitude on the part of the AUCECB leadership, so they must move forward and attempt to stabilize their own position by forming themselves into a more permanent body.

Thus an Enlarged Conference of the Action Group met in February 1962 and their proceedings were as follows:

ACTION GROUP FOR THE CONVENING OF AN EXTRAORDINARY ALL-UNION CONGRESS OF THE EVANGELICAL CHRISTIAN AND BAPTIST CHURCH IN THE USSR

Proposed Agenda of the Congress

1. Report of the All-Union Council of Evangelical Christians and Baptists.
2. On the unity of the Evangelical Christian and Baptist churches and a united leadership.
3. Adoption of new statutes for the Union of Evangelical Christians and Baptists.
4. Election of new members to the All-Union Council of Evangelical Christians and Baptists.

By authorization of the Action Group for the Convening of an Extraordinary All-Union Congress of the Evangelical Christian and Baptist Church in the USSR,

Presbyters: A. F. Prokofiev
              G. K. Kryuchkov.

The conference noted the following:

1. The work of the Action Group should not be considered as propagated by its leadership, but as the result of God's answer to many prayers of his people who have felt such a need everywhere.
2. The desire for the convocation of a congress has been transformed into a serious and widespread movement for the restoration of godly principles in the life and service of the church before God, according to his teachings.
3. Despite our repeated offers to co-operate in the matter of the convocation of a congress, the leadership of the AUCECB has adopted

a consciously hostile attitude to all our planned measures, which are pleasing to God and the ECB Church.

N.B. The decision on the AUCECB will be reported separately.

On the basis of the above statements and guided by the word of God and the will of the church, the conference of the Action Group adopted the following decisions:

1. In connection with the conclusion of the preliminary period and the change-over to the organizational period for convening an Extraordinary Congress of the ECB Church in the USSR, and for the purpose of safeguarding the steps planned, it was decided to form an Organizing Committee of the ECB Church, the main purpose of which is to prepare its organizational and spiritual condition for conducting a congress according to the will of God.
2. Members of the Organizing Committee are located in all regions of the USSR, depending on the number of ECB believers.
3. A presidium of five members is to be elected to supervise the work of the Organizing Committee.
4. The presidium of the Organizing Committee is to work out the procedure for nominating representatives to the congress and the conduct of voting on behalf of the ECB communities.
5. Members of the Organizing Committee are responsible for the correct nomination and discussion of representatives to the congress and for the voting procedure.
6. They will report to the presidium of the Organizing Committee on any irregular activities in preparing for the congress.

By authorization of the Enlarged Conference of the Action Group:

Presbyters: G. K. Kryuchkov
A. F. Prokofiev.

In view of the fact that the statutes of the ECB Union in the USSR, which are in effect at this time, have not been approved by an ECB congress and the application of these statutes causes great harm to the work of God and of the church, they should be considered as a draft.

The following changes should be introduced into the statutes and submitted for approval to the ECB congress.

N.B. The text of the present statutes is being given in its entirety.

It is found in Appendix I with the draft emendations printed in parallel columns.

COMMUNICATION
ON THE FORMATION OF THE ORGANIZING COMMITTEE
OF THE EVANGELICAL CHRISTIAN AND BAPTIST
CHURCH IN THE USSR

On 25 February 1962 the Enlarged Conference of the Action Group, attended by presbyters and workers of the ECB Church, completed its programme. The conference offered sincere prayers of gratitude to our Lord for the blessings given to the work of our Action Group and to the life of the church during the whole period since 18 August 1961.

'If ye love me, keep my commandments ... He that loveth me not, keepeth not my sayings.' (John 14. 15–24.)

Decision of the Organizing Committee on the anti-church activities of the AUCECB

Dear Brothers and Sisters in Christ,

We give thanks to God that the powerful movement in our church, begun under the influence of the Holy Spirit, for its purification and awakening from deadening Laodicean indifference, has expanded through the mercy of God and has attracted more and more of God's true children.

However, the Church of God is facing a great deal of work before it can achieve the desired goal. All this requires a continuing spiritual struggle, the combined efforts of all God's people and their steadfast prayers.

The Enlarged Conference of the Action Group, attended by presbyters and churchmen of registered and unregistered ECB communities, which was concluded on 25 February 1962 adopted the following decisions:

To set up an Organizing Committee for the convening of a congress of the ECB Church and to authorize it, on the basis of information concerning the activities of the AUCECB examined at the conference, to express a serious warning to the Council concerning its conscious deviation from the truth and the continuation of its persistent anti-church activities.

You all know that for the past eight months the Action Group has appealed to the church to sanctify itself and to unite, and that the Group is working for the preparation of a congress. We have gratefully noted that this appeal has met with a wide response in all our communities.

During this whole period we have repeatedly addressed the AUCECB leadership, inviting them to repent and to co-operate in the great cause of restoring evangelical principles to the life of the church. However, they not only have not given their consent, but have even begun to work actively against the measures undertaken by the Action Group. For this purpose the AUCECB called a special conference of senior presbyters at the end of November 1961. This conference approved the activities of the AUCECB and adopted a disgraceful decision aimed at the suppression of the movement begun under the influence of the Holy Spirit for the purification and restoration of the church.

The question is: who was at this conference and what is their spiritual attitude, if they say that 'black is white' and approve all the serious misdemeanours of the AUCECB?

We raise our voices for internal church freedom, purification and the unity of all God's people.

Our watchword is: 'All ECB communities in our country are a single brotherhood in Christ!' Therefore we must condemn the two principal documents of the AUCECB, i.e. the *New Statutes* and the *Letter of Instructions*. The church has been forcibly guided by these documents against the will of God.

These documents contradict the spirit of the New Testament, they disunite the church, take away all its rights and banish its true churchmen, introducing dishonesty and confusion. Therefore, in the name of God, we witness that anyone who accepts them as normative for the church defies the New Testament (Gal. 1. 8–9).

That is why I. G. Kargel wrote in a certain letter to Ya. I. Zhidkov:

'Any church which removes God's foundations and places its own decisions in their place loses the right to be called Evangelical'

and:

'... only a carnal and blinded person should be found in those ranks, but not a Christian.'

Since then over 30 years have passed. Many times the Lord has condemned the AUCECB leaders. However, they have not repented but have deviated even more from the truth, forcing the church to accept anti-evangelical statutes and instructions.

It was stated in a communication from the Kiev brothers sent to the Council for the Affairs of Religious Cults attached to the Council of Ministers of the USSR:

'The now existing religious organization calling itself the AUCECB (in Moscow) has not been elected by the local ECB churches, has not been authorized by them and does not represent them. Members of the AUCECB have long since cut themselves off from the masses of believers, have followed the path of dictatorship, and have abolished the rights of local churches to self-determination.'

We wish to make the following definite statement: the Church of Christ does not need any changes of external circumstances or a new teaching, but it requires purification and it has to follow the commandments of Christ, since the strength of the church lies not only in knowing the word of God, but in applying it practically to life (I John 2. 3–5; II John v. 9).

Therefore, the Organizing Committee, together with the whole church, accuses the AUCECB:

1. Of putting into effect anti-evangelical documents not confirmed by the church — the *New Statutes* and the *Letter of Instructions*.
2. Of including in the union only one-third of the communities (registered), while two-thirds (unregistered) have not been recognized by it.
3. Of conducting hostile activities against the convocation of an all-union congress, in opposition to the demands of the whole church.

In the light of the above statements, and also guided by the word of God, particularly Heb. 12. 15; I Cor. 5. 12–13; Gal. 5. 10 and 12; and the words of Christ, we declare:

'But if he neglect to hear the church, let him be unto thee as an heathen man and a publican.' (Mat. 18. 17)

In the name of God and also in the spirit of all God's people, the Organizing Committee warns the members of the AUCECB as well as the republican, regional and some local presbyters who are introducing the above-named AUCECB 'documents' into the life of the church and are carrying out its programme, that unless they repent openly before God's people for their deliberate anti-church activities and declare their intention to serve God and his people faithfully in the future, they will be excommunicated from the church in fulfilment of God's will.

The register of people to be excommunicated will be published in a special document. We remind the AUCECB of Rev. 2. 21:

> 'I gave her space to repent.'

We recommend to communities and groups that you should transmit directly to the Organizing Committee lists of those churchmen who, in your opinion, should be excommunicated with an indication of the place where your community or group is located and the number of members who agreed with this decision.

The time until the publication of the document regarding excommunication from the church should be spent by all God's children in serious spiritual meditation and prayer, so that God may influence our whole church and especially the hearts of the AUCECB members. We wish no-one to be excommunicated who has the spirit of God, but no-one, not a single churchman, should remain in the ranks of the church if he has consciously deviated from the truth.

This measure should not be an arbitrary human decision, but the result of work of the Holy Spirit. For this purpose a general day of fasting and prayer is to be held throughout the church on 6 May 1962.

We ask you, dear brothers and sisters, to pray for us so that the Lord may help us to act in his name for the good of God's people.

We greet all those who continue to love our Lord.

> The presidium of the Organizing Committee, your brothers in Christ.

22 March 1962.[24]

The evidence we have now presented in this chapter and Appendix I suggests that <u>from its earliest stages the reform movement was so bedded on a rock of expertise in Baptist constitutional matters that its challenge to the established leadership would be extremely serious.</u> At the same time, this document proves that the questions under discussion were internal ones for the church alone in which the state could have no legal jurisdiction. We seem to have here a reliable guide to the true nature of Prokofiev's activities, and we are thus able to offset the

D

picture of him in the Soviet press and suggest that his leadership was responsible, not hostile to the state and based firmly on New Testament teaching. Whatever doctrinal differences there may have been between the AUCECB and the 'Pure' Baptists, we are now able to state with some confidence that these were not a point at issue when the aims of the Action Group were made a matter for discussion in the ECB Church.

3 Towards a Congress

We shall now assess the situation as it stood between the AUCECB, the reformers and the state during 1962 and early 1963.

Most of the evidence we have presented so far gives the reformers' case against the AUCECB and the state. We lack knowledge of the real feelings of those Baptists who remained loyal to the AUCECB, and, more seriously, we do not know what were the inner motives of the official leaders which led them to act as they did in trying to suppress the reform.

To fill this gap we are reduced to a careful study of the official reactions as they appear in the pages of *Bratsky Vestnik*. The leadership was certainly more seriously worried by the 'new and stronger attempts to divide our brotherhood'[1] than it had ever been by earlier movements. The official Baptist view was to deny that the essential aim of the Action Group was to reform the leadership of the church and to revitalize it spiritually; instead the movement was represented as the latest in a series of tendencies whose chief aim was to accomplish a schism in the ECB Church. This view was propounded explicitly by A. L. Andreyev, Senior Presbyter of the Ukraine, but it should be emphasized that it can in no way be reconciled with the real intention of Prokofiev and Kryuchkov as expressed in the documents at the end of the previous chapter. Indeed, Andreyev's account expressly states that in its earliest stage the movement was seen to be calling for reform, not schism:

In the past two years in the Ukraine we have been experiencing new attempts at dividing our brotherhood in several of our congregations. These attempts originate from the followers of the so-called 'Action Group'. Although in several congregations in individual regions of the Ukraine detachments of Action Group supporters have actually been formed, nevertheless the overwhelming majority of our societies are preserving unity and supporting our fraternal union of the AUCECB. One should note that in a number of regions in the

39

Ukraine the Action Group has not attained success and has not founded its groups in a single congregation. Such regions are Chernovtsy, Transcarpathia, Ternopol, Volynia, Rovno and others, and in several more (for example, Kherson, Nikolaev, Dnepropetrovsk, Lvov, Poltava, etc.) there are no more than two or three groups in each. The influence of the Action Group is mainly in Donetsk, Kharkov, Lugansk and some other regions.

The work of the followers of the Action Group was at first not understood and several believers, not penetrating to the heart of the matter, did not see anything bad in the calls to fasting and prayer for the cleansing of the church. But many quickly understood that the cleansing to which they were being summoned was in fact a division of the church and was a matter unpleasing to the Lord.

Dear brothers! We should not forget that for many years the children of God in our country thirsted for unity, prayed and waited for it. Then in 1944–45, the Lord gave us unity—and how we should thank him for this. Can it be that now, at the summons of the Action Group, we should again choose the path of division instead of strengthening unity and founding peace in the churches? Has the Lord really not called us to unity? Many churches understood that the dangerous work of the Action Group leads to division, and would not follow them.[2]

One cannot analyse the true motives behind this AUCECB reaction without attempting to read between the lines. Yet this is a highly speculative undertaking, one in which every student of the situation is likely to reach a different conclusion. If we take his words at face value, Andreyev seems to be saying that guarding ECB unity is the highest goal, therefore no attempt at reform along the lines advocated by the Action Group can be entertained because this would immediately result in the division of the church. It might, however, be possible to interpret his insistence on unity as an indirect way of saying that the Baptist movement in the USSR exists only on the sufferance of the state. The movement would be suppressed totally if it allowed these open challenges to renewal to play a dominant part in its life. To hold with such a view it would be necessary to believe that it is possible in present Soviet conditions for a totalitarian government to extirpate a movement of which it disapproves and which affects half a million people (at the very least).

Any church existing in a communist country (or for that matter, in an industrialized Western society or an emergent state of Africa) exists in a situation of greater or lesser compromise. We do not wish, therefore, to pass a moral judgment on the compromises which Russian church leaders have accepted in order to continue organized Christian life in their country. We wish merely to present the evidence which is available, with the simple word of warning that a pronouncement in *Bratsky Vestnik* may conceal hidden currents of thought about which we lack evidence. Any statement in it will be read by the communist authorities as well as by the faithful and may not be intended to convey an identical impression to both.

In an official communication to all member congregations in 1963, the AUCECB leaders stated:

We caution all our brothers and sisters against various sorts of letters, which contain attempts to place our brotherhood in an aggravated position with the authorities and government of our country, because this is dangerous and harmful for the entire work of the Lord in our country. Not only is it harmful to our entire brotherhood, but it also contradicts the whole spirit of the gospel and the teaching of our Lord Jesus Christ.[3]

There does seem to be an element of hostility present in such a reaction — and Prokofiev and Kryuchkov specifically complained of this in the document which we presented at the end of the last chapter. Even so, this hostility might possibly be attributable to fear of state reprisals rather than to malice caused by the threat to the leaders of having their own position undermined.

In June 1962 the Enlarged Conference of the Organizing Committee met again. This record of its proceedings refers to several other documents which are not available, but it seems to summarize the position accurately as it stood in the summer of 1962. The conference arose out of the request to the communities to furnish the names of those who they consider should be excommunicated.[4] This list, we are told, is not complete, but it should not be assumed that the inclusion of a name on it necessarily means that the person concerned has betrayed the gospel. Some may have chosen the path of co-operation with the state, genuinely believing it to be the best way of witnessing as Christians in the given circumstances. We do not set out here to pass moral judgment on anyone, but simply present the evidence available:

Whatsoever you bind on earth shall be bound also in heaven . . .
(Mat. 18. 18)

PROCEEDINGS No. 7

of the Enlarged Conference of the Organizing Committee of the Evangelical Christian and Baptist Church held on 23 June 1962

Remembering the words of the Lord: 'Whatsoever you bind on earth shall be bound also in heaven . . .' (Mat. 18. 18) and seeing, more precisely, that the church has a basic right to authorize and forbid, it is the purpose of the conference, in fulfilling the will of God, to examine the proceedings and reports of individual communities and of republic Evangelical Christian and Baptist brethren which have been sent to the Organizing Committee, and thereby to disclose the will of the church, in order that the questions below be resolved, not in their name, but in the name of the Evangelical Christian and Baptist Church.

In this connection, the following questions were examined:

1. How does the church regard the AUCECB in connection with the warning given it (see decision of the Organizing Committee of 22 April 1962)?
2. The place of the Organizing Committee in the Evangelical Christian and Baptist Church.

In discussing the above questions, the conference noted:

The anti-church activity of the AUCECB has been evident and has been set forth in detail in the foregoing documents (see the first and second despatches, reporting on the work of the Action Group and the decision of the Organizing Committee of 22 April 1962), and it has also been confirmed by a large number of documents from local sources.

How the activity of the AUCECB is regarded is attested to by the evidence of the statements below:

For example, in the statements of the brethren in Western Siberia and the Altai region is was noted: 'The AUCECB, which exists to serve God, has departed from truth and created a depraved system of ministers alien to the church and to God, including senior presbyters who have ensnared the church with all kinds of endearments and eloquence and have seduced the hearts of the unsophisticated... They are well organized and united apostates (Acts 7. 51–53).'

Similar statements are characteristic also of other declarations.

But despite the warnings of the Organizing Committee on behalf of the church, the AUCECB officials not only have not repented, but they have held to their former attitudes which are alien to the spirit of God. According to the testimony of the believers of the Gorky region: 'On the contrary, they have taken up arms against God's word and the will of God even more resolutely.'

In their declaration the believers of the city of Zhdanov say directly that 'henchmen-ministers passionately persecute true children of God, disdaining nothing, to the detriment of the work of God'.

It is noted in the declaration of the Kiev brethren: 'In the matter of the suppression of the truth they display special interest and personal initiative. They do not stop even from restraining the spiritual intentions of members of congregations who speak out against the *New Statutes* and *Letter of Instructions* of the AUCECB.'

In all the other documents which have been sent to the Organizing Committee from registered and unregistered churches of the Evangelical Christians and Baptists of Moldavia, the Ukraine, Belorussia, Tataria, the Caucasus and Trans-Caucasus, the Urals and Trans-Urals, Northern Kazakhstan, the regions of Western Siberia, the Altai region, and other areas of the USSR, there is unanimous testimony to the fact that members of the AUCECB have long deprived themselves of the right to be members of Christ's Church. There is witness to this in passages in the Holy Scriptures:

'Whosoever denieth the Son, the same hath not the Father' (I John 2. 23);

'Now if any man have not the spirit of Christ, he is none of his' (Rom. 8. 9).

Having considered the above demands of the Evangelical Christian and Baptist Church in the USSR for the excommunication of those servants who long ago abandoned God and who are alien to the church, the Organizing Committee fully subscribes to them and in fulfilment of God's will declares that it does not recognize for the AUCECB and its officials:

1. the right to be ministers of the Evangelical Christian and Baptist Church
2. the right of representation and maintenance of relations within the USSR
3. the right of representation and maintenance of relations with foreign organizations.

We further declare the excommunication from the Evangelical Christian and Baptist Church of the following ministers:

1. Ya. I. Zhidkov — Chairman of the AUCECB
2. A. V. Karev — General Secretary of the AUCECB
3. I. G. Ivanov — Treasurer of the AUCECB

Members of the AUCECB:

4. I. I. Motorin
5. A. I. Mitskevich
6. G. M. Buzynin
7. S. G. Shchepetov

Senior presbyters:

8. A. L. Andreyev
9. P. A. Karchevsky
10. N. N. Melnikov
11. F. R. Astakhov
12. K. S. Veliseichik
13. N. N. Germanovich
14. V. I. Yermilov
15. T. S. Kasaev
16. I. Ya. Tatarchenko
17. A. V. Gaivoronsky
18. I. Ye. Yegorov
19. I. A. Yevstratenko
20. R. R. Podgaisky
21. D. D. Shapovalov
22. A. B. Rusanov
23. K. L. Kalibopchuk

24. D. I. Ponomarchuk
25. I. Ya. Kalyuzhny
26. Ye. N. Raevsky
27. D. M. Andrikevich — assistant senior presbyter.

Supplementary lists of the excommunicated will be published as the declarations are received.

The Organizing Committee has received a large number of reports about the excommunication of the presbyters in local communities which were considered in this conference:

The conference considered it advisable to let the local churches themselves carry out excommunication of local presbyters and ministers.

We remind all churches that the officials of the AUCECB in being excommunicated will be like Saul who was cast out by God, but the Lord will strengthen the House of David (II Sam. 3. 1). We implore the church to cleanse itself of unworthy servants, knowing that every congregation which leaves unworthy or excommunicated servants in office is thereby responsible to God, and being deprived of blessing, brings upon itself condemnation (I Cor. 5. 13).

The second question on the agenda was brought up and discussed for this reason: the above-cited documents of the registered and unregistered congregations and groups of the ECB Church which have come to the Organizing Committee contain declarations that these communities recognize the Organizing Committee of the ECB Church as its sole central leadership. They state that the activities of this committee are pleasing to God and reflect the interests of the church; further, the Committee acts unanimously in taking upon itself this service.

In connection with this, the Organizing Committee thanks God and all the children of God who have put such faith in it, and seeing a real need for this, it declares that:

1. The Organizing Committee, which manifests the authority and confidence of the church, will take upon itself the leadership of the ECB Church in the USSR in the future until the congress.
2. The guiding principle of the ECB Church is the word of God.[5]
3. The resolution of the third letter remains in force: all AUCECB meetings, their decisions and documents, and the calling and conducting of a congress without the participation of the present Organizing Committee are to be considered invalid.

4. The church does not recognize as valid the excommunication of believers for support of the movement to sanctify the church.

The Organizing Committee entreats the Lord for the granting of his blessing, powers, abilities, and wisdom to it from above for the carrying out of this great labour, desiring to keep itself pure and dedicated to God until the end: it requests all the children of God to support its work with prayers and personal participation, having faith that with God's help the whole church will achieve purity and divine order for the welfare of God's people and to his glory.

Blessings on all those who are constant in the love of the Lord. Amen.

On behalf of the conference the following presbyters have signed the Proceedings:

G. K. Kryuchkov

A. A. Shalashov

N. G. Baturin

Moscow, June 1962.[6]

There are other points of importance which should be noted in this document. It gives impressive testimony on the nation-wide character of the reform movement,[7] and it claims that the true leadership of the ECB Church has now passed to the Organizing Committee. The absence of Prokofiev's name from the signatories should not cause surprise, because he was under severe pressure by this time.[8]

Further evidence on the relations between the reformers and the AUCECB in the first half of 1962 is contained in the following extract from *Bratsky Listok*, Nos. 2–3, 1965:

Have these anti-evangelical instructions[9] remained on paper only or have they become a practical reality?

What does your activity show you to be?

The Organizing Committee considers you to be a body for the control of the brotherhood instituted not by God nor by the church, but carefully selected and set up by the Council for the Affairs of Religious Cults and other bodies which specialize in destroying the work of the church.

Facts testify that you have not only given instructions, but have also zealously put into practice the atheist programme of destroying God's church from within . . . [10]

How has the vigilant church reacted to your deviation?

The Lord has seen it all! So have the true children of God and the Holy Spirit has moved his ministers to come to you with their criticism and request that you turn from this path of destruction on which you now find yourselves and return to the way of truth.

In August 1961 in order to improve the situation, the Action Group suggested that you agree to call an Extraordinary All-Union Congress of the ECB Church, but you gave no answer and never even considered our criticisms. We approached you with the suggestion that an Organizing Committee, which would include your representatives, be appointed, but even to this you gave no answer. When the Action Group began its work independently and addressed a 'letter' to the church in August 1961, when God's people were consumed with zeal, you proclaimed from your Moscow pulpit that this was 'the fire of Satan'. You brazenly announced in your letter to the church of 20 June 1962 that this work of the Action Group was inspired by 'the enemy of God's work'. You instigated a cruel campaign against the movement for a congress and the cleansing of the church, again and again causing offence to the Holy Spirit.

In spite of all this the vigilant church tried to do all in her power to convert you (James 5.19–20).

However, working in close contact with the Council for the Affairs of Religious Cults you continued to force upon the church the *New Statutes* and *Letter of Instructions* and removed any who opposed these.

When the church saw that amongst all senior presbyters not one responded to the call to return to the way of truth, but all to a man continued to destroy the work of God, when the church saw that the whole organization of AUCECB was utterly corrupt and evil, and not susceptible to renewal, then the church and the Organizing Committee completely rejected the AUCECB as a central religious leadership. In Proceedings No. 7 they informed you that they no longer recognized the AUCECB and that you had been excluded from the ECB Church.[11]

It is important to establish how widespread was the support which the reform group was able to command. From the amount of attention it had in the Soviet press in 1966 (see Chapters

6 and 7), one would expect it to be very large indeed. Yet there is a widespread tendency to play it down. A. L. Andreyev, in the speech quoted earlier in this chapter, stated that 'the overwhelming majority of our societies are preserving unity', while more recent estimates of the percentage of Baptists supporting the reforms have been given as 5 per cent[12] or 8 per cent,[13] while in another source an absolute figure of 15,000 has been put forward.[14]   Nevertheless, as we saw in Chapter 1 where we discussed registration, these figures are virtually meaningless, because they can apply at best only to registered communities.

Leaders of the reform movement assert that two thirds of all communities are unregistered,[15] and indeed there is no evidence to suggest that this statement is inaccurate. We also know that the greatest support for the movement has come from the unregistered communities:

The demagogues from the Organizing Committee, the followers of Prokofiev, took it upon themselves to 'protect' these unregistered Baptist groups from the AUCECB and from the 'satanic authorities'.[16]

Fortunately, where so much is unclear we are able to give precise statistics about one particular community in Belorussia:

In 1960 the Brest ECB congregation united with a similar one at the village of Vulka-Podgorodskaya (Brest district). But only about 100 of the 380 believers went to Vulka. The rest, incited by their spiritual pastors, Matveyuk, Shepetunko, Kotovich and Fedorchuk, began to organize illegal gatherings in private houses in the town.[17]

There are several features of outstanding interest here. Firstly, we should remind ourselves that according to Soviet legislation on religion, any group of twenty believers has the right to form a congregation and to apply for registration.[18] This, then, is a clear account of an obviously thriving congregation in a major population centre being illegally expropriated from its place of worship and being forced to unite with a weaker parish whose place of worship was relatively inaccessible. If the AUCECB was unwilling or unable to take up the case of the Brest Baptists, then a potentially schismatic situation already existed. The most valuable information of all is that only just over a quarter of the whole congregation continued to support the AUCECB:

> The others, with Matveyuk and his confederates at their head, pronounced an anathema on that organization and declared themselves to be 'true Christians' and supporters of the so-called 'Organizing Committee'.[19]

It is not possible to make any statistical deductions from an isolated example, and it might be claimed that a proportion of those who supported Prokofiev in this particular instance did so because of the practical inconvenience to which they had been subjected by having to go out of town if they wanted to continue to worship legally. At the same time, the figures do have some significance, if for no other reason than that the community of Brest was not the only one to be disbanded or amalgamated at this time, and what happened there could well be a typical reaction in such circumstances.

The same article also gives strong evidence on the way in which Prokofiev himself travelled before his arrest, so that he could persuade people to support him through personal contacts with them. Under his influence, the Brest Baptists themselves worked most assiduously for the cause:

> They actively mimeographed and disseminated 'appeals', 'addresses' and 'protests' of the Organizing Committee, not only among the Brest Baptists, but they even made missionary journeys to 'the brothers and sisters in Christ' in the Kamenets and Kobrin districts, at Pinsk and even in the Orenburg region.[20]

The latter is some 1,200 miles from Brest, and so we have here an early hint of the truly remarkable way in which the reform movement was able to maintain its organization over the years to come. These Baptists also made tape-recordings of religious broadcasts from abroad and paid especial attention to influencing the young.

Whereas the AUCECB leaders tried to quell the movement for reform by moral persuasion and failed, the state stepped in and attempted to suppress it by force.

Prokofiev was not able to lead his movement for long. After

cataloguing his crimes, the attack on him in a Moldavian newspaper quoted in the last chapter went on to state:

At the end of last year in Zhdanov the adventurer A. F. Prokofiev was condemned to five years imprisonment, to be followed by a further five years exile. The obscurantist has got his deserts.[21]

According to another report he was imprisoned in August 1962, and he was then about 50 years old.[22] The reform movement now had its first well-known martyr figure.

There were others left to carry on Prokofiev's work:

And we would not have bothered to talk about him in such detail but for the fact that he had found sympathizers in Moldavia.[23]

Some, like these two girls, Volodina and Sokolova, expressed their sympathy in a way which was guaranteed to draw attention to the movement. This incident concerning them occurred in a village near Tula:

The girls had declared a fast! If one were to believe the letter, it was already about twenty days since they had eaten.[24]

The *Izvestia* correspondent who wrote this hastened to the scene and talked to the girls, one of whom said:

'Yes, we are ready to die for justice and our faith' ... 'They'll fast until atheist persecution against us ceases', interrupted Vera's mother ...

The writer continues by referring at this point to the other chief initiator of the demand for reform, about whom we have gathered less information than about Prokofiev at this early stage in the movement:

Presbyter G. Kryuchkov left his job in the central electro-mechanical workshops and went away. But he did not forget his flock and continued to lead the sect by written instructions . . . They pasted up leaflets in various places and dropped envelopes into the letter boxes of local people. They made demands and threats. In all these countless letters there was an ultimatum: either complete freedom of action for the Baptists or death for Volodina and Sokolova ... The houses where the girls were lying became a regular Baptist headquarters. Every day they gathered there, encouraged the fasting girls and discussed new provocations.[25]

An ambulance was ultimately brought to the girls and their lives were saved, despite attempts of their relatives to prevent any treatment being administered.

Although Kryuchkov appears to have remained a free man at this time, despite this attack on him, repression of the reform movement was promised:

The vain attempts of the supporters of the obscurantist Prokofiev do not of course command great sympathy amongst the Evangelical Christians and Baptists of Moldavia. But public opinion cannot countenance even the droplets of spiritual poison which they dispense. We must isolate these latter-day 'apostles', prevent them from having the opportunity of spreading their baneful influence even on individual Soviet people, and especially on children and adolescents.[26]

The 'isolation' meant the rounding up of many of the more active sympathizers with the Organizing Committee during 1961–64 and the number of known arrests totalled 197.[27] Many of the names collected by the 'Temporary Council of Prisoners' Relatives' (whose activities we shall be describing in the next chapter) are corroborated by a series of articles which appeared in the Soviet press at this time.

In January 1962 five leaders of an 'illegal Evangelical congregation' at Dedovsk in the Moscow region were exiled. Their crimes were listed as using tape-recorded sermons to influence believers, living well off the income from collections among members of the sect and keeping at home 'books with religious and anti-social contents'.[28] These five also happen to be the first names on the list compiled by the Temporary Council of Prisoners' Relatives, where we are informed that their deportation was for five years.[29]

There were a number of trials in December 1962. Yakov Peters was given four years imprisonment at Ivanovka (in the Chui district of Kirgizia) for engaging in active youth work — though this is not specifically stated to be in connection with an illegal Baptist group.[30]

A young girl, Vera Arent, is reported to have denounced her parents at a trial at Semipalatinsk (Kazakhstan), but the details of the accusations are decidedly unclear. The names and exact sentences of those imprisoned are not stated, but N. Krivosheyev and V. Rudnev are said to have been 'deprived of parental rights',[31] and the information from the Temporary Council of Prisoners' Relatives (95 and 96 on the list) makes it clear that they were given five years each in a strict-regime camp.[32]

I. E. Grunvald, a Belorussian, was sentenced to three years imprisonment merely for leading an illegal Baptist sect and making converts in and around Alma-Ata (Kazakhstan). The most serious crime listed was that he enticed his own son into the congregation.[33]

The four leaders of the Brest congregation whose activities we discussed above were imprisoned.[34] They appeared as prisoners 88–91 on the list compiled by the Temporary Council of Prisoners' Relatives, and their sentences were stated to be from three to five years.[35]

The leaders of an unregistered Baptist sect were brought to trial at Namangan (Kazakhstan) late in 1963, where three women faced the court. They were accused of paying undue attention to the sick and trying to win them for their congregation, circulating religious texts from books printed in Tsarist Russia, and trying to 'attract the whole world' into their ranks. They were sentenced to two years imprisonment each. A certain Georgi Vekazin was tried at the same time and given eight years for allegedly raping a 14-year-old girl whom he was trying to attract into the sect.[36]

During these years there were also a number of recorded arrests of Pentecostals and *Tryasuny* ('Shakers'), an allied sect. These were not allowed to exist legally unless they joined the AUCECB.[37]

Despite this series of events, the methods which the state had decided to employ were no more successful than the subtler ones of the AUCECB in curbing the activity of the Organizing Committee. Kryuchkov seems to have remained a free man and the Committee stood its ground during 1962–63, sending a whole series of appeals to the government, the texts of which have not reached us. However, we do have the climactic document of the series, which is here published in full for the first time.

It will be noted that this document goes back over recent history to explain why the present situation has come about. It gives more convincing details on the AUCECB's compromise with the state than we have found elsewhere. We decided, however, that the document would more effectively convey its message if presented as a whole rather than split into parts and inserted at the most relevant points in our history.

COMMITTEE FOR CONVENING AN ALL-UNION ECB CONGRESS

To the Chairman of the Council of Ministers of the USSR, Comrade N. S. Khrushchev, and the Government under him.

Esteemed Comrade Chairman,
Esteemed Members of the Government,

For the seventh time the Organizing Committee of the ECB Church appeals to the government of the country. Over the last two years we have made requests for permission to convene a congress of the ECB Church in letters addressed to the Council for the Affairs of Religious Cults, to the Procurator General of the USSR, Comrade Rudenko, to the Chairman of the Supreme Soviet of the USSR, Comrade Brezhnev, and most recently on 2 January 1963 to you personally, Nikita Sergeyevich. All these have been left unanswered and because of this the question of the congress is becoming a serious problem. A lawful and just internal church movement for the convening of a congress is being crushed by the state with repressive measures, which is evidenced by the court proceedings against ECB believers over the last two years throughout the country.

At the outset of its activities the Organizing Committee knew that the ECB Church had been made the victim of injustice, and we knew that an unlawful administrative and even a physical campaign was being conducted against it. However, the Committee considers it as its aim to go as far as possible on the path of reducing this aggravation.

It was with this purpose that the Organizing Committee made a special point of the existence of humane laws in our country in the appendix to its report of 22 September 1962. Thus we tactfully reminded and indicated to those who create and defend lawlessness how much they are contradicting the spirit and the letter of the existing legislation by their actions and how far they have gone along the

E

road of arbitrariness and illegality. However, this unlawfulness continues.

The interests of the church do not permit us to limit ourselves merely to unsuccessful petitions, but we have been brought to the point where we must express ourselves more candidly on the present situation of the church in our country.

All doubts have now been removed that the church, which should be separated from the state, is completely under the illegal control of various state authorities. Apostate ministers have entered into illegal deals and collaboration with government bodies and the KGB,[38] who have thus been granted both clandestine and unconcealed access into the church.

In order to understand how this could happen it is important to remember how the foundations for these illegal relations between church and state were laid.

To you, Nikita Sergeyevich, it is well known that the massive repressions directed against believers, which had begun soon after the death of Lenin, had by 1937 attained such a form and dimension that in all the country not a single God-fearing minister and hardly a true professing believer was left at liberty. Only an insignificant number of congregations were left under ministers who, because of the terror which prevailed, had accepted compromise and collaboration with the state authorities.

Many of those sentenced for their faith never came back from their places of imprisonment. They were executed or they perished in the incredibly severe conditions of their imprisonment and camp life. Those who were released but remained firm in their faith were soon given new sentences.

So as to implement persecution on such a scale and in order not to seize believers at random, but to select the more active ones, the agents of GPU, NKVD[39] and later the KGB penetrated all facets of church organization. Here, under the threat of repressions, they enlisted shaky and weak ministers of the church, as well as ordinary believers. The interest of government agents led to the following questions being asked:

Where is the next church service to be?
Who will preach?
Who are the members of the church council?
Which preachers have come from outside?

Who made any trips and to where?
Who preached a call to repentance?
Who prayed for the imprisoned brethren?

And so on.

For over 30 years thousands of completely innocent Christians have suffered while such 'work' has continued.

In the war years, 1943–44, the Council for the Affairs of Religious Cults attached to the Council of Ministers of the USSR was created, and this is now the special supreme authority over the church.

At about the same time the AUCECB was created to be a leading body. It was not elected by the church, but was brought into being by the state authorities and consisted principally of churchmen who had consented to deviate from Evangelical doctrine and agreed to an illegal collaboration with various state authorities. For this purpose some of them were released from detention before their terms were up.

It is quite obvious that after all these massive repressions and because it had been penetrated by a mass of various government agents the church was already in fact under illegal state control. Government authorities were moulding church councils for local congregations as though they were of clay; they were appointing senior presbyters for regions and republics from among their own trusted men, and then they subordinated them to the AUCECB.

During the war when churches were reopened believers at large greeted this event and the attendant appointment of ministers with such enthusiasm that they did not foresee the deception and the danger. They reasoned that if these men had agreed to accept leadership in God's cause at such a hard time, then they must obviously be men devoted to God.

Registration of ECB churches was accepted for only two years (1947–48). During this time only a small proportion of churches were registered and they were turned into a special showcase for freedom of conscience. Behind this, the majority of churches were left without any rights and in spite of repeated appeals they remained unregistered. Obviously this was so that at any time they could be classified as illegal and subjected to persecution, with the purpose of liquidating them.

In this way, in the years when arbitrariness and lawlessness ruled and under the threat of extreme repressions which were continuing, the foundations were laid for consolidation of the illegal ties between church and state, so that the former could be disintegrated from within.

Direction and control over the church came from two main channels, one (more overt) through the representatives of the Council for the Affairs of Religious Cults; another (clandestine) through the thousands of strands of the dense net of official and unofficial KGB agents.

In your speech to the 22nd Congress of the CPSU you said:

> 'It is our duty to investigate cases connected with misuse of authority ... We can and we must work to clear them up and to tell the truth to the Party and to the people ... This must be done in order that similar occurrences should never be repeated.'

We would not talk about this if these illegalities were not continuing, and if the illegal liaison between church and state, which has resulted in so many victims, were a matter of the past which has left only nightmare memories. But this liaison has been carefully carried over into present-day practice, and it is not only guarded as a precious heritage but is being reinforced and conveniently used in the struggle against believers as a means of repression.

The difference here consists only in this: that in order to carry out persecution in the past the fatal Article 58 of the Penal Code of the RSFR used to be applied in closed judicial proceedings, while now Article 227⁴⁰ is used, and in the other republics of the Soviet Union the corresponding article is applied. But ECB believers have never been guilty of breaking any of these articles. However, judging from the way Article 227 has been applied since its promulgation, it can be definitely stated that it is in fact intended to accomplish the same results in its application to believers as was Article 58, which had no bearing on them but which took many thousands of lives.

One characteristic aspect of the present repressions must be noted: namely, that judicial proceedings are now conducted with 'open doors', but the audience is basically picked from communists, Komsomol members and auxiliary police. They are incensed against believers and gathered together by invitation tickets, and the persecutions of today are preceded by the cultivation of public opinion.

It is common knowledge that before an act of persecution the whole arsenal of ideological persuasion, such as newspapers, radio broadcasts, television, lectures, is fed to people's minds in increased doses. These are decked up with slander and sometimes outright lies about believers. These attacks on believers go under such vilifying titles as 'Monsters',

'Scum', 'Obscurantists', 'In the Snares of Sectarians', 'Poison of Religion', and so on. Prayer meetings of believers are called 'mob gatherings', churchmen are called 'extortionists and parasites', believers are pictured as 'blood-thirsty people who sacrifice their own children, forbid them to study and lash them with a chain for the slightest misdemeanour'.

After such psychological belabouring and incitement to animosity and after all such 'ideological' work, people are brought to the point of anti-religious ecstasy and fanaticism and it then becomes possible to pronounce anything against believers without any apprehension of arousing public indignation. Then persecutions commenced and have been continuing up to the present. Prayer meetings of unregistered and sometimes even of registered congregations are being dispersed under the direction of the KGB by the auxiliary police, who do not baulk at taking physical action. Suffice it to mention the beatings of believers at Zhivoto (Vinnitsa region) and Kharkov, where those arrested were sentenced to 10–15 days imprisonment. The KGB also instigated the beating-up of scores of believers at Kiev.

There have been cases where church buildings have been demolished with bulldozers in raids by groups of youth and auxiliary police, especially after incitement by the authorities, for example at Tashkent, Brest, and Vladivostok. People have also been exiled to the remote areas of Siberian encampments, they have been put into concentration camps and their property has been confiscated. The court proceedings against groups of ECB believers at Tashkent, Yangi-Yul, Dedovsk, Khmelnitsky, Shepetovka, Kharkov, Odessa, Kirovgrad, Shakhty, Brest, Semipalatinsk, Barnaul, Kazan, Kursk, etc., are blatant examples of illegality, as are the cases against individual believers at Zhdanov, Novomoskovsk, Uzlovaya, Vitebsk, Omsk, Slavuta, Osinniki, and in many other towns.[41]

Believers are being discharged from employment, expelled from universities and from technical schools, their homes searched, musical instruments, tape recorders, religious literature and personal correspondence confiscated.

All this is being done in a most gruesome way. For instance, at Kharkov when a newly completed private home was confiscated a pregnant woman with her weeping children was literally thrown out in the rain, and food which they were not allowed to cook for their meal was thrown out after them. Their house was converted into a public library named after Dobrolyubov. Homes of believers have been confiscated and designated as libraries and for other purposes at Dedovsk, Kazan, Barnaul and in many other towns.

At Dedovsk (near Moscow) during the search of a believer, Ruma-chek,[42] his savings account book was discovered in a pocket of his coat. To snatch it from him before the eyes of his weeping children the searchers put his arms out of joint, took the savings book and confiscated his savings for the state.

In Semipalatinsk a mother of eight children was separated from her husband who had been sentenced as a believer. After the court proceedings the prosecutor demanded that seven of the eight children be separated from the mother because she was exerting a religious influence on their upbringing. Neither is this an isolated case. Children of believing parents have been taken away from them in Smolensk, Kazan and in other cities.

Some defenders of these extreme persecutions further the deception by saying that all this is being done in accordance with the laws of the land. But is it? Are not our laws humane? Is it lawful to reduce the ideological struggle against religion to a campaign of mockery and slander against believers? And to inflict universal repressions on them? To accept this assertion would mean to accept that Article 58 has been applied lawfully, that thousands of our dear and innocent brothers and sisters have suffered and many have been liquidated lawfully, while the few who were rehabilitated came back unlawfully. It would also mean accepting that Article 227 and the May decree are being applied lawfully, that arrests, deprivation of freedom, banishment, confiscation of homes and the separation of children from their parents are all lawful.

It is common knowledge that the struggle against religion must be conducted ideologically and by ideological means only. However, it is not from ideological battlefields that ECB believers have been taken as prisoners of war to serve their sentences in prisons and concentration camps. The dead in the prisons and in the camps are not enemy casualties in an ideological war; the confiscated homes, tape recorders, harmoniums and religious literature are not trophies captured in victories of ideological warfare, but are evidence of terrible illegality.

The Council for the Affairs of Religious Cults which has been specially created for the purpose of regulating the relations between church and state knows better than anyone else all the violations of the law by the state authorities; yet it not only does not remedy the situation, but even commits basic violations of the law itself, both centrally and through its local representatives. For example, in a consolidated

action by an extensive network of special representatives of the Council
for the Affairs of Religious Cults, the churches are being forced to
accept as their ministers men pleasing to those representatives who
operate through them to disintegrate the church. On the basis of
what law is this done? According to what law do the representatives
of the Council demand from the ministers of churches lists of church
members and persons baptized, and information on those who have
expressed interest in the church or who wish to repent? But as for
believers who defend the purity of Evangelical doctrine, the state
generally has them on a special index.

We feel it urgent to call your attention to one further serious problem. Occasionally we are pictured as political enemies of the state,
in order to stir up hatred in people and to justify any illegal action.

However, it is rather surprising that in answer to such hatred,
persecution and the complete injustice meted out to the ECB Church,
we remain unshaken in our relationship to the state. The above-
mentioned actions have not provoked in our midst any political
opposition or discontent whatsoever against the existing political
regime.

We have already stated that the ECB Church does not need any
changes in external conditions. ECB believers have been and continue
to be good citizens of their country and are active participants in all
good and useful enterprises, whatever the circumstances. Yet this
does not mean, either, that we are satisfied with any conditions in our
church life and that we should admit 'the powers of this world' into
leadership of our church. Whatever state law might be, the church
must remain free from the interference of the world and the secular
authorities in her internal life.

Therefore the Organizing Committee has been seeking and is
determined to find ways and means of purifying the church, of re-
establishing an Evangelical internal church order for separation of
church and state and of uniting all ECB believers (in registered as well
as unregistered congregations) into one brotherhood in Christ with
the gospel as its only rubric.

The state is now exerting a definite and unlawful opposition to this
precise task of purifying the ECB Church, which compels us to appeal
to you to make a more thorough analysis of the deprivation of rights
to which the ECB Church has been subjected in our country. We
are now compelled to appeal by force of necessity, because when we
deal with internal church matters and reveal who are the apostate

ministers, we inadvertently come in contact with the state representatives who have infiltrated into the church and have very close illegal and unjustifiable ties with the church.

The congress which we are petitioning to have convened should resolve all these problems and at the same time it must liquidate the unlawful relations between church and state,

If it were not for interference by the state authorities in this matter, if the state had not declared a war with new persecution, if it were not backing its planted men, the church itself would quickly, painlessly and without any complications re-establish the necessary internal church order by removing the unrepentant officials. By this it would break the essential link in the criminal chain binding church and state. In this way the illegal relationship would be liquidated without mentioning the state in so much as a word at the congress. All this could be attained painlessly.

We have manifested great forbearance and have done everything possible to achieve this reasonable goal. Our task was not to transgress any law, even though we have paid very dearly for this, for we have striven to remain within the limits of the existing law.

Now, firstly, no-one will accuse us of any illegal activity; and, secondly, during this period of time any remaining doubts about the existence of the ties between church and state have been completely dispelled. The relationship which existed in disguised forms has become obvious,

'for nothing is secret that shall not be made manifest.' (Luke 8. 17).

Now it has been fully defined what goals the AUCECB is called upon to pursue.

It is no secret to anyone that the government and the Party are not interested in the prosperity of the church and that they are waging a struggle against it. But by rejecting the petitions of thousands of ordinary believers (that is, the whole church), and by using persecution to suppress their movement, the state authorities are shielding the AUCECB ministers, despite the fact that this is a violation of the law.

Such unanimity has been established between the AUCECB and the state authorities that any expression of opinion against the AUCECB is looked upon by both as opposition to the state. This is conclusive proof that the state needs the AUCECB to disintegrate and liquidate the church from within and that the interests of the AUCECB and of the church are directly opposed to each other.

In summing up what has been said, the Organizing Committee comes to the following conclusions:

1. At present the official part of the church under the AUCECB (the registered congregations) is under the complete illegal and unjust direction and control of the state authorities.
2. The AUCECB and its staff are the principal link in this illegal relationship. They have betrayed the principles of the gospel and have been excommunicated by the church, but they are holding on, supported exclusively by the state.
3. The press, the procuracy, the courts, the Council for the Affairs of Religious Cults and the KGB are all acting extremely unlawfully in regard to believers. They ignore and break not only the Soviet Civil and Penal codes, the decrees on the separation of church and state and the constitution of the USSR, but also the Declaration on Human Rights.
4. The links between church and state are being utilized exclusively for the struggle against the church by disintegrating it from within and by persecuting it.

The Organizing Committee believes as before that a congress of the ECB Church, as set out in the letter sent to you on 2 January 1963, would be the best means of re-establishing lawful and normal relations between the church and the state, and therefore we do not have any other requests, except as outlined in the letter mentioned above.[43]

To you, Nikita Sergeyevich, it is well known that the history of the ECB Church in Russia, except for a short period of time, has been a history of a people doomed to life-long suffering, a history of camps and imprisonments affecting fathers, children and grandchildren. It is a sad and thorny road washed by the tears of mothers and children, a road created by arbitrariness and illegality in a country of humane law and constitutional principles specifying freedom of conscience.

However, it is not our desire to rid ourselves of persecution which compels us to address you.

We are not campaigning against the authority of the state, for according neither to the word of God nor to the secular law is the state subject to our jurisdiction. Moreover, persecutions are not detrimental to the future of the true church. But as witnesses for God, in our appeal to you we once more wish to remind you that the judgment of God awaits all who do injustice. For this the main responsibility falls on you as the head of the Soviet government.

Avail yourself of the forbearance of God whose name you abuse, but to whom, nevertheless, belongs all authority in heaven and on earth.   Thus may our people lead a quiet and peaceable life, which in all ages has been the foundation of prosperity and peace.

God is the witness between ourselves and you.

Respectfully,

Chairman of the Organizing Committee of the ECB Church,

G. K. Kryuchkov

Presbyter and member of the Organizing Committee of the ECB Church,

A. A. Shalashov.

13 August 1963

Appendix I

Excerpt from the latter addressed to N. S. Khrushchev, 2 January 1963:

'... the Organizing Committee authorized by the church requests you:

1. To permit an all-union congress of the ECB Church to be convened and held under the leadership of the Organizing Committee.
2. To permit the establishment of an office for the work of the Organizing Committee at one of the ECB churches (preferably Moscow). The staff should consist of released presbyters and preachers and it would prepare for the congress.
3. To give an order to the Council for the Affairs of Religious Cults to prevent neither the registered nor the unregistered ECB congregations and groups from having their religious services anywhere on the territory of USSR.
4. To give an order to release the ECB believers sentenced under different pretexts for their support and help in organizing the convening of a congress, and also to give an order to suspend arrests in connection with this activity for convening a congress.'

Appendix II

At present more than 200 people are in prison, almost all of them sentenced under Article 227, Par. I.   This article has been introduced into the Penal Code only recently, and I do not know its full contents, but briefly it is directed against 'Anti-social activity under the pretext of preaching religion'. This article is very broadly interpreted. Here is an example of how two of our brethren who were tried in Odessa in August 1962 were incriminated.

'Bondarenko and Shevchenko are accused under Article 209, Par. I, of the Penal Code of the Ukranian Soviet Socialist Republic.[44] The accused have subverted youth from participation in social life, made speeches against the arts (films, radio, theatre, games and literature), travelled to other churches (congregations) for the purpose of agitation. The accused Bondarenko was arrested on a bus where he was active in religious propaganda, distributing leaflets and preaching renunciation of the arts. He proposed to create a 'Fraternal Council for Young Christians', he organized young people's groups for Bible study and conducted exams on biblical subjects, for example:

1. The creation of heaven and earth
2. The creation of man
3. Abraham, hero of the faith
4. The recitation of biblical verses.

He held young people's meetings with singing, recitals of poetry and the playing of musical instruments. The accused Shevchenko made his home available for illegal meetings, and he baptized young people until the moment of his arrest.'

Even though it was never proved that the accused had preached the 'renunciation of art', and this was not corroborated by any witness, I. D. Bondarenko was sentenced to five years in prison, with subsequent exile of three years. Shevchenko was sentenced to four years in prison and three years of exile.

In approximately similar ways the administration of 'justice' was carried out in other cases.[45]

Here follows a list of 42 prisoners (their names are listed in Appendix II at the end of the book). This register contains the ages of 22 of them, and it is notable that of these no less than fifteen were under the age of 40 at the time the document was compiled in 1963. Thus, contrary to the frequent communist assertions that religion has now almost died out among young people, the reform movement has gained very strong support among the rising generation. This has its parallels in the field of literature, for example, where the chief thrust for throwing off the inherited shackles of the past has come from the young.

The point had now been reached where the AUCECB was forced to act decisively in order to try and prevent a full-scale and permanent schism within its congregations.

A most moving insight into the minds of the reform Baptists is provided by this hymn which was appended to the Kryuchkov-Shalashov document. Here is a profound Christian answer to modern materialism and a successful attempt to put recent scientific achievement into the context of man's spiritual development.

Man

1. Man, whose life is a perpetual struggle,
   For whom life means a conquest,
   You have subdued all in this world,
   But you have failed to subdue yourself.

2. You have gained fame as a ruler on land,
   You have penetrated the depths of the sea,
   You have reached the heights, but you are still a slave
   Of your own base passions.

3. You have split the invisible atom,
   You even know how to conquer space,
   You have reached the age of great discoveries,
   But you have failed to conquer yourself.

4. Yes! You are strong and at the same time weak,
   You are great, as well as insignificant,
   By the power of your mind you are a god,
   But by your lust you are a slave.
   You were high, but how low you have fallen.

5. In your selfishness you scorned the Creator,
   You did not find him in the stratosphere,
   You returned to earth victoriously like God,
   Robbing him of his glory.

6. You are firmly resolved, as in past ages,
   To make your name immortal,

And have forgotten the Tower of Babel
In your senseless struggle with God,

7. What of it that you can soar above the earth,
With transient glory on your mortal brow?
You will take off into space again,
But you will still die here on earth.

8. The hosts of planets, in lofty majesty,
Follow their courses above you.
But it was decreed to mankind: No!
You will not reach a single one of them.

9. Oh, unfortunate, haughty, and earthly man!
Give glory to the Supreme God.
Only with him can you be truly happy,
With him you will reach the region beyond the clouds.

10. Without your space-ships and all your efforts,
The Lord will transform your body.
In the first Resurrection, he will give
An immortal body to the faithful saints.

11. God is spirit, and the eternal ruler of the stars,
And if you want to reach the starry sky
You must fall down before him, earthbound man,
And you must conquer yourself in this life.

Amen.[46]

In the next month (19 September 1963) the leaders of the Organizing Committee sent a letter to the President and General Secretary of the Baptist World Alliance, which was designed to acquaint Baptists in the West with the stand which was being taken by many of their co-religionists in the Soviet Union. This unpublished document contained the following information not found in other writings of the reformers:

In May 1961 an Action Group was formed from among ECB churchmen, the aim of which was to convene an All-Union ECB conference. On 13 August 1961 the group came to the presidium of the AUCECB with the proposition that the latter should co-operate in calling a general conference. . . . At this time a considerable number of the registered churches have declared their non-recognition of the AUCECB as the central leadership of the ECB Church.

4 The 1963 Congress and After

In 1963 there was an occasion on which a reconciliation between the AUCECB and the reformers might have occurred, but it led instead to a deepening of the schism.

In October 1963 an ECB congress took place in Moscow. It elected a new AUCECB and adopted a new constitution. Prokofiev's sympathizers did not receive support.[1]

Such is the laconic report from an atheist source on the Evangelical Christian and Baptist congress which took place in Moscow just two months after the appeal which Kryuchkov and Shalashov had written to Mr. Khrushchev. *Bratsky Vestnik* gives us the official record in fifty pages of text,[2] with the introductory remarks:

The congress, at first called a conference, was attended by 210 delegates with deciding votes, 45 with deliberative votes and 195 guests with no right of vote; in all there were 450 people present at the All-Union Congress of Evangelical Christians and Baptists.[3]

There are, however, serious gaps in our knowledge of the proceedings, many questions which cannot be adequately answered on the basis of our present knowledge. We miss the atmosphere of the discussion on the elections and the adoption of the new constitution. It is possible, indeed, that there was no opportunity to deliberate on the latter, for it was adopted 'unanimously'[4] at the end of a day which had begun with a series of reports which bore the whole weight of the congress,[5] after which there can have been little time for such a complicated matter to receive adequate airing.

Most seriously of all, we do not know whether any single representative of the Organizing Committee was there to express the views of the reform movement to the congress. If so, *Bratsky Vestnik* devotes not as much as a word to such a speech. The

66

indications are that only the official view was represented and our atheist sources do not help.[6] It seems certain, therefore, that there was no adequate representation by the Organizing Committee.

The reasons why Prokofiev's supporters were not there are various. Firstly, as we saw in the last chapter, a decisive break with the AUCECB had already occurred and a Soviet source published six months before the congress talks of the reformers as pronouncing an 'anathema' on the official body.[7] Secondly, physical restraint was used. Probably about 150 of Prokofiev's most prominent sympathizers were in prison at the very moment when the congress was taking place,[8] which could hardly have encouraged free expression of the movement's views, no matter who represented it at the congress. *Bratsky Listok* (No. 2–3, 1965) suggests that the 'great majority' of the group's leaders, the Organizing Committee, were under arrest and so could not come,[9] and elsewhere it is suggested that this was simply to ensure that the people already put in office by the state should retain their posts.[10] A final reason which would explain the absence of the reform leaders who were not in prison is that they were simply not told that the conference was going to take place.[11]

Of the 255 named delegates none is known as being a Prokofiev supporter; if the other 195 without voting rights contained a single one, there is no mention of it in the congress report, although the 'Free Baptists' were apparently represented by a former adherent, M. Ye. Zyubanov, who recounted his return to the main stream of church life.[12] The most important speech on the Organizing Committee was by A. L. Andreyev, who was critical of its work, but proposed some concessions in its favour.[13] We quoted extensively from this speech in the last chapter. If others expounded their difficulties in this connection, it was not reported. S. P. Fadyukhin, for example, gave no hint that there was anything wrong in his congregation at Tashkent,[14] yet less than a year later *Bratsky Vestnik* reported:

The church in Tashkent has for a long time suffered from divisions. The Lord has blessed the labours of the presbyter, Brother Fadyukhin, and more than 400 members have returned to the church for common work.[15]

The conference elected a new ten-man council,[16] of whom nine were identical to those who had previously served,[17] and the tenth, I. Ya. Tatarchenko, senior presbyter of the Donetsk region, was filling a vacancy which had occurred through the death of M. A. Orlov in 1961.[18] There was clearly no concession to the Organizing Committee here.

Of much greater significance were the modifications made in the AUCECB statutes. A. L. Andreyev reported his dissatisfaction with some aspects of the work of the AUCECB and made particular reference to displeasure at the activities of senior presbyters which had been expressed locally. This almost certainly is an oblique reference to the 1960 regulations on senior presbyters. Andreyev said:

Our future desire for the new constitution of the AUCECB is as follows: at the proper time to give attention to urgent questions of the societies which cannot be decided locally as they arise; to exercise stricter supervision over the work of individual senior presbyters, so that their activities should not evoke censure from individual congregations served by them and so that their work should strengthen unity.

From the AUCECB report it is evident that the AUCECB has attended insufficiently to internal activities, as is noted in the report itself. Therefore the AUCECB in future should give serious attention to this and provide workers who will give it exclusive attention. We hope that these measures will help to remove differences of opinion and will give practical help to our congregations in these questions and needs.[19]

N. A. Levindanto introduced the new constitution with a short speech, the text of which was quoted by the Organizing Committee and will be found in their assessment of the achievements of the congress.[20]

A careful study of the text of the new constitution as compared with the *New Statutes* of 1960 is most revealing,[21] and the widespread nature of the concessions to the reformers is a matter of some surprise, considering the refusal to co-operate with the new movement on the part of the AUCECB. Indeed, there are so many concessions, at some points even with verbal correspondence, that not only do we have proof of the extreme pressure which the reformers had exerted, but we must also postulate a genuine desire, at least on the part of some AUCECB officials, to meet the reformers half-way. At the same time, serious defici-encies still remained in the 1963 constitution, which we shall point out as we go through it. It can hardly be stated emphatically enough, however, that while the All-Union Congress fails to represent unregistered ECB communities, such reforms as these are democratic on paper only.

In the new §1 a concession was made over the point that the ECB Union should be 'voluntary'.

§3 makes the vital concession that the ECB Congress should become the supreme authoritative body of the church and that the AUCECB should exist only to carry out its wishes. The new principle is adopted that it must meet every three years, which is, of course, too infrequently to guarantee effective control. Many functions which had belonged to the AUCECB are now trans-ferred to it: financial control (though a comparison with §14 suggests that it will merely rubber-stamp the work of the Audit-ing Commission); the right to change the constitution; election of the AUCECB (which had before been the task of an obscure 'special conference of responsible representatives'). The demand for the 'worthiness' of AUCECB members to be guaranteed was not included. A comparison with §§4, 18, 19 and 20 of the 1960 *Statutes* shows how significant these concessions were.

§5 affords a partial concession: the AUCECB is to hold a plenary session at least once a year (the reformers had demanded a minimum of twice a year).

§6 demonstrates one of the best features of the 1963 constitu-tion: it has simplified its predecessor's definition of AUCECB duties and substituted a much more workable one. This replaces the old §§10, 12 and 13 and excises the tortuous qualifications of the last two. It includes a new and (from the religious point of view) valuable positive principle of 'spiritual and organizational help', which occurs again in §7 and §15 (a). It does not, how-ever, mention 'the word of God' as being the ultimate authority (cf. §12 of the Prokofiev–Kryuchkov revision). The contentious feature that the AUCECB has dealings only with 'registered'

F

communities is dropped here, as in the new § 15, but the reformers' demand for the AUCECB to keep in touch with 'groups' is not adopted.

§7 is a partial concession to the reformers' demand on the old §21 for a full democratic election of senior presbyters. However, the new version is unsatisfactory here, for it is by no means clear what is meant by 'the agreement of the communities' over these appointments, nor who basically makes them.

§9 does not concede on guaranteeing a supply of religious literature to the parishes, but §10 makes a verbatim agreement to invite 'foreign spiritual leaders' to the USSR. The reformers had criticized the word 'accurate' in the records of the communities kept by the AUCECB (§14 of the 1960 *Statutes*), but this clause has now gone altogether, as has the next one, where the reformers had demanded full training of ministers under AUCECB guidance.

§15 and §16 simplify the regulations on senior presbyters, who no longer control such local affairs as the admission of new members, the character of services and the enforcement of 'strict discipline', all of which omissions were specifically demanded by the reformers. However, an unclear compromise is reached over their role in appointing ministers for the congregations. Previously, as now, ministers were 'elected by the community' (§35 of 1960 and §22 (b) of 1963), yet the senior presbyter formerly had to see that they were 'made available'. The reformers demanded the removal of this ambiguity, but the new version makes the unclear proviso that senior presbyters now 'share' in choosing ministers. Contrary to the demand of the reformers, regional conferences are not given any control over the work of senior presbyters, nor is there any democratization of their appointment. As the old clause on their appointment by the AUCECB (§23) is removed altogether, there is great confusion here.

§17 substitutes a profession of faith for a trial period of two–three years as a condition of entry into the ECB Church, but the reformers' further demand that teenagers should not be excluded is not accepted. §18 removes the stricture on winter baptisms, but 'verbal' testimony is not regarded as sufficient for admission. A new point is the 'suitable examination' of candidates for baptism, and it is not stated by whom this is carried out.

In §19 the reformers failed to carry their demand on religious meetings in private houses (i.e. unregistered worship), but they gained a point on extra week-day services in §20, and §21 makes a partial concession on increased local control over the timing and frequency of the breaking of bread.

§22 fails to reflect the reformers' demand that the three-man executive in charge of local affairs should be done away with, and the new function of the three as a 'church council' is unclear.

§23 does not yield on the demand for increased attention to children, nor on the possibility of laymen leading worship as a regular practice (not just during the illness of the minister).

§24 is an almost total concession on the possibility of laymen preaching, though it is the minister and three-man council, not the community, who decide upon which laymen may fulfil this function.

§25 upgrades the church council (as opposed to the 'executive body' of 1960) and the stipulation that records of all meetings in the community should be kept is abolished. A new point is that preachers should be given a say in spiritual matters.

§26 greatly simplifies the rules on music in worship. In accordance with the demands of the reformers, the ban on pay for the choir is removed and it is no longer illegal for choirs to visit other churches and sing in them. Strictures on 'religious concerts' and the use of instruments other than an organ and upright piano are also removed.

§27 introduces a new principle of financial support for the AUCECB and senior presbyters.

The 1963 constitution was a very great improvement over its predecessor, particularly where it exhibits greater simplicity and displays hints of a spiritual approach to church government (which had been singularly lacking in the 1960 version). The partial concessions to Prokofiev and Kryuchkov would undoubtedly have gone some way towards a successful re-uniting of the church if a representative group from the Organizing

Committee could have been present to discuss them fully in an open session of the 1963 congress, if many of its members had not been in prison, and if the congress itself had not just represented communities affiliated to the AUCECB. However, steps were taken at this point towards a theoretical democratic structure which would be of the highest value, should all registered and unregistered communities be allowed to nominate representatives to a future All-Union Congress.

At first the AUCECB affected high hopes that there would be a reconciliation:

> We should go from this place with a balm of consolation and peace for our churches, for there are no further reasons for arguments and mutual recriminations.[22]

A 'Fraternal Letter' was immediately sent to all Baptists, Evangelical Christians, Pentecostals and Mennonites,[23] including those who were not members of the AUCECB.[24] The AUCECB promised to continue sending about 20,000 letters a year to its member congregations and to receive their delegates in Moscow, numbering on average about 150–200 a month. It further promised the following help:

> ... in applications for the registration of churches and for receiving and preserving prayer houses; in defending the rights and interests of individual churches and presbyters before authority.[25]

This bold promise must certainly have given new hope to congregations which had been exposed to illegal administrative measures. The mind of the congress was also that senior AUCECB officials should pay more frequent visits to local congregations.[26] Such visits were undertaken, as when I. I. Motorin visited Siberia and included Barnaul on his itinerary,[27] where there had recently been a great deal of trouble with the authorities and about which we shall be giving full details later in this chapter.[28] A. I. Mitskevich spent over a month travelling around Central Asia.[29] This was not a new feature, for Ya. I. Zhidkov, chairman of the AUCECB, had undertaken a journey to Siberia as recently as December 1962.[30] Even so, not all congregations

were quickly visited (and indeed as a physical task this was impossible); it was eighteen months after the congress before the
same Mitskevich went to Moldavia, and there he was greeted by
the request for more frequent visits from Baptist leaders.[31]

Hints that the 1963 congress had not achieved its goal of end-
ing disunity soon came in abundance. Already in February 1964
there was news of an unregistered group still active in Tashkent.[32]
The second issue of *Bratsky Vestnik* in 1964 complained that
Pentecostals were still holding aloof.[33] The enlarged AUCECB
plenum which met in Moscow on 2–3 September 1964 had to
give attention to the continuing problem,[34] and Ya. I. Zhidkov
stated at the concluding service:

> I do not wish to go into details, in order not to cast reproach on
> anybody. I would not wish it to happen that some believers should
> support the constitution accepted at the congress, while others have
> another opinion, but I wish to say that we have considered how to
> make of two opinions one and in which manner to destroy the element
> of enmity and misunderstanding caused by preconceived thoughts
> which has been a barrier across our way.[35]

The introductory message to all congregations from the AUCECB
in the last number of *Bratsky Vestnik* for 1964 stated:

> Unfortunately, it is necessary to say that the enemy of men's souls
> can never look calmly at the unity of the children of God and has al-
> ways tried to scatter them like wheat. He has not been slumbering
> with respect to our dear brotherhood and one must say with grief that
> some brothers and sisters in our churches busy themselves with sowing
> not the seeds of peace and love but the bad seeds of enmity and
> separation.[36]

These words show a very strong concern for the well-being of
the Christian community as a whole, and they surpass anything
that was printed in the proceedings of the conference of the
previous year. They demonstrate that the desire of the AUCECB
for unity is heartfelt and not dictated purely by political considera-
tions. Nothing could be more sincere and moving than the
review of Baptist achievements in the field of unity which is

found in the same introductory message to the congregations:

We argued about our name — and now we have one and the same name: 'Evangelical Christians and Baptists'. We disagreed over the question of who could baptize, preside over the breaking of bread and solemnize marriages — now we agree that these must be performed by ordained presbyters, and only in their absence may any of these be carried out by members of the congregation, and then only at the command of the church.

These words had originally been written twenty years ago at the formation of the AUCECB,[37] and it is significant that they are repeated now.

Despite these internal appeals, the reaction from the Organizing Committee was negative, as we see from what members wrote about the congress in an issue of *Bratsky Listok* (Nos. 2–3, 1965):

In your constitution adopted in 1963, there is no mention of the most important point: for what purpose the ECB Union was created and what are its aims. For you (the AUCECB) have rejected the basic purpose of the church's presence on earth, which was always set out in the opening paragraphs of the constitutions of both the Evangelical and Baptist Unions:

'The Union of Evangelical Christians has as its aim the task of spreading the gospel . . .'

And again:

'The Union of Baptists in the USSR . . . strives to fulfil the tasks laid by the Lord upon his disciples, namely taking the gospel "to the whole of creation" — that is, to all people, regardless of their nationality, sex and age.' (Mark 16. 16.)

Such were the constitutions of our unions in the 30's, based on the commandments of Christ which said: 'Go ye therefore, and teach all nations, baptizing them in the name of the Father and of the Son and of the Holy Ghost: teaching them to observe all things whatsoever I have commanded you.' (Mat. 28. 19–20.)

The Apostle Paul says: 'But none of these things move me, neither count I my life dear unto myself, so that I might finish my course with joy, and the ministry, which I have received of the Lord Jesus, to testify the gospel of the grace of God.' (Acts 20. 24). . . .

How did you react to the church's decision to excommunicate you?

It is well known that excommunication from the church has two ends in view: firstly, to cleanse the church of those arbitrarily sinning (Heb. 12. 15, 1 Cor. 5. 13); and secondly to arouse in the sinner the realization of his responsibility for his personal salvation and lead him to repent and be saved.

But you showed no contrition or repentance after your excommunication. You continued to sin and undermine the work of God even more. When the great majority of the original members of the Organizing Committee had been imprisoned you called a pseudo-congress, without letting the Organizing Committee know, a congress which had the support of this world's rulers and at which you formally approved all your work of destruction and condemned the activities of the Organizing Committee.

Seeing that the church condemned and refused to accept the *New Statutes* of 1960 because of the way they led to a deviation from the commandments of God, you decided to announce at this pseudo-congress that the *New Statutes* were no more than a draft. How could you commit such deceit?

In his report at this pseudo-congress N. A. Levindanto said the following with reference to the *New Statutes*:

'The 1960 *Statutes* of the AUCECB were not considered to be final and permanent and therefore they were referred for discussion to our communities . . . after which significant suggestions and good wishes for making changes in the statutes of the AUCECB were received from a great many of our congregations.

After studying all this and the new possibilities which had opened up for us, the AUCECB now invited the congress to consider and ratify the revised statutes of the AUCECB, which we will now call the constitution of the ECB Union.' (*Bratsky Vestnik* No. 6, 1963.)[38]

How customary it has now become for you to lie!

When you had foisted these documents on the church, A. V. Karev said, when speaking to the young people of the Moscow church in 1961:

'The *Statutes* and the *Letter of Instructions* are the substance of two guiding lines which our brotherhood is now following. They are founded upon the law. To refuse to recognize these documents is to refuse to recognize the law; this in its turn entails refusal to recognize the Soviet State, which is the same as to oppose it.'

And now, when hundreds of believers have lost their freedom, and some even their lives, because of their refusal to recognize these anti-evangelical documents, you now say that they were merely a draft. However, if you ask all of our brothers and sisters who have suffered as a result of these documents, they will tell you whether the *Statutes* of the AUCECB were merely a draft or an active weapon used against the Church of Christ.

You may say that the *Statutes* of 1960 and the *Letter of Instructions* no longer exist and that therefore there is no point in discussing them. Yes, you have hidden the *Statutes* now, but you have not rejected the main point: that, as you have remained the same, willing to act on and agree with any unlawful transaction with atheism against the church, so your corrupt alliance with the world is still in existence, just as before. And this alliance is unlawful, impure and evil!

We do not wish to say that ministers of the church must be opposed to lawful, honest and open contacts with the representatives of the authorities, contacts about which one can openly speak from the pulpit to God's people; but we do say and insist that alongside this the principle of the church's full independence from the state and the complete absence of interference in the church's affairs by any government body must be observed.

When you work in league with atheism to destroy the word of God, when you carry out its instructions which contradict Christ's commands, when you communicate in the minutest detail all that is going on in the church, then these connections of yours are treacherous and are a betrayal of Christ and his church.

You do not only continue in your collaboration with atheism, but in all kinds of ways you try to justify and defend it.

At your pseudo-congress in October 1963 you were concerned over maintaining the possibility of preserving your friendship with the world even in the future. To this end you set about falsifying the seven Evangelical and Baptist principles, accepted by our brotherhood throughout the world. You distorted them beyond recognition: you both preserved the number seven and at the same time entirely excluded three; moreover, you excluded those very ones which were hindering you from sinning, namely:

1. The independence of the local church.
2. Preaching the Gospel or bearing witness of Christ as the main task and basic calling of the church.
3. The separation of church and state.

You were not even afraid to publish the principles which you had distorted in your 'Fraternal Letter' of 16 October 1963.

When you rejected the Evangelical and Baptist principles and adopted new ones, you provided documentary evidence that you had cemented your breach both with the teaching and with the church of the Evangelical Christians and Baptists.

Thus you have fully revealed the way in which you have completely and consciously deviated from the truth and thrown away your salvation.

Yet, despite the fact that rejection of the truth leads to death (James 5. 19–20, Heb. 10. 26–27) you (the AUCECB) have up to now shown not the slightest concern for repentance and the winning of eternal life. All this witnesses to the fact that many of you have obviously completely lost your belief in eternal life.

Such is our general view of you as a central religious organization.[39]

If the aim of the AUCECB to heal the schism had been severely damaged by the state's judicial procedures against prominent Prokofiev sympathizers before the 1963 congress, then the situation was further exacerbated immediately afterwards and the church was given no real opportunity to hammer out its differences in an atmosphere free from hysteria.

Further convincing evidence that the situation had deteriorated even more since the congress emerged from the case of the unregistered congregations at Barnaul and Kulunda (Altai region of Siberia). From it we learn that the state had decided to introduce even sterner measures against those who would not accept the new AUCECB constitution.

The basic text on this case was published in a Soviet legal periodical:

Feoktist Ivanovich Subbotin, Lyubov Mikhailovna Khmara, the brothers Nikolai Kuzmich and Vasili Kuzmich Khmara were brought before the court. The court proceedings lasted four days. For four days the judges of the Altai regional court painstakingly investigated the activities of the Kulunda sect.

The accused pleaded 'not guilty', announcing that they had committed no crime whatsoever, after which they refused to give evidence on the substance of the accusation.

They carefully concealed from the court the contents of sermons preached at their services. However, as a result of the witnesses' testimony and the evidence collected during the investigation, they were convicted of bringing up minors in isolation from social life by drawing them into their group, of calling on believers to reject their responsibilities as citizens; they were convicted of inciting citizens to disobey the auxiliary police, to refuse to join trade unions and in general to avoid all forms of social activity. They held illegal prayer-meetings at night, in insanitary conditions and with minors present. The senior sanitary inspector of the Kulunda district presented his findings, stating that the building in which the prayer-meetings had taken place was unsuitable for the religious services held by this congregation, according to the accepted standards of sanitation and hygiene (the cubic capacity of air was insufficient and there was no ventilation). In Kulunda an unregistered community of Evangelical Christians and Baptists had existed for a long time. This community had preached the Bible and observed the religious practices laid down by the AUCECB. Since 1961 all kinds of addresses, notices and other texts criticizing the AUCECB had begun to appear amongst the Baptists. From this time the activities of some of the community's members have taken on a reactionary character.

In November 1962 the chairman of the Kulunda Settlement *soviet* demanded that the community either be registered or cease holding meetings.

The older members obeyed, but the younger ones, with Subbotin at their head, broke away. They began holding illegal meetings at night. This section of the Baptists refused to recognize the official AUCECB statutes and evaded the control of the laws on religious cults in force in the Soviet Union.

Subbotin organized an illegal school for training young Baptists. After the course examinations were held during which they were given cards with such questions as: 'On which day did God create the world?', 'On which did God create man?'. Yet the day on which Subbotin began to harm the state, our society and citizens (including believers themselves) was of no interest to him.

The Criminal Court of the Altai region sentenced Subbotin, the organizer of the reactionary Kulunda Baptists, to five years imprisonment, the brothers N. and V. Khmara to three years and gave L. Khmara a conditional sentence because of extenuating circumstances.[40]

A much fuller version of this case, and its sequel, was written up by 120 Baptists from Barnaul and Kulunda:

To all children of God who constitute the church of Our Lord Jesus Christ, to all Evangelical Christians and Baptists living in our land from east and west, and from north to south: 'Grace be unto you and peace from him which is and which was and which is to come' (Rev. I. 4).

Beloved Brothers and Sisters in Christ:

We have decided to inform you of the sad events of which we have been eye-witnesses, since the sorrow of which we shall tell is our common sorrow, since all of us who constitute the one church make up the one Body of Christ (I. Cor. 12. 26).

On 11 January 1964 Sister Maria Ivanovna Khmara who lives in the town of Kulunda (Altai region) received notification from the prison in Barnaul that her husband had died. The telegram meant that now she was left a widow with four children, aged from thirteen to one month.

Her husband, Brother Nikolai Kuzmich Khmara (born 1916), joined the church in the summer of 1963, together with his wife.

This brief life in Christ is a clear example of conversion for all those who knew his former years of uninterrupted drunkenness. The Kulunda church, of which he was a member, witnesses to the fact that he sacrificially loved our Lord and sought to serve him with all his household; he greatly loved the hymn:

'I am called to work in the world,'

and especially these words:

> 'Struggle against all idols,
> Pay no attention to critical friends,
> Be a witness before the world,
> Fear not the judgment of men.'

And so, from 24–27 December 1963, together with Brothers F. I. Subbotin, V. K. Khmara, a brother in blood and spirit, and Sister L. M. Khmara, he came before the court and, like them, he was sentenced for defending the name of Christ and because he had acted according to his conscience. After the verdict he lived only two weeks in the prison, and then came the word about his death. On 13 January his wife and relatives, along with us, received from the prison the corpse of Brother Nikolai Kuzmich Khmara. At the court relatives and friends had seen him in completely good health and courage. But what did we see now when we received him dead?

On his hands was the evidence of handcuffs; the palms of his hands were burned, as were his toes and the soles of his feet. The lower part of his abdomen showed marks of deep wounds made by the insertion of a sharp jagged object; his right leg was swollen; the ankles of both legs seemed to have been beaten; on his body were black and blue bruises.

Seeing all of this, we were overcome with mixed emotions, with deep sorrow and yet joy. We grieve that our dear brother, Nikolai Kuzmich, had to undergo such horrible torture and to die in prison; we grieve for the unseen wounding of the hearts of children committed by the hands of the godless, not for evil deeds but for good, — for the love of mankind, for the Lord and in his name. Nikolai Kuzmich stood it all as a good soldier of Jesus Christ, showing himself loyal to him to the end.

We were filled with great sorrow at seeing his widowed wife and her children standing at the grave and hardly able to take in the fact that their father had died. Yet we comforted them and were ourselves comforted by the fact that we all have a Father for orphans and widows, and that there is a righteous judge — Jesus Christ.

For four days and nights many brothers and sisters from near and far came to the bier of the fallen brother, as they rendered homage to the Lord. The funeral services took place on 16 January 1964, in the afternoon, with a procession through the town; they sang hymns and repeated gospel texts, such as:

'For me life is Christ and death is gain,'

'Fear not those who can kill the body but cannot kill the soul,'

because they had seen him who had been beaten to death for the word of God.

When we had given the body of the fallen brother to the earth, we returned each to his place with grateful hearts and the desire more zealously to serve the Lord and, like our brothers, to be loyal to him unto death.

Beloved Brothers and Sisters, we know that the first question to come to you will be, 'Why?' What were the official charges brought against him at the court, and why was he condemned to death? In reply we give an excerpt from the judgment rendered by the Altai Regional Court on Case No. 142, where it is stated that a group of Baptists conducted meetings illegally and in insanitary conditions, and brought young people and minors into a sectarian group. Under the guise of 'purifying', the group conducted propaganda against the

AUCECB and its statutes, and maintained contact with similar illegal groups. There were other allegations of the same kind.

In the concluding accusation are the words:

'The guilt of the accused person is confirmed by the following evidence. As regards reactionary activity harmful to society, certain people declared that the group of sectarians headed by Subbotin and his active colleagues, N. K. Khmara, V. K. Khmara and L. M. Khmara, analyzed various biblical texts, permitted arbitrary and incorrect interpretations, criticized and did not accept the new constitution of the AUCECB.'

There you have all the evidence given about reactionary activity harmful to society. One might think that the witnesses were members of the Holy Synod, people with higher theological education, well versed in biblical truths and called to defend their purity. But not at all!

Dear Brothers and Sisters: the fact is that the world cannot be permitted the illegally acquired right atheistically to interpret the Bible to us; we cannot be forced into the church of its servants which is controlled by their 'constitution'.

Vengeance must not be taken on all the ministers who have been appointed by the Lord and elected by the church. Yet they do this very simply. Since in the Penal Code there is no article against incorrect interpretation of the Bible, the prosecutor called it reactionary activity, harmful to society. Thus he put the 'incorrect' interpretation of the Bible and criticism of the constitution of the AUCECB under Article 227 of the Penal Code. The Altai court did the same, and this is also done by other courts all over the country.

Such was the decision of the court, according to which Brother F. I. Subbotin was condemned to five years of severe regime imprisonment, the two brothers, Vasili and Nikolai Khmara, were condemned to three years ordinary imprisonment and Sister L. M. Khmara was given a two-year suspended sentence.

Were those who appeared before the court really criminals? Not at all. They are no more guilty than any of us who believe in the Lord Jesus Christ. Their entire guilt consists of the fact that they did not hesitate to hold meetings, to allow youth to attend them, and to have contact with other congregations, and to speak out against the AUCECB and its constitution. But perhaps the judges were exceptional, then? No, the judges themselves were quite ordinary, modern judges, the same as those who are conducting similar 'courts of justice' and condemning plainly innocent believers.

We do not want this letter to create in you a feeling of hatred toward the persecutors. Even though this evil is done by wicked persons, but unimportant ones, they could not have done it by themselves. They do that to which they are led and in which they are encouraged.

No less guilty of this murder are those who unceasingly publish lies in the papers, on the basis of which court proceedings are begun and wild hatred is stirred up against believers. This is the collective sin of the world.

Let us look upon the persecutors as Christ taught us:

'But I say unto you, love your enemies, bless them that curse you, do good to them that hate you, and pray for them which despitefully use you and persecute you.' (Mat. 5. 44.)

The Lord says:

'Rejoice, for great will be your reward in heaven.'

They condemn us not for evil deeds or for breaking the law, but for good deeds, for not recognizing the AUCECB and its constitution, which destroys the church, but which is of such advantage to the courts for the condemnation of the faithful that they continue to render judgment on the basis of the constitution even though it has been 'rejected'. The judges of this world condemn the children of God because the AUCECB has destroyed the church and its true ministers to the world, in the same way as the high priests, scribes and Pharisees betrayed Jesus Christ to Pilate.

Such is the true image of the AUCECB. Hundreds of brothers and sisters suffer in prison and exile because of the AUCECB. The courts, with full force, support the AUCECB and they accuse and condemn all who do not support it. It is not only that the betrayers of truth and the church have caused many tears and sufferings among the children of God but, by continuing their shameful activity and sin against God, they add to the measure of illegality, as is witnessed by the death of our dear Brother Nikolai Kuzmich Khmara.

Yes, even in our day the 'unexpected' happened. Pay attention to this, take counsel and speak up. Tell this to all the people who love the Lord. Tell all, great and small, in order that all in whom there is the fear of God and who thirst to meet with Christ may in one spirit turn to him, defending and holding fast to the truth. Say to him:

'And now, Lord, behold their threatenings; and grant unto thy servants that with all boldness they may speak thy word.' (Acts 4. 29)

16 February 1964

(Signed by 120 persons, Brothers and Sisters in Barnaul and Kulunda).[41]

These two texts corroborate each other completely and form one of the most notable instances of material from the reform Baptists being confirmed in Soviet sources. The Baptist letter pre-dates the Soviet press report by three months. The most disturbing accusation in the letter of the 120 is that the local court made itself an arbiter between the AUCECB and an unregistered congregation on matters of a purely religious nature — and this is made almost explicit in the Soviet printed version.

One of the results which followed the arrests of Prokofiev sympathizers between 1961 and the early part of 1964 constitutes a remarkable development in the recent history of opposition to the Soviet regime. The relatives of those who had been imprisoned were able to form themselves into a group with the aim of meeting to decide on common action on behalf of those who had lost their freedom. They also made it their duty to collect detailed information about all those imprisoned and to tabulate it. We have a series of documents which prove that such a group was not only formed, but that it has managed to maintain its organization for over three and a half years from early 1964. We have documents covering the early part of its activity, and an article in the Soviet press in August 1967 suggested the group was then circulating very recent lists of prisoners.[42]

APPEAL

of the participants of the All-Union Conference of ECB Prisoners' Relatives in the USSR

To the whole ECB, saints and faithful in Jesus Christ: happiness and peace to you from God our Father and the Lord Jesus Christ.

Beloved Brothers and Sisters, St. Paul, in his Epistle to the Philippians, wrote:

'... my bonds in Christ are manifest in all the palace'

and

'the things that happened unto me have fallen out rather unto the furtherance of the gospel' (Phil. 1. 12–13).

It happened to St. Paul in the first century, but today it is happening to our relatives and ourselves, although it is now the twentieth century.

We, the relatives of the prisoners, also desire that what happens to us may serve the furtherance of the work of God and, therefore, we want the imprisonment of our relatives to become known to all of you, so that you may be participants in that body about which it is said that it is 'fitly joined together and compacted by that which every joint supplieth' (Eph. 4. 16).

St. Paul requested Timothy, the servant of the Church of Christ:

'Be not thou therefore ashamed of the testimony of our Lord, nor of me, his prisoner' (II Tim. 1. 8).

'Remember my bonds',

he asked the church in his Epistle to the Colossians (4. 18).

At this time, your own brothers and sisters beg of you:

'Be not ashamed of us, remember our bonds.'

We thank God for you, that because you serve him, we, though persecuted by the world, are not left alone; through you God satisfies our needs according to his word. And we ask you that in your prayers to God you should always remember your brothers and sisters in prison.

How sad it is to read about what happened to the prophet Jeremiah (Jer. 38. 13–15). The only man who remembered the bonds of the prophet, who was in a dungeon, was the heathen Ebed-melech, the Ethiopian; but among the children of Israel, for whom the prophet Jeremiah had shed tears (Jer. 9. 1) and whom he wished all the best with his whole heart, nobody remembered his sufferings in the dungeon. Today the blood of Jesus Christ our Lord has united us in one body and, therefore, if one member suffers, the whole body suffers; when one member is praised, the whole body is praised with him.

We wish to share in suffering and to enjoy together the comfort of Christ and all the saints who constitute the Church of God and of Christ!

Therefore, if there is someone else who is in a similar situation to ours, having brothers, husbands or sons imprisoned for the word of God, let us know about them and we shall notify the church.

The church, in its prayers, will convey the message to its Head, Jesus Christ, who will soon send his protection.

Our Lord is not indifferent to the sufferings of his church, as the scripture says:

'What toucheth you, toucheth the apple of his eye.'

Therefore we shall not hide our sufferings from the Lord and from the face of his church. We shall say with St Paul that we, too, glory in our tribulations (Rom. 5. 3). We also want to share with you the sorrows which we, the mothers, bear since our children have been taken away from us.

We loved them and followed the word of God, 'that the generations to come might know them, even the children which should be born' (Ps. 78. 4–7). We also received a direct command from God (Heb. 6. 4) to bring up and educate our children according to his teaching. For this we have been separated from our children.

Only you can fully conceive this sorrow, as you are the members of one living body of the Church of Christ, which is also threatened with such sharing in suffering.

We implore you, our brothers and sisters in the Lord Jesus Christ and in the love of the Spirit, to raise with us your prayers to God for our relatives who are in prison and are listed in the information we are enclosing herewith. Please pray also for us and our children.

God bless you!

Yours in Christ, brothers and sisters, relatives of prisoners for the word of God.

At the direction of the All-Union Conference of ECB Prisoners' Relatives in the USSR.

23 February 1964.

1. Govorun (Smolensk)
2. Yastrebova (Kharkov)
3. Rudneva (Semipalatinsk)

G

REPORT

on the activities of the All-Union Conference of ECB Prisoners' Relatives,
23 February 1964

On 23 February 1964, an All-Union Conference of ECB Prisoners' Relatives took place and conducted its business according to the following agenda:

AGENDA

of the All-Union Conference of Relatives of ECB Prisoners sentenced for the Word of God

1. Collection and specification of information concerning ECB prisoners sentenced from 1961 up to February 1964, after the introduction of the *New Statutes* of the AUCECB.
2. Establish for what reason and on what charges our relatives, brothers and sisters who are now in prison and in places of deportation, have been sentenced.
3. Establish for what reasons children are being taken away from believing parents.
4. Our relationship, as relatives of prisoners, to officials and authorities.
5. Our service, as relatives of sentenced persons, to the church and our service to God in our families.

THE COURSE OF THE CONFERENCE

The All-Union Conference of Prisoners' Relatives, remembering the words of the Holy Scripture (Heb. 13. 3), studied the reports which had arrived from local churches concerning ECB prisoners sentenced from 1961 up to February 1964; it edited them and established the following:

1. Full reports have been received concerning 102 prisoners.
2. Supplementary information (incomplete) was later received concerning 53 prisoners.
3. The total number of prisoners is 155.
4. Of this number, ten were released after serving their time or for other reasons.
5. Four people died during the investigation, before or after trial, in prisons and camps.
6. The total number of people in prisons at February 1964 (on whom reports were received) was 141.
7. The number of dependents in the prisoners' families is 297.
8. Of this number, 228 were children of pre-school and school age.

9. The oldest prisoner is Yu. V. Arent, 76 years of age.
10. The youngest prisoner is G. G. Gortfeld — 23 years old.
11. Families sentenced: Lozovoi: father, mother, son;
    Zhornikov: father and mother; children of school age were placed in institutions.

The conference studied the question of why our relatives, brothers and sisters have been sentenced and came to the following unanimous conclusion:

1. All 155 ECB prisoners have been sentenced not for violating the law or for crimes against society or the state, but for their religious belief, for the word of God, in defiance of the existing laws of our country.
2. The reason for their arrests and trials was the introduction in 1960 of the *New Statutes* of the AUCECB and their dissatisfaction with them.

This is supported by an analysis of the trials. Thus, for example:

(1) The sentence of the people's court of the Zmiev district (Khar-, kov region) on 1 May 1962, in the case against Ye. M. Sirokhin states:

'The reactionary character of the illegal community headed by the defendant in the village of Sokolovo is implied in the fact that the community expressed its dissatisfaction with the existing *Statutes* of the AUCECB, and with the activities of its executive body.'

(2) In the writ of indictment in the case against F. I. Subbotin, N. K. Khmara, *et al.* (village of Kulunda, Altai region) it is written:

'Under the pretext of performing religious services and executing religious rites, they committed acts directed towards the criticism of the officially valid *Statutes* of the AUCECB',

and it is written in the sentence in the same case (Case No. 2–142, of 27 December 1963), that a group of believers, under the guise of 'purification', conducted propaganda against the AUCECB and its *Statutes*.

The conference also considered the question of children taken away from ECB parents, and established that reports were received concerning five families from which nine children had been taken away. It was found that the reason for the taking away of the children was their religious upbringing in their families. The conference noted that both according to the word of God and the laws of our country, those ECB believers had the right to bring up their children in a religious way. This is stated in the decree on the separation of church and state of 1918, Art. 9:

'Citizens can teach and learn religion privately',

and in the 'Convention on the fight against discrimination in the field of education (Art. 5) approved by the Presidium of the Supreme Soviet of the USSR on 2 July 1962, and which came into force on 1 November 1962:

'Parents and, in appropriate cases, legal guardians, should have the possibility of ensuring religious and moral education of their children according to their own convictions.'

The conference noted that, in connection with so much persecution and oppression of ECB believers for their faith in God, a feeling of hostility towards their persecutors might appear in some of them.

The conference deems it essential to remind all the faithful that they should not admit a feeling of hostility towards the oppressors and should pray for those accusing and persecuting them. (Mat. 5. 44)

On the question of our serving the church as relatives of those imprisoned for the word of God, the conference passed a resolution establishing a Temporary Council of ECB Prisoners' Relatives, set down its objectives and tasks, and elected a Temporary Council.

OBJECTIVES AND TASKS OF THE TEMPORARY COUNCIL OF ECB PRISONERS' RELATIVES

1. Continuous information to the ECB Church on those imprisoned for the word of God and on the children taken away from ECB parents, and calling for prayers for the prisoners and children.
2. Petitioning the government for the review of all court cases concerning ECB believers sentenced for the word of God since 1962, with the purpose of setting them free and fully rehabilitating them; also petitioning the government for the return to their families of children taken away from their parents.

3. In order to fulfil the tasks set forth under 1 and 2 above, the Council shall keep a complete record and files of all information concerning all ECB prisoners sentenced for the word of God, and concerning all children taken away from their ECB parents for having brought them up in a religious way.

4. Only members of the ECB Church who have ECB relatives imprisoned for the word of God in the USSR can be members of the Council. The members of the Council shall be elected at an All-Union Conference of ECB Prisoners' Relatives.

The conference directs the Temporary Council of Prisoners' Relatives to select from among themselves representatives for a personal visit to the head of the government and to submit to him the appeal of the All-Union Conference of ECB Prisoners' Relatives. The conference decided to turn to the whole ECB Church community in our country with a special appeal, asking for prayers for the prisoners and for the children taken away from the ECB believers as a result of being brought up in the word of God; and to publish information concerning ECB prisoners and children taken away from ECB parents.

CONFERENCE OF THE TEMPORARY COUNCIL OF ECB PRISONERS' RELATIVES

1. The Conference of the Temporary Council considered the question of its representatives visiting the head of the government, and they selected from among themselves a delegation composed of three people:

Govorun (Smolensk)
Yastrebova (Kharkov)
Rudneva (Semipalatinsk).

The Temporary Council turns to the whole church and to all ECB believers with the request:

(a) To submit to the Council full information on all ECB members imprisoned for the word of God who are not listed in the published record. Also we ask them to send us corrections and supplementary information on ECB prisoners, if there are errors or incomplete information in the record.

(b) To send to the Council information concerning the children taken away from their parents because of their religious upbringing and concerning all court decisions in such matters.

(c) To send to the Council information concerning released brothers and sisters, along with the reasons for release.

(d) To send to the Council information concerning all brothers and sisters who have died during investigation or court proceedings, as well as after trial, in prisons, camps or places of deportation.

'... And others had trial of cruel mockings and scourgings, yea, moreover of bonds and imprisonment' (Heb. 11. 36)

'Remember them that are in bonds, as bound with them' (Heb. 13. 3).

Here follows complete information on 102 prisoners and fragmentary information on a number of others. In the first category are stated the name, date of arrest or trial, article under which sentenced, length of sentence, place of residence before arrest and a list of dependents (see Appendix II).

The proceedings of the next meeting of the Temporary Council are as follows:

'For the Lord heareth the poor, and despiseth not his prisoners' (Ps. 69. 33).

To our brethren and sisters, Evangelical Christians and Baptists, who compose the church of Christ in our country, from the Temporary Council of ECB Prisoners' Relatives in the USSR:

APPEAL

Children of God, beloved in the Lord!

Again, we wish to give praise and gratitude to our beloved God for your sharing in our sufferings and the consolation wherewith we are comforted by God (2 Cor. 1. 7; 1. 4).

God left his word for our consolation and he speaks by the Holy Spirit through St. Paul:

'Comfort one another with these words' (I Thes. 4. 18).

We wish to console you with the scriptural words:

'For the Lord heareth the poor, and despiseth not his prisoners' (Ps. 69. 33).

The Lord also listens to your prayers. We, as well as our prisoners with whom we meet, however rarely, can testify to this. Due to your prayers, God gives them so much joy and courage that one of them, when hearing at a meeting about the great awakening among the people of God caused by their bonds, said:

'I would be pleased to stay here for my whole life if this would ripen the cause of the purification and sanctification of the church.'

Such is also the spirit of the other prisoners. For some of our friends God opened the prison doors following the prayers of our church, so that they might praise Jesus Christ at liberty. This fills us with joy and pleases us, because God himself said:

'Ask, and ye shall receive, that your joy may be full' (John 16. 24).

Yet we do not want to hide this joy from all of you:

'that for the gift bestowed upon us by the means of many persons, thanks may be given by many' (2 Cor. 1. 11).

At the same time, we inform you about new prisoners so that you, imitating God as his beloved children, may not neglect his prisoners in your prayers; pray for them as well as for everything that they and their families need.

Dearly beloved: we ask you to send information on releases from prison and new imprisonments of our brethren and sisters to the Council of ECB Prisoners' Relatives.

Take heart, friends. God is with us in all our ordeals by fire. Amen.

THE TEMPORARY COUNCIL OF ECB PRISONERS' RELATIVES

At the direction of the Temporary Council of ECB Prisoners' Relatives — members of the Council:

1. Rudneva
2. Yastrebova
3. Govorun

5 July 1964.

'And others had trial of cruel mockings and scourgings, yea, moreover of bonds and imprisonment' (Heb. 11. 36).

'Remember them that are in bonds, as bound with them' (Heb. 13. 3).

Here follows full information on 48 more prisoners, with incomplete details of a further 47.

1. Information has been received concerning 150 prisoners.
2. Additional (incomplete) information has been received concerning 47 people.
3. The total number of ECB prisoners sentenced between 1961 and June 1964 is 197.
4. Five people died during the investigation, before or after trial, in prisons and camps.

> '... and others were tortured, not accepting deliverance; that they might obtain a better resurrection' (Heb. 11. 35).

   1. N. K. Khmara (died on 9 January 1964, in the prison of Barnaul).
   2. K. S. Kucherenko (died during the investigation, 22 January 1962, at Nikolaev).
   3. O. P. Vibe (died in prison on 30 January 1964).
   4. M. F. Lapaev (died in prison in 1963).
   5. Ryzhenko (died at a place of deportation, 1963).

5. Out of this number the following persons were released after serving their time or for other reasons:

   (22 names follow).

6. The total number in prisons, places of deportation or under investigation is 174.
7. Number of dependents in the families of prisoners is 442.
8. Of this number, 341 are of pre-school or school age.
9. Sisters sentenced for the word of God and under investigation: 15.
10. In addition to list No. 1, the following children were taken away from their parents for having been brought up as Christians and for being faithful Evangelical Christians and Baptists:

   1. Lyubov Yevgenievna Sirokhina — 14 years old.
   2. Nadezhda Yevgenievna Sirokhina — 11 years old.
   3. Raisa Yevgenievna Sirokhina — 9 years old.

They were taken away in April 1964, according to a court decision at Sokolovo (Zmiev district, Kharkov region). Their father is a disabled veteran of the Second World War (first group) and is blind in both eyes. He was sentenced to three years regular imprisonment for managing the ECB Church at Sokolovo and for bringing up his children as Christians.[43]

Even though this Council worked assiduously, it failed to gather all the names of Prokofiev supporters arrested.[44] Its achievement was nevertheless a remarkable one, not least in the insistence that these tragic happenings should not be used to foster hatred or anti-Soviet activities.

Despite the apparent concessions made to the Organizing Committee in October 1963, there would seem to be little doubt but that the last few months before the downfall of Mr. Khrushchev were exceptionally bitter ones for Russian Christians. The most intensive activity of the All-Union Conference of Prisoners' Relatives relates, in so far as we have information about it, to that time, and probably reflects the prevalent atmosphere. That the situation did indeed become worse early in 1964 is fully corroborated from Soviet sources.

Despite all that had happened in the previous four years, Leonid Ilichov wrote a 24-page article in the first number of *Kommunist* in 1964 calling for a stepping-up of the anti-religious campaign. As Ilichov was Mr. Khrushchev's chief ideologist and *Kommunist* is the theoretical and political journal of the Central Committee of the Communist Party of the Soviet Union, the voice could hardly have been more authoritative. At the outset, the author tries to kill the idea that there can be any rapprochement or dialogue between Christianity and communism. He goes on to review the history of religion in the Soviet Union since the Revolution. He complains about the privileges which the church acquired during the Second World War, but says that the underlying justification for the recent attack on religion was simply that these privileges were acquired illegally and had now been annulled.

Ilichov particularly urged that more attention should be paid to leading women away from the church and to counteracting illegal religious activity among Muslims and Baptists, who were still succeeding in organizing evening religious activities for young people. Using immoderate language, he went on to call for the intensity of the campaign to be stepped up in education:

We cannot, we must not remain indifferent to the fate of children, upon whom believing fanatical parents are carrying out what is virtually spiritual rape.[45]

Thus the situation in the months after the 1963 AUCECB congress was even worse than it had been in 1962–63.

5 The Reformers' Challenge to the State

The question we have to ask in this chapter is whether the introduction of a new regime in the USSR after the fall of Mr.
Khrushchev had any immediate effect on the lives of the Baptists
who had been pressing for reform.

We noted at the end of the last chapter that 1964 was in-
augurated with a call for increased intensity in the anti-religious
campaign and it seemed that a firm decision had been taken to
try to extirpate religion from Soviet life once and for all. However, only a few months were left for this intensification to pass
from theory into reality before Mr. Khrushchev fell from power
in October of the same year, and his demise was followed by that
of Ilichov in March 1965. One of the questions asked at this
time both in the West and in the Soviet Union was whether these
events presaged a change in the Ilichov line on religion.

The Soviet press is of little help here. There were no articles
calling for a basic reappraisal of the existing anti-religious policies,
though there does seem to have been a temporary lull in the spate
of atheist articles in the press. *Nauka i Religia* remained the only
publication in Russian devoted solely to atheism; it changed its
format in January 1965 to take on a more popular look and its
circulation went up in conjunction with this (161,000 in January
1964, 200,000 in the same month of 1965). Its tone became
distinctly milder than it had been. According to the document
from Kiev which we print at the end of this chapter, a number of
those Baptists who had been imprisoned were released and open
repressions associated with the Khrushchev 'cult of personality'
ceased.[1] An article in a legal periodical originating from no less
a source than the Supreme Court called for a more correct interpretation of the laws on religion.[2]

This respite was only temporary, at least as far as the reform
Baptists were concerned, and after the 23rd Party Congress

(March–April 1966) the situation became much worse again.³   In
the Kremlin itself there never had been any suggestion, as far as
is known, of listing Mr. Khrushchev's policy towards religion as
one of the factors contributing to his downfall, and the basic
anti-religious policy of Soviet communism was never called in
question.   Early in 1967 the authoritative voice of *Pravda*, the
organ of the Central Committee of the CPSU, issued a call for
improvement in training atheist specialists to work in all fields of
education:

> Moreover, there are still many serious deficiencies in the training of
> atheist cadres.   The institutesof the Academies of Sciences of the
> USSR and the Union Republics fail to show proper concern over the
> formation of scientific cadres in the sphere of atheism.   The Ministry
> of Higher and Specialized Secondary Education in the USSR shows
> little concern for improving the atheist training of students or for their
> study of the principles of scientific atheism in depth.   This applies
> especially to graduates of pedagogical, agricultural and medical
> institutes, upon whom much of the responsibility rests for conducting
> atheist work, especially in rural areas.⁴

At the same time voices were now heard in public which dis-
sociated themselves from the 'administrative repression' which
had been practised under the Khrushchev regime:

> As has been said in official statements, disbanding a congregation
> does not make atheists of believers.   On the contrary, it strengthens
> the attraction of religion for people and it embitters their hearts
> besides.⁵

Nauka i Religia took up these words and showed what they
meant in a concrete situation.   The Yukhimchuk family were
Adventists living in a village near Kovel, in the Ukraine.   When
they rebuilt their house after a fire they quite legally allowed it
to be used for religious meetings in return for a loan from the
Adventist congregation to cover part of the construction costs.
However, Faddei Yukhimchuk was brought to court for building
the house with 'stolen materials', evidence was brought which
was 'an utter and complete fabrication', and he lost the case.
The author comments:

In the village the Yukhimchuks were known as an honest and hard-working family; no-one, of course, believed that they were good-for-nothings and swindlers. It was clear to all that if they hadn't been Adventists there would have been no lawsuit in the first place and no-one would have confiscated their house. In people's eyes the sectarians were right and the authorities wrong. Which won in that instance — religion or atheism? ... It was not concealed from Faddei Yukhimchuk that if he left the sect all his difficulties would immediately be at an end and his house would quickly be returned.[6]

The slogan of 'personal work with believers' had been prominent since 1957. It was a kind of atheist evangelism which was a gross invasion of the privacy of the individual. It was now elevated even higher, and was supposed to replace 'administrative measures' against religion. It was expressed in terms such as these:

The chairman of the collective farm, F. Kopkin, the Party organization and all atheists arrived at a decision: to begin a struggle against religious prejudices not by means of theoretical condemnation, but by practical action ... After such preparations they made a frontal attack and began individual visits to Baptists at their homes, on the farms and in the fields, inviting them to lectures and concerts.[7]

This theme was insisted upon during succeeding months,[8] and was eventually expressed much more strongly:

Besides the Nikolaevs' house, in Shchuchinsk and its district there are still quite a number of families into which atheist agitators must boldly penetrate and not leave the premises until the believers have forgotten the road to the church.[9]

Even so, the anti-religious press in 1965, led by *Nauka i Religia*, lost some of the overall vehemence which it had had between 1960 and 1964.

Possibly in the belief that there was hope of real success to be gained through democratic action, the leaders of the Baptist reform movement began a new phase of their work. We know much about their relations with the AUCECB at this time from the pages of *Bratsky Listok*:

'Grace to you and peace from God our Father and the Lord Jesus Christ' (Phil. 1. 2).

Thanks be to God, who through the death of his son Jesus Christ has extended his grace to us and given us salvation and eternal life!

We rejoice, beloved brothers and sisters, that in spite of circumstances which are so extremely difficult for the church, you are continuing in prayer and standing firm in all towns and villages, defending the truth of God. Your prayers and steadfastness in faith support our hands and give us approval in our service to God (Ex. 17. 11–12).

We wish to remind you likewise that both the success of the personal life of each one of us and the success of the life and ministry of the whole people of God depends solely on whether God's blessing rests with us; it will do so only when we are zealous for purity and sanctity. Be zealous for purity and the indwelling of our Lord Jesus Christ in our hearts through the Holy Spirit! Be zealous for the purity of each congregation, for the purity of the whole people of God unto his glory, and God will be with us all! (Ps. 24. 4–5). Amen.

By the grace of God we also continue to fulfil our duty towards him, trying to fulfil all that he has revealed to us by his Holy Spirit in his word.

We have to inform you, brothers and sisters, that in February of this year the Presidium of the AUCECB sent us a letter calling us to a reconciliation. In particular it said:

'In sending you this letter we wish to express our desire to meet with you and talk about the question of reconciliation and the future relations between us.'

Similar letters were sent to all communities and to many believers by the AUCECB, and all of you, obviously, are already acquainted with the contents of this letter.

To this letter of the Presidium of the AUCECB the Organizing Committee sent a written reply, the text of which we quote below:

To the Presidium of the AUCECB

'... in Christ's name, we implore you, be reconciled to God!' (2 Cor. 5. 20).

Your letter, sent on 12 February 1965 to brothers G. K. Kryuchkov, S. T. Golev, A. S. Goncharov, S. G. Dubovoi, S. Kh. Tsurkan, G. I. Maiboroda and G. P. Vins, was discussed from all points of view at a meeting of the Organizing Committee of the ECB

Church, as well as at meetings of the ministers of the ECB Church in many regions and republics, so that we might give an answer which had taken into consideration the opinion of God's people.

Since we have a quite definitely established attitude to you, the Organizing Committee considers it essential once again openly to remind you of our relationship with you in general and of the reasons and motives which underlie our position as regards reconciliation with you.

The Organizing Committee looks at you in two different ways:
1. As a central religious leadership, which you consider yourselves to be, and
2. as people with immortal souls, as you in fact are.

Considering you as a central religious leadership, the Organizing Committee has once again thoroughly studied the basic questions about which there are serious disagreements between us.

First of all we asked ourselves the following question:

What does the AUCECB show itself to be by its doctrine?

Considering this in the light of God's word, the Organizing Committee drew the conclusion that you (the AUCECB) have rejected and do not recognize the basic principles of Evangelical Christian and Baptist teaching.

It is enough merely to point to one of seven Evangelical Christian and Baptist principles, by destroying which you have been led to destroy all the others. The principle is:

'the separation (independence) of church and state.'

On the observance of this principle depends the following: will the church belong to Christ as to her one and only Head, or will it belong to the state, as a corollary to which it will cease being the church and will prostitute itself in a pact with the world (i.e. atheism)?

The teaching of the Evangelical Christians and Baptists demands the complete separation of the church from the state. It reads thus:

'We believe that the Church of Christ, unlike the state, is a kingdom not of this world (John 18. 36).

'By its very existence the church, recognizing Christ as its Head, cannot be under the authority of a secular power . . . Church and state must be independent of each other (Mat. 22. 21)'
(*Doctrine of the Evangelical Christians*, Chapter XVI).

And again:

'We believe that the powers that be are ordained of God (Rom. 13. 1–2), and that he gives them authority to protect the good and punish the evildoer (Rom. 13. 3–4).

'We therefore consider that we must needs be unconditionally subject to their laws (Rom. 13. 5–7, Titus 3. 1, I Peter 2. 13, 14, 17) on condition that these do not restrict our free observance of the duties incumbent upon us as Christians. (Mat. 22. 21, Acts 4. 19–20, 5. 29–42).'
(*Baptist Christian Doctrine*, Section VIII.)

In violation of God's word and Evangelical Baptist teaching you, as a central religious leadership, have not only completely given your-selves over to the government authorities, but you even instruct the people of God to do the same. To prove that the church must be subject to the state, you of the AUCECB often quote in your letters the words of Christ to Pilate, which are irrelevant to this case:

'Thou couldest have no power at all against me, except it were given thee from above' (John 19. 11).
(The AUCECB report of 10 September 1964.)

By this you are trying to prove that the world has been given power from above to govern the Church of Christ.

Pilate had the power to crucify Christ, but no-one has ever doubted, nor ever will, that Christ was subject to his Heavenly Father alone and did not carry out any orders opposed to his will.

Unlike Christ who never flinched before Herod and Pilate, you are crudely distorting the meaning of Christ's words in order to justify the way in which you have destroyed the principle of the church's independence.

By destroying this basic principle, you of the AUCECB have rebelled against obedience to Christ and accepted the authority of the secular state, a step which has led you to destroy all the remaining Evangelical and Baptist principle.

In order to be quite sure of this we have only to quote another very important principle adopted by our brotherhood throughout the world; it reads thus:

'Preaching the gospel or witnessing for Christ is the basic task and calling of the church.' . . .[10]

Before deciding the question of our reconciliation 'for the sake of co-ordinating our efforts', as you write in your report of 10 September 1964 (p. 2) we think it important to clarify:

Where is the AUCECB going?

in order to ascertain afterwards whether those who seek to inherit eternal life can be on the same road as the AUCECB.

And we again came to the conclusion that if we follow the path of conscious deviation from the truth, as the AUCECB is doing, then we will never inherit the Kingdom of Heaven (Is. 1. 28, Rev. 21. 8).

After a full discussion of your letter of 12 February 1965 the Organizing Committee sees that the very call to reconciliation once more proves that you yourselves not only set no value on salvation and eternal life, but through reconciliation are trying to lead us back to the path of transgression and death — to lead us who are the vigilant church and the followers of our Lord. Through this many thousands of God's people would perish.

As a result of everything set out above, the meeting of the Organizing Committee adopted the following resolution:

THE RESOLUTION OF THE ORGANIZING COMMITTEE OF THE ECB CHURCH, MADE AT ITS CONFERENCE ON THE LETTER FROM THE PRESIDIUM OF THE AUCECB OF 12 FEBRUARY 1965

Taking into consideration:

1. that despite the commandments of God's word, the AUCECB has made a close and unlawful alliance with the powers of this world (John 18. 36, Acts 4. 19, 5. 29, James 4. 4);
2. that, to please the world and contrary to the word of God, the AUCECB has deviated from the truth and rejected the basic principles of Evangelical and Baptist teaching (Gal. 1. 8–9, Titus 3. 10–11);
3. that as a result of its deviation from the truth, the AUCECB is implementing destructive activities in the ECB Church;
4. that because of such action against the church the AUCECB has been expelled by the church and that, as a religious organization, it can no longer be renovated or reformed (Mat. 7. 15–19);
5. that in such cases the word of God forbids all God's children to

H

have any communion with those expelled (Eph. 5. 11, II Cor. 6. 17);

6. that if the Organizing Committee and the AUCECB are re-united, then this reunification would only confirm the AUCECB in its apostasy and finally sever it from the possibility of repent-ance and lead it to ultimate destruction;

7. that, finally, if the reconciliation and reunification of the Organizing Committee with the AUCECB takes place, then the Organizing Committee itself, as part of the AUCECB, would be allied with the world, and in conjunction with this it would be deprived of communion with the Lord and would be subject to God's judgment (Rev. 18. 4).

The conference of the ministers of the ECB Church comprising the Organizing Committee adopted the following decision:

1. In all relations with the AUCECB to be guided by Proceedings No. 7,[11] based on the word of God and passed by the Enlarged Conference of the Organizing Committee on 23 June 1962, i.e. not to recognize that the AUCECB has the right to control the ECB Church and to consider the AUCECB ministers listed in Proceedings No. 7 and 7(a)[12] as excommunicated.

2. All conversations and conferences with the AUCECB on questions of ministry and reunification should be considered as inadmissible and contrary to the Holy Scriptures and to the will of God. With this we bear in mind God's warning:

'Woe to the rebellious children, saith the Lord, that take counsel, but not of me and who make a league but not of my spirit ...' (Is. 30. 1).

3. The question of receiving back into the church those 'ministers' of the AUCECB who have been excommunicated should be decided individually, after their sincere repentance, according to the usual conditions applicable to all those who have been excommunicated.

By this resolution we express our attitude towards you as a central religious leadership which pursues the sinful goal of corrupting the church, and at the same time we are grievously concerned for you, both as immortal souls and as people who have thrown away their salvation and eternal life.

We do not seek our own gain, as God is our witness, but as people who know what is the truth and life, we look upon you from the point of view of eternity, and for this reason we reveal our concern for your souls and call you to public repentance and reconciliation with God.

The fleeting days of your human fame will soon pass, since all the things of this world pass away, but the works of man are not erased. Each of you will stand before the judgment seat of Christ,

> 'that everyone may receive the things done in his body, according to that he hath done, whether it be good or bad' (II Cor. 5. 10).

Moreover, your life-span is short and the opportunity to repent and turn from your ways which you now have will not come to you again. Oh, take advantage of this fortunate opportunity! Come to your Advocate, Jesus Christ, who is able to justify you before the judgment seat of God Almighty.

God is impartial. Do not rely on having wrought great service — his ministers not only will not receive any indulgence in punishment for sin, but even 'the angels which kept not their first estate ... he hath reserved in everlasting chains under darkness unto the judgment of the great day' (Jude 1. 6).

Great was the prophet David before the face of the Lord, but when he sinned before God then he knew that he had lost all, for he understood what retribution follows sin. Therefore was he grieved and so contrite that even now his groaning and wailing in repentance are to be heard:

> 'Cast me not away from thy presence; and take not thy Holy Spirit from me' (Ps. 51. 11).

We sincerely want you to be saved, and we wish to cry out to you: Yakov Ivanovich,[13] Alexander Vasilievich[14] and all who are with you! Run to save your souls! Do not be embarrassed if the world, in whose glory you now partake, mocks you; forget all that is around you, and do not look upon each other, but run with repentance to Christ and find a refuge in the shrine of Christ's Church, for:

> 'the great day of the Lord is near, it is near and hasteth greatly ... the mighty man shall cry there bitterly!' (Zeph. 1. 14).

Oh, will you really not hear? Have you become so hard of heart, your ears so deaf that you cannot hear?

Who knows whether the Lord may be knocking at your door for the last time (Rev. 3. 20)? And so we 'pray you in Christ's stead, be ye reconciled to God' (II Cor. 5. 20).

23 March 1965.   Organizing Committee of the ECB.

Beloved brothers and sisters! We hope that after reading our reply to the AUCECB and having the wish to live honestly you will all be in complete agreement with us in this reply, for we know you under-stand that the day when we are reconciled with the AUCECB would be a day of the greatest misfortune for God's people. It would be a day when we would be deprived of the grace of God, when the false and inscrutable world would fill the hearts of many with a joy behind which the cunning serpent would be lurking, gloating over his victory in depriving ministers of communion with God.

May the Lord preserve us from this!

We know that by refusing to accept this worldly central religious leadership we may suffer many storms bearing tribulation with them, but the Lord will be with us. To walk without the Lord leads only to destruction. Therefore it is better not even to take the first step in an enterprise than to run one's race without the Lord. Moses said to the Lord:

'... if thy presence go not with me, carry us not up hence' (Ex. 33. 15).

It is better not to lay the first stone of a divine building than to build without the Lord, for

'except the Lord build the house their labour is but lost that build it' (Ps. 127. 1).

We surely know that the Lord will dwell amongst us, we believe in him, we believe in his Holy Church, in the prayers of our wives and children, in the prayers of all God's people. And we know that if we faint along the way he will bear us up in his arms (Ps. 91. 12, Is. 40. 29–31).

When the Lord has helped us to fulfil all he has vouchsafed us, to-gether with all his faithful warriors we shall lay our armour at the feet of Jesus Christ, we shall bow before him and say:

'We are unprofitable servants: we have done that which was our duty to do' (Luke 17. 10).

Then we shall cry out:

'Not unto us, O Lord, not unto us, but unto thy name give glory' (Ps. 115. 1).

For

'Thou art worthy, O Lord, to receive glory and honour and power' (Rev. 4. 11).

So, beloved in the Lord,

'Cast not away therefore your confidence which hath great recompense of reward' (Heb. 10. 35).

Praise be to the Lord and may he be with us all. Amen.[15]

The frustration of the Organizing Committee in its failure to carry their case with the AUCECB leaders is probably reflected in a document dated 14 April 1965 addressed to the highest government authorities, and in particular to Mr. Brezhnev in his capacity as president of the commission which was drafting a new constitution. The main attention of the Organizing Committee now turned away from the AUCECB leaders to the state, and a determined effort was initiated to secure reform of the legislation on religion. The authors of this impressive exercise in constitutional history were Gennadi Kryuchkov and Georgi Vins, president and secretary respectively of the Organizing Committee. They show a grasp and mastery of the subject and demonstrate that the reform movement had now moved from the sphere of narrowly ecclesiastical importance to take its place in the modern political history of the Soviet Union.

To the president of the Commission on the Constitution,
Comrade L. I. Brezhnev.

Copies to:

the Presidium of the Supreme Soviet of the USSR,

the Draft Bills Commission of the Nationalities' Council of the Supreme Soviet of the USSR,

the Draft Bills Commission of the Union Council of the Supreme
Soviet of the USSR,

the Supreme Soviet of the USSR,

the Presidium of the Supreme Court of the USSR.

'Woe unto them that decree unrighteous decrees, and that write
grievousness which they have prescribed; to turn aside the needy
from judgment and to take away the right from the poor of my
people . . . ' (Is. 10. 1–2).

In connection with the fact that at the present time a new Constitution of the USSR is being drawn up, we, Christians of the Evangelical
and Baptist faith, beg you to consider our needs as Christian citizens
and to include in the new Constitution an article which would guarantee for citizens true freedom of conscience and would serve as reliable
means of achieving a just peace, agreement and order, not only between
church and state, but also between people of different outlooks.

We are approaching you with this request not because no such
article exists at present. There is an article on freedom of conscience
in the present Constitution, but in spite of its existence we have for
several decades now not only been unable to benefit from this freedom
in practice, but have also been victims of systematic constraints and
repressions. Persecution has become hereditary — our grandfathers
were persecuted, our fathers were persecuted; now we ourselves are
persecuted and oppressed, and our children are suffering oppression
and deprivations. Such is the real situation today.

§124 of the Constitution of the USSR which coexists with all this
is unfortunately quite powerless to change the situation.

This clause is ineffective not by chance, but because it has been
intentionally made so. The clause was not like this at the start, but
after being altered twice its democratic character was weakened and
it has come down to us in a degraded and ineffective form.

A well-defined aim was in view when the wording of the article
was altered; that is, it was essential to formulate the article in such a
way that, while the right to freedom of conscience was left on paper,
in practice it should be possible through various instructions, administrative pressure and repressions to deprive believing citizens of this
right. And it must be said that in this respect the article has entirely
fulfilled its purpose.

In the history of the Soviet state there was a time when citizens enjoyed freedom of conscience.

It was first proclaimed in the Decree of the Council of People's Commissars on the 23 January 1918, 'On the Separation of Church and State'. This decree not only proclaimed freedom of conscience, but at that time also had a practical effect in its application to life, in accordance with its meaning — and this gave citizens real freedom of conscience.

One would hope that this provision for freedom of conscience was neither a mistake nor an act of excessive liberality on the part of the state; even more, one hopes it was not a democratic measure temporarily permitted in order to achieve certain aims of propaganda.

On the contrary, what was put into practical effect was contained in the promises and the programme of the Russian Social Democrats many years before the Soviet government came into being.

As early as 1904 the Social Democrats, lamenting the absence of freedom of conscience and the status of the sectarians who had no legal rights in Tsarist Russia, wrote that after the revolution the workers would be guaranteed complete freedom of conscience.

'The Russian Tsars showed no mercy on schismatics and sectarians,'

wrote the Social Democrats,

'they persecuted, tortured, drowned, executed them, they pilloried them, threw them mercilessly into prisons and dungeons and drank their blood. And so it has gone on until now, when the mentality, laws and customs of people have become less severe. No longer are sectarians and schismatics executed before the very eyes of the people. Now they are merely put on trial, arrested, exiled, imprisoned.

Sectarians are now banished . . . and fined, . . . their children . . . are taken away from them and they are mocked in every possible way . . .

Soon the day will come, and is indeed already near, when all people will have the right to believe in what they want, observe whatever religion they prefer. The day will come . . . when the church will be entirely separated from the state. Everyone will have the right to meet freely, to speak freely and everywhere to propagate whatever views he likes. Everyone will have the right freely to print and disseminate whatever he wishes anywhere in the world.

. . . Sectarians! the hour of freedom is at hand and it is drawing nearer.'

(V. D. Bonch-Bruevich, *Selected Works*, Vol. I, pp. 197–98, Moscow, 1959.)

In 1903 V. I. Lenin wrote in a brochure, *On Rural Poverty*:

'The Social Democrats go on to demand that each individual should have the full right to confess any creed whatever quite openly . . . In Russia . . . there still remain disgraceful laws against people who do not hold the Orthodox creed, against schismatics, sectarians, Jews. These laws either forbid the existence of such a faith or forbid its propagation . . . All these laws are most unjust and oppressive, they are imposed by force alone. Everyone should have the right not only to believe what he likes but also to propagate whatever faith he likes . . . No civil-servant should even have the right to ask anyone a single question about his beliefs: this is a matter of conscience and no-one has the right to interfere.'
(V. I. Lenin. Vol. 6, pp. 325–92.)

The demand for freedom of conscience was included in the 1903 programme of the second Russian Social Democratic Workers' Party congress, in which it is stated in particular that the Constitution of the Soviet Union must guarantee the following:

§5. Complete freedom of conscience, speech, press and assembly.
§7. Complete equality of rights for every citizen, regardless of sex, religion, race or nationality.
§13. The separation of church and state.
      (*The CPSU in its Resolutions*, Part I, Moscow 1954, pp. 40–41.)

From the above quotations it may be seen that the whole question of conscience revolves around two basic propositions:

1. The right of each citizen freely to propagate his beliefs, and
2. The right of the church to be separate from the state.

As of rural poverty, so of the urban intelligentsia; everyone understood that, regardless of how the law on freedom of conscience should be formulated, these two propositions should be its basis and should penetrate the whole legislation like a golden thread.

This was why, after these demands and promises on the programme, the Decree of 23 January 1918 announced:

'Every citizen may confess any religion . . .'

The words 'confess a religion' signify:

'openly to proclaim one's religious convictions, openly to witness to one's faith.'

This is why §13 (on freedom of conscience) based on the decree and the first Soviet Constitution of 10 July 1918, proclaimed:

'In order to guarantee complete freedom of conscience for the workers, the church is separated from the state and the school from the church; the right to religious and anti-religious propaganda is recognized for all citizens.'

It would appear that this article, which openly set forth complete freedom of conscience and democracy, should have been unshakable.

However, if in time it had to be altered, then the change should have been one of enlargement only, and in no circumstances of limitation on freedom of conscience.

In fact, to change an article in the direction of restriction on citizens' rights entails betrayal of all one's pronouncements, of all one's promises and of one's programme. This means deceiving the people. Yet this has actually happened! The above article did not remain in force for long.

In order to carry out the intention of an administrative and physical struggle to destroy religion and the church, on 8 April 1929 a special resolution was passed by the All-Union Central Executive Committee and the Council of People's Commissars, 'Concerning religious societies', which aimed at reducing freedom of religion to nothing. This resolution should have given a concrete juridical interpretation to the Decree and the Constitution, it should have been based on them, as well as upon the supreme legislative acts. However, it deprived citizens of the possibility of enjoying the right to freedom of conscience.

Thus in its §7 this resolution gave all registering bodies the right arbitrarily to refuse to register religious societies, while according to §4, religious societies are not allowed to function without being registered.

According to §12 of this resolution, meetings of the society and of groups of believers can take place only with the permission of the relevant state authorities.

§14 gives the registering bodies the right to dismiss members of the executive body without stating a reason, and this gives them the right to appoint executive bodies of communities in their place, as they see fit.

All this contradicts the principle of the separation of church and state. This resolution gives government organs the right in certain cases to declare a place of worship to be subject to demolition without obliging them to provide an equivalent one in its stead ...

There are a number of other such restrictions. It is quite understandable that the article on freedom of conscience in the first Constitution should have presented a serious obstacle in the way of this resolution. So it became necessary to change the article of the Constitution. Only 40 days later, that is on 18 May 1929, the article of the Constitution on freedom of conscience was altered, after which the article read thus:

> 'In order to guarantee true freedom of conscience for workers, the church is separated from the state and the school from the church, while all citizens are recognized as having the right both of religious confession and of anti-religious propaganda.'

But even this version did not remain unchanged for long and after a second amendment §124 as it is now in force reads thus:

> 'In order to guarantee freedom of conscience for all citizens, the church in the USSR has been separated from the state and the school from the church. The freedom to hold religious services and the freedom of anti-religious propaganda is acknowledged to all citizens.'

Those who have not suffered or experienced the consequences of such amendments of the article will say:

> '§124 is not so bad, you know. It guarantees freedom, in spite of having been amended.'

But what is really behind the emendation of the article and with what aim was it altered? A tree is known by its fruits and from the results of the emendation one can see the sort of rod arming the hand which brought about this change. It is quite clear that if after the amendment to the article in 1929 there followed the first horrors of the 30's, then after the amendment of 1936 there followed 1937, the infamous year which has gone down for ever in history as a year when unheard-of repression and arbitrariness reached their culmination.

Now the present §124 does not correspond to the Universal Declaration of Human Rights, adopted by the General Assembly of the U.N. on 10 December 1948, and signed by the governments of the world, including ours. This declaration proclaimed the basic rights of the

individual and in particular the right of each to freedom of conscience.
The declaration reads thus:

Article 18:

'Every man has the right to freedom of thought, conscience and
religion; this right includes the freedom to confess one's religion or
convictions either . . . individually or collectively, both publicly
and privately in teaching, at worship and in the observance of
religious rites and rituals.'

Article 19:

'Every man has the right to freedom of conviction and to express
this freely; this right includes the freedom to uphold one's convictions without hindrance and the freedom to look for, receive and
propagate information and ideas by any means and independently
of all national frontiers.'

§124 of the Constitution does not even correspond to the convention, 'Concerning the struggle against discrimination in the field of
education', adopted by the U.N. in 1960, so that by not providing for
the right to engage in religious propaganda, §124 gives grounds to
atheists to prevent believers bringing their children up in the religious
tradition, whilst the above-mentioned convention states:

Article 5:

'Parents . . . should have the opportunity to . . . guarantee the
religious and moral upbringing of their children in accordance with
their own convictions.'

The present convention became effective in the USSR on 1 November 1962 (*Vedomosti Verkhovnovo Soveta SSSR* ('Gazette of the Supreme
Soviet of the USSR') No. 44 (113), Article 452, p. 1047).

The apparently insignificant amendment to the article enabled a
programme of mass repression to be practically applied. The outcome was the death of thousands of believers. They died in thousands
in prisons and concentration camps. Their children, wives and relations waited in vain for them and do not even know where they have
been laid to rest. The Lord God alone knows where are the mass
graves of our brothers.

Can we now say that all these nightmares are now behind us? No!
Such criminal activity has not yet ended! It still continues. And here
is living proof of this: at this moment, as you read our letter, many

hundreds of believers have been illegally deprived of their freedom, they are in prison, in concentration camps and in exile, while some have died a martyr's death; the children of believers have been taken from them, thousands of ECB communities have no legal status, their meetings take place in private houses, where there is only room for 25–30 per cent of the members of the congregation; moreover, even in these conditions, believers cannot gather in peace, because often these meetings of the faithful are dispersed by the regular and auxiliary police and the houses are confiscated.

All this gives evidence that this criminal activity has not come to an end! But it can and must be stopped!

And we consider that this must be done at once. Now that a new Constitution is being drafted, what moment could be more opportune for bringing to an end injustice and illegality towards Christian citizens?

We address ourselves to you, as you have the right of initiating legislation, and in the name of all ECB citizens we beg you:

1. to re-establish the meaning of the decree 'Concerning the separation of church and state' and its previous objective interpretation (in its practical application);
2. to repeal the resolution of the All-Union Central Executive Committee and Council of People's Commissars made on 8 April 1929, 'Concerning religious societies', because it contradicts the spirit and letter of the basic legislation of the decree, and also to annul all instructions and resolutions which contradict the decree;
3. to give maximum clarity and precision of formulation to the article on freedom of conscience in the Constitution now being worked out by you, so that the clause contains a guarantee of true freedom of conscience, i.e. to include freedom of religious propaganda, without which there can be no question of true freedom of conscience.

Today the fate and future well-being of hundreds of millions of people lie in your hands. The new Constitution must show whether the government of our country will take up a position of freedom, equality and brotherhood towards believers and the church, or whether as before, it will follow the road of arbitrariness and force, which lead not to well-being but to retribution from the Lord which will weigh heavily on the people.

As people who have themselves experienced the full position of believers who have no rights, and as people who have been appointed by God as witnesses to the world, we are obliged to say to you that as rulers you are guilty before God not of breaking the canons of the church, but of breaking the natural laws of truth, freedom, equality and brotherhood. Therefore we consider that by addressing ourselves to you in this letter, we have openly and honestly fulfilled our duty before God and before you.

Accept our sincere wishes for success in establishing justice by embodying it in the relevant principles of the new Constitution.

With respect and by the request of the Christian citizens of the Evangelical and Baptist faith,

> Chairman of the Organizing Committee of the ECB Church, G. K. Kryuchkov;
>
> Secretary of the Organizing Committee of the ECB Church, G. P. Vins.

14 April 1965.[16]

When no satisfactory answer to this letter was received, the Organizing Committee held a further conference. One of its aims seems to have been to finalize the break with the AUCECB in name as well as in fact — in other words to set up a rival organization claiming to be fully representative of the ECB Church of the USSR:

> Finally, an All-Union Conference of the followers of Prokofiev was held on 18 19 September 1965 in Moscow, where a new Baptist sect was established, namely the 'Council of Churches of the Evangelical Christians and Baptists' (CCECB). In December 1965 the CCECB began to circulate its statutes.[17]

In connection with this new move there was an intensification in the activities of the reformers. An *Izvestia* correspondent described the course of events in these terms:

> For some time now certain petitioners have been appearing in the reception rooms of offices in the provinces, in the capitals of the republics and even in Moscow. They call themselves Baptists, but they emphasize at once that the present Baptist Church 'does not conform to Christ's teachings' and that they are now in schism with it.

These petitioners behave in an aggressive manner, at times clearly trying to provoke those around them. The petitions they hand over to the officials contain illegal demands (not requests, but demands!). They are built around two points.

Firstly, they request that their so-called 'Organizing Committee' should be permitted to call an All-Union Baptist Congress which would remove the present leadership of the community and replace it by that of the Organizing Committee. Secondly, they ask that there should be no more interference by school and state authorities in the upbringing of believers' children.

It was with such a petition that they approached the Council for Religious Affairs and other official bodies. Everywhere they received the patient explanation that calling a congress of believers was an internal affair of the religious communities, since church and state are separated in our country. It would be illegal for the state authorities to suggest to the present leadership of the ECB Union that a conference should be called and it would be even more illegal to issue instructions about which leaders should be removed and whom put in their places.

It was also explained that we have a law on universal compulsory education; every child must receive a secular education, regardless of its parents' own convictions.

When the more literate of the petitioners are asked why they are not satisfied with the leadership of the Baptist community, they answer more or less in terms like these: 'We recognize only the laws of God, whereas the present Baptist leaders recognize earthly laws as well.'

This, then, is the substance of the matter. The people who are behind these petitioners do not want to recognize the laws of the Soviet state and do not wish to take into account the fact that sectarians are not only believers, but also Soviet citizens. Our laws protect the rights of believers, and also the freedom of their confession of faith. However, the law obliges believers as well as atheists to carry out their duties as citizens, as stipulated in the Constitution of the USSR, and to observe Soviet laws. Essentially, the leaders of the Organizing Committee are acting against the law, but they do recognize some laws, however. They regularly receive their pensions and are glad to accept paid holidays and other benefits of our society, against the establishment of which they protest.

The petitioners are instructed to demand satisfaction for their illegal demands by every possible means, even to the extent of creating an uproar. Their leaders convince them that this is a 'struggle for the true faith'. Usually, however, the petitioners themselves have only a poor understanding of the subtleties of their requests. Their leaders simply prepare them to 'stand up for their faith' and to 'endure hardships' for it. For this they travel to provincial centres and to the capital.

Recently I had an opportunity to talk with two such petitioners. What were they defending so stubbornly?

Anna Fyodorovna Istratova works in a Tula factory as a charwoman, she is 52 and unmarried. She left her job and in obedience to instructions from her sectarian leaders she came with a petition. Istratova had only the vaguest idea of what was written in it: 'I am concerned that the others, the registered Baptists, shouldn't oppress us, because there is no truth in them.'

Akim Ivanovich Bobylev (aged 62 and receiving a very good pension) travelled from the Bryansk region fully convinced that his objective was to effect the registration of his congregation with the representative of the Council for Religious Affairs. He was most surprised when it became clear that he was petitioning for just the opposite — for the abolition of the sect's legal mode of existence.

Behind these generally backward and shamelessly deceived people there is a group of adventurers, composed of members of the Organizing Committee, who are trying to seize power over the Baptist community and lay hands on its money. This group is led by a certain Gennadi Kryuchkov and Georgi Vins. These two brief the petitioners and control them from their hiding-places, urging them to come forward as though they were acting 'in the name of the people'. In fact they have no right to speak even in the name of the Baptist community, since they have managed to deceive and carry with them less than 5 per cent of all Baptists.

Having suffered defeat inside the community, members of the Organizing Committee have developed turbulent underground activities. Supporters have been recruited by deceit and have been incited to impudent and provocative acts. Now they need 'victims of persecution' and 'martyrs for the faith', so as to fan into flames the cooling interest which believers are showing in them.[18]

We read of such delegations from *Bratsky Listok*, too, and learn that they began as early as May 1965:

We bring to your notice that on 25–26 May 1965 Brothers G. K.

Kryuchkov, G. P. Vins and N. G. Baturin visited the reception room of the Presidium of the Supreme Soviet of the USSR. Here they again presented a request that a delegation of the Organizing Committee of the ECB Church should be received by the Chairman of the Presidium, A. I. Mikoyan, in order to discuss the factual position of the ECB Church in the USSR and the decision to convene an All-Union ECB Congress ...

Independently of the above-mentioned delegation of the Organizing Committee, at the beginning of 1966 there was in Moscow a delegation of 26 people from among those brothers and sisters who had just been released from prison and exile. The Lord moved them, in accordance with his teaching to lay down one's life for one's friends, to address an appeal to the Procuracy of the USSR and to other government bodies for the release of the other brothers and sisters who were still in prison and for the full rehabilitation of all ECB believers who had been sentenced; also they petitioned for the cessation of the local persecution of believers and for permission to call a congress under the leadership of the Organizing Committee.[19]

Another such deputation eventually did achieve an interview:

In September 1965 Mr. Mikoyan received a delegation from our church and the promise was made that our complaints would be investigated, but after this the position for believers did not at all improve.[20]

There is full official confirmation for this interview:

More than once the leaders of the Organizing Committee of the 'Council of Churches' have been refused legal recognition for their organization, and they have not been granted permission to hold an All-Union ECB Congress. It has been made clear to them that it is for believers themselves to solve their leadership problems ... This was the answer given to supporters of the Organizing Committee when they were received by the highest authority of state, the Presidium of the Supreme Soviet of the USSR, in September 1965. Always at the same time the leaders of the Organizing Committee have been warned about their responsibility for the continuation of anti-social and illegal activity.[21]

As the demands of the reformers were still not met, the scale of such demonstrations increased. There was considerable activity in Moscow in May 1966, and we have abundant evidence about this from various sources. News about it reached the West extremely quickly, because foreign correspondents reported on what was happening. *The Times*, for example, quoted a Reuter report describing the events of 22 May:

A group of break-away Baptists held a quiet demonstration outside Communist Party headquarters here to demand recognition of their split from the officially-recognized Baptist Church, it is reported. Some members sat on the pavement and asked to see Mr. Brezhnev, the Party leader.[22]

Nauka i Religia seems to refer to a more impressive occasion, but despite its inflammatory tone no additional evidence is adduced to disprove Reuter's statement that it was a quiet sit-down demonstration:

Despite all this, self-appointed representatives of the Action Group started to assemble large gatherings of believers and send them to Moscow, in order to put pressure on government bodies for the satisfaction of their illegal demands. The last instance of such a group visit to Moscow by supporters of the Organizing Committee of the 'Council of Churches' led to a gross violation of public order right at the entrance to a government building. The arm of the law had to take appropriate measures to re-establish order.[23]

Fortunately, fuller information about these events is available from supporters of the reform movement and it fully corroborates what we have said about their peaceful nature. It would also seem that the Reuter account printed above was merely of one incident in a series of demonstrations which occurred when the petitioners assembled in Moscow:

On 16 May 1966 a delegation of about 500 from many parts of the country, having continued in prayer and fasting, came to Moscow in order to gain an interview with the head of the Communist Party, L. I. Brezhnev, and review the problem of Christian persecution in our country, as in the USSR conditions of life for believers had become intolerable. The delegates handed over an application from all our brotherhood to the Central Committee of the CPSU. The application contained a request for permission to hold a free All-Union ECB

Congress (both of registered and of unregistered communities); it requested that the CCECB, the organization actually controlling many Evangelical and Baptist communities, should be officially recognized, that repression and persecution of believers should cease, that those imprisoned for their faith in Jesus Christ should be liberated, that citizens should have the right to teach and be taught religion and that atheist interference in church affairs should be stopped. Rumours being circulated that this application contained a request that believers should be excused military service are untrue.

However, the meeting with the head of the ruling Party never took place. The delegates were not received. They waited in vain all day long at the main entrance. They spent the night in the open in the court-yard of the Central Committee building, as they had nowhere to go and sleep and anyway it would have been dangerous: separated one from the other they could have been caught and arrested. The next morning yet more believers from the Moscow church came to the Central Committee building (in all there were about 600 people). Soldiers, police and KGB detachments arrived to disperse the believers. Around mid-day a government representative announced that ten leaders could be received and he ordered the remainder to disperse to their homes. After a wait of one and a half days, such an announce-ment seemed suspicious (all the more so because the KGB had for several months been hunting for the leaders of the sect). The believers therefore announced, 'We shall quietly wait for our brothers here by the building'. They prayed in the square in front of the building, encircled by a ring of auxiliary police. A great crowd of people gathered. The authorities drove up buses and forcibly tried to put the believers into them. The latter took each others' arms and formed a human chain — but of course no-one actively resisted. 'For the Evangelical faith' — these were the words of the hymn which could be heard all over the square. The believers also sang:

'The best days of our life, the radiant strength of our young spring we shall dedicate to Jesus . . . Many perish in sin, but we shall bring them the good news.'

A detachment of people in civilian clothes pushed the believers into buses, hitting them with their fists. So passed the day of 17 May 1966, somewhat reminiscent of 'Bloody Sunday' (9 January 1905).

The believers were taken into the courtyard of the police stables, surrounded by walls. There they held a service — they sang, read the word of God, and read poetry aloud. This was a thanksgiving service offered as a witness to the police detachments standing in the courtyard. The believers were then put into different prisons. Some were allowed to go the next day after questioning, some were sentenced to ten or fifteen days in prison, and then freed.[24]

Another account confirming these events in Moscow is provided by a document originating from Kiev which goes on to tell us what happened to supporters of the reform movement in the Ukraine shortly after the first demonstration in Moscow and on the same day as the one reported by Reuter.

APPEAL

On 16 May this year an all-union delegation of the ECB Churches gathered outside the building of the Central Committee of the CPSU. It represented more than 130 towns of the Soviet Union and consisted of more than 500 people, of whom eleven were emissaries of the Kiev congregation.

Believers of the Soviet Union were compelled to send their representatives directly to Moscow because of the fact that for five years the government has entirely groundlessly been refusing ECB believers the legal right to avail themselves of the opportunity to call and conduct a free democratic congress with a wide representation. For several decades the ECB Churches, under the leadership of the initiators of the movement for this congress (the CCECB), have been deprived of their rights of resolving these internal church questions. This has happened with the knowledge and on the instructions of the central government authorities. This is testified by these facts: systematic repressions, assaults, arrests, trials, searches, destruction and confiscation of prayer houses, removal of children, breaking up of services, discrimination against believers in factories and educational institutions, the incitement of public opinion against believers by false and libellous concoctions in the press, etc.

And all these illegalities were for the first time rendered openly legal by the Presidiums of the Supreme Soviets of the Republics in March this year[25] and approved by the 23rd congress of the CPSU. This did not occur even during the time of the cult of personality.[26]

Instead of receiving and hearing out the requests of the churches' delegates, who for a number of days remained in the open and out in the rain on the tarmac beside the Central Committee building, the latter body of the CPSU, under the command of Comrade Semichastny, Chairman of the Committee of State Security, gave orders for KGB officials, soldiers and police to surround the delegation of believers on 17 May this year and brutally assault them. They tore their clothes, beat their heads against a wall and on the tarmac, suffocated them, hit them over the heads with bottles, etc. All this happened before the eyes of a large number of people who had assembled. Then the delegation was arrested, including the representatives of the Kiev congregation, and they were sent off to the Lefortov prison in Moscow. Some of them returned home, but the fate of most members of the delegation, including seven of our men, is not known.

This violence at the Central Committee building set the tone for other similar actions by local authorities, of which a clear example was the pogrom carried out against the Kiev ECB congregation.

On Sunday 22 May this year, the Kiev ECB congregation was holding its usual regular service in the wood by the junction to the Darnitsa railway carriage repair factory. The Kiev congregation has been gathering at this place for three years during the spring and summer season, and the local and central authorities had been informed about this each year. The unusualness of the choice of place to meet is connected with the fact that the private houses and flats of believers cannot accommodate all the 400 who wish to attend, and our places of worship at 53 Lenin Street and 104 Zhelyanskaya Street were confiscated during the years of the personality cult. We cannot at present meet at the registered place of worship at 70 Yamskaya Street, because of the way in which the principle of the separation of church and state is broken there.

From the very beginning of this service believers were surrounded by the KGB, regular and auxiliary police who had come there in special cars and buses; their total exceeded the number of believers who had assembled. Without giving an opportunity for the concluding prayer to be pronounced, Major-General Degtyarev of the MVD and leader of this operation gave the signal for all the KGB and police forces organized for the reprisals to launch themselves at the believers from the thick of the forest. They carried out a similar assault on them to that which had been meted out to the delegation in Moscow. The sadists, both uniformed and ununiformed, indiscriminately beat not only men, but also women, children and old women, tore their hair, threw them to the ground, kicked and punched them, trying to drive off the believers into the depths of the forest away from the railway platform, and thus prevent witnesses from observing their criminal and foul conduct. They struck our fellow-Christian, Daniil Titov, until he lost consciousness and in that state they threw him into a car. They wrenched the arms of other people, throwing them into the cars and beating them. Electric trains were stopped until this shameful 'operation' had ended. The arrests similarly continued on the platform, and altogether about 30 people were arrested.

The scale of this shameful and illegal reprisal can be gauged from the fact that the central station at Kiev, to which the believers who remained after the pogrom returned, was cordoned off by an operational police regiment which had been mobilized by an alarm signal, several military cars and hundreds of auxiliary police and KGB men. This was a precaution taken in case they had not been successful in bringing the reprisal to a conclusion in the woods. The day after these events (23 May) the believers decided to go to the Procurator of the Republic with a complaint. However, the believers were not permitted access to the Procuracy building, let alone to the Procurator himself. The entrance to the building was blocked by policemen and the adjacent sector of Kiev was cordoned off by a great number of auxiliary police and KGB men. Because of this the believers had to return and assemble at the flat of their fellow-Christian, G. S. Magel, in order to pray.

When literally only fifteen minutes had elapsed after the believers had assembled, dozens of cars drew up to the flat, led by the same Major-General Degtyarev. They began to take out the believers in groups from the flat, they photographed them, took down their names and took them away in special cars to preparatory detention cells.

A large crowd of people assembled to witness what occurred. With the aim of lending a façade of legality to their illegal actions, and also to arouse in people hatred and anger against believers, the leader of this degrading operation, the above-mentioned Major-General, appealed to the people in a provocative and libellous speech in which he depicted believers as criminals against the state, debauchees, thieves, drunkards and murderers. In his speech he brought up instances of rape and child murder which were well-known to the whole town and he created the impression on people that all this lay at the hands of believers. In conclusion and without any logic he pronounced these words:

'Citizens, protect your children, for statistics show that recently juvenile delinquency has been on the increase.'

It is clear from the speech what this man and the people invested with legal authority are capable of doing, for it is they who gave the orders to carry out this unprecedented reprisal.

As a result of this vile operation about 100 believers were arrested in two days. The majority of them were sentenced to fifteen days in prison, some of them were fined 50 roubles and have already been released. Among those fined most were old women dependent on relatives or receiving a pension of about 20 roubles a month.

On release the believers were threatened with being fined until they stopped praying.

But this was not the end of the illegalities. According to the testimony of our fellow-believers who have already been released, it has become known to us that in the course of interrogating some believers torture was used. It is known that criminal proceedings are being hurriedly concocted against some believers.

Moreover, the Kiev KGB has now set up secret but obvious monitoring of believers' homes and shadowing of their movements. There has even been direct pursuit of individual believers.

Representatives of the Kiev authorities and Comrade Sikhonin, an official of the Council on Religious Affairs, declared that all these moral, economic and physical measures would continue until believers stop believing in God, go over to the congregations which acknowledge the AUCECB or become Orthodox converts.

All this is not happening in some underdeveloped colonial country, and not under a fascist regime, but in a country where it has already been proclaimed to all the world for fifty years that the most just, democratic and humanitarian society has been built, and that there is equality of all people, irrespective of race and creed.

But from all that has been set out above it is evident that all these declarations and slogans are only a sham calculated to deceive the people and world opinion. In fact it is completely clear that the CPSU, as a party of atheists, has adopted the direct course of creating in our country such conditions for believers that they cannot even live, let alone confess their faith. The course has been adopted of physically exterminating believers.

This course was not overtly proclaimed before the 23rd Congress of the CPSU and open facts of repression were condemned and ceased after the unmasking of the cult of personality. Evidence of this is found in the rehabilitation of many of our fellow-believers who had been condemned for their faith in God in the 1961–64 period and also in the exposition of the correct interpretation and application of the laws on the cults which the bench of the Supreme Court wrote in the journal, *Sovetskoye Gosudarstvo i Pravo*[27] ('The Soviet State and Law'). Since the 23rd Congress this course has been openly proclaimed and the work of 're-educating' believers by force has been conducted centrally and in a calculated, organized way.

All these acts which are being put into effect in our country at this time are quite simply a very grave crime against humanity. They are genocide.

For the two thousand years of its history the Church of Christ has endured many and various cruel tribulations, but despite all the efforts of persecutors, Christians still exist and will exist on earth until Christ's second coming. Not one weapon or means used against them shall be successful (Is. 54. 17).

History has branded with shame the names of those who have persecuted Christians in all centuries, and God's wrath and punishment have justly descended upon the countries in which Christians have been persecuted. Neither will God's chastising hand pass by any of the persecutors of the 20th century.

'Seeing it is a rightous thing with God to recompense tribulation to them that trouble you; . . . in flaming fire taking vengeance on them that know not God, and that obey not the gospel of our Lord Jesus Christ: who shall be punished with everlasting destruction from the presence of the Lord, and from the glory of his power' (II Thes. 1. 6, 8–9).

But we who believe in the living God are ready to suffer and to sacrifice all in this world — even life itself — rather than renounce our firm faith in Christ's teachings.

We also believe that Almighty God can save his church from the strongest and most malicious persecutors, but if this were not so, then

'Be it known unto thee, O King, that we will not serve thy gods, nor worship the golden image which thou hast set up' (Dan. 3. 18).

As citizens of our country, however, we who are undergoing all these excessive and unceasing persecutions bear ourselves towards you with respect, as to rulers ordained by God to govern the people entrusted to you in a just and humanitarian way.

But taking into consideration that you, as immortal souls, must inevitably give an account of your rule before Almighty God, as an impartial and just judge, and also considering that nations or a people who allow persecution of those who believe in God have always experienced God's punishment, we believers of the Kiev ECB congregation suggest that you should follow the path of reason and justice for the sake of your own good and the good of our people.

We make the firm request that:

1. Freedom of confession should be guaranteed in practice, in accordance with the laws and international acts accepted by the government of our country.
2. Permission should be given for the calling of a free congress of the ECB Church. It should be held under the leadership of the Council of Churches of the ECB (the Organizing Committee).
3. All believers who have been arrested in Kiev should at once be freed; the fabrication of criminal proceedings against them should cease and the imposition of fines for attending worship should stop immediately.
4. Members of the all-union ECB delegation arrested outside the reception room of the Central Committee of the CPSU on 17 May this year should be immediately released.
5. All those who have been condemned for the word of God in recent years should be freed.

The Kiev ECB congregation sends its respects to you.

In the name of the congregation of about 400 members, 116 signed.

24 May 1966.[28]

The reprisals against the Kiev ECB congregation brought a glare of publicity to focus on the most recent Soviet policy towards the reform movement. There now came a spate of articles in the Soviet press which showed that these measures were not confined to any one area, but were being taken on a national scale. Yet the tenor of the Kiev document demonstrates that the ECB believers were still hoping to put their case openly before the government, and despite the physical provocations against them they still refused to call their followers to rebel against the Soviet regime.

6 The Reform Movement as seen in the Soviet Press

In the last chapter we built up a picture of the activities of the Organizing Committee in the post-Khrushchev period, relying mainly on material written by its members and sometimes circulated in the USSR in mimeographed form. Now we take our account further by using our other principal source, the recent Soviet press. The sole reason for the publication of these articles, it must be borne in mind, is to blacken the reform movement and falsely accuse its leaders of fostering an anti-Soviet campaign, yet the detail with which these Baptist activities are sometimes revealed is astounding. We are often able to discern the truth quite clearly behind the atheist 'interpretation' of it. Throughout this chapter the Kiev document printed at the end of the last chapter should be used as a yardstick against which to judge the Soviet version of recent developments.

Whereas the original intention of the Action Group and of the Organizing Committee had been to reform the AUCECB, the Council of Churches of the Evangelical Christians and Baptists constituted in September 1965 at once announced its presence by stepping up its evangelistic campaign. The huge geographical area covered by its influence is remarkable, with Central Asia and the Ukraine being mentioned again and again. Activities have been recorded at Frunze,[1] Karaganda,[2] Tashkent[3] and Sokuluk[4] in Central Asia, at Krivoi Rog,[5] Kiev,[6] Lvov,[7] Zaporozhie[8] and Lugansk[9] in the Ukraine. Other republics affected are Azerbaijan,[10] Georgia,[11] Estonia[12] and Moldavia.[13] In the RSFSR activities have been widespread: Cheboksary,[14] Ryazan,[15] Mtsensk,[16] the Polar regions[17] and, in the extreme south, Rostov-on-Don, which was the centre for a mass evangelistic campaign affecting the surrounding areas.[18]

The intense zeal of the CCECB in spreading the gospel is even more remarkable than the geographical distribution of the areas it has influenced. It almost seems to reflect a spirit of elation at throwing off the shackles imposed by the restraining influences of the AUCECB.

The spearhead of the whole programme was undoubtedly the determination of the reformers to guarantee and expand religious education for children whose parents desired it. They pressed ahead with this resolve, despite the increasing likelihood of being persecuted for doing so under Article 227 or, after March 1966, under Article 142, which was specifically amended to prevent the organization of Sunday schools.[19] Every one of the seventeen major articles which appeared on the reformers' activities in the Soviet press in 1966 mentions religious education and more space is devoted to it than to any other aspect of the movement. *Komsomolskaya Pravda*, the youth newspaper, summed up the situation in these words:

Recently in the Adventist, Pentecostal and especially the Baptist church there have appeared advocates of a 'universal system' of religious education. In the opinion of these people there is a legal provision for the religious education of children. They are demanding that special religious schools should be created and that the catechism should be introduced into the Soviet school curriculum.[20]

This is what was happening at Sokuluk, in Kirgizia:

Grossly violating Soviet law, Yelena Chernetskaya and Maria Braun created an illegal religious school for children of infant and junior age ...

At the trial Vera Kudashkina, a girl in the tenth class of the Novo-Pavlov school, stated: 'I once met Yelena Chernetskaya with a group of children from our school at the bus station in the town. She was treating them liberally to ice-cream.'

A. I. Reshetova, the headmistress of the Novo-Pavlov secondary school, recounted: 'In order to dispose children favourably to her and to entice them into a religious school, Chernetskaya organized games for them and took them on excursions. Then she distributed to the children note-pads which had a drawing of a flower imprinted on them — a kind of conventional sign of the sect. Beside the flower an oath was reproduced: "I will sing to the Lord all my life, I will sing to my God while there is breath in me". '

In 1964 Chernetskaya and her confederates managed to attract over 80 children of pre-school and school age into a religious class. The 'Sunday school', as it was called, was organized according to a definite routine and principles. The children were divided into age-groups in which a strict attendance register was kept. Lessons took place in various believers' houses. Usually they began with a prayer from Yelena Chernetskaya, Maria Braun and Yevgeni Shmidt, the group-leaders. Then the children learnt songs which extolled the 'next world' and depicted life on this earth in a completely hopeless light. This would alternate with the recounting of biblical legends and invariably for homework they were set to learn poetry or a prayer.[21]

At Cheboksary the picture is not much different:

The teachers arrived at Nikita Vasiliev's house on Sunday. The activities of the 'circle' were in full swing. The children were sitting at a table learning prayers and psalms under the direction of Nina Bykova. A Bible was lying open on the table and in front of every child was an exercise book or a pad into which he was copying out 'texts'.[22]

In Baku seven members of the 'youth corps' of the illegal Baptist church were named, and it was noted that they were intelligent children old enough to think for themselves.[23] In Rostov-on-Don there is a special 'children's congregation' for catechism instruction.[24]

As well as Bible classes the children are given plenty else to occupy them:

Out-of-town excursions are specially timed for 1 and 9 May and 7 November . . . During these 'excursions' there are sermons in which (it goes without saying) there isn't a word about national holidays and everything dear to Soviet people is called 'of the devil'.[25]

Among other activities, there are 'sewing classes' in which children embroider 'samplers with religious texts',[26] but by far the most popular activity of all is music:

A guitar is striking up the rhythm of a slow waltz, creating an atmosphere of gloom and sadness. A girl's voice quietly starts up the song:

> On stringed instruments
> We extol him

> Who saves us from troubles and misfortune,
> Who gives life and joy to all.

Children's voices discordantly take up the refrain:

> Sing, guitar, oh sing!
> Of the wonderful works of God.
> Sing, guitar, oh sing!
> Of the wonderful teaching of Christ!

Then the children sing of how 'God created the flowers and the birds', 'My house is in the heavenly country', etc.[27]

It is interesting that even though the writer of this article attempts to depict this singing as a despondent activity, he does not refrain from quoting these words which so obviously radiate joy. Here is a further example of the part music plays:

> Then these soul-snatchers hit upon the idea of organizing their own school — specially for religious music. Here under the pretext of learning to play string instruments the children were taught psalms. The 'brothers' generously gave their pupils musical instruments. The religious imposition on the children grew and they even had to do homework which they were given at their new school. A circle of Christian adolescents aged 10–16 was formed here.[28]

All this is depicted as serving to instil hatred into the children:

> The investigator who talked to Irochka, a young Sunday school pupil, was struck by the look in the little girl's eyes when, with un-childlike hatred, she said to him: 'Unbelievers are our enemies!' The words do not belong to her. They come from her Baptist 'tutors'.[29]

These articles do not often represent the children as being any other than willing participants in what was going on, and one is reminded of the bravery of the girl at Chernogorsk who was prepared to stand up and defend her faith before the whole class.[30] A boy at Mtsensk was 'persecuted in school for his faith', according to the written testimony of his mother,[31] and here is yet another who is prepared to stand up for her beliefs:

> Lena's elder sister, who has spent all her life with Christian relatives,

obediently took off her Pioneer neckerchief and destroyed it under the influence of those at home.[32]

Certainly other children would have psychological difficulties because of the conflicting influences of home and school:

> In school he has to accept everything his teachers say. Then, at home, everything he has learnt is contradicted. Is this not the beginning of a tragedy? But the day of enlightenment will come when we shall really have to choose between life and death.[33]

This is, incidentally, the theme of the writer Vladimir Tendryakov's story, *The Miraculous Icon*.[34]

This conflict may even take a physical form:

> In April the older son, Vanya, was admitted into the Pioneer organization. Maria snatched off his neckerchief. She forbade her daughter, Lyuba, in the first class, to wear the star of the October Revolution. She then went to the school and declared that her children were believers and could not join the Pioneers and the October children's group.[35]

Some children do apparently manage to rebel against Baptist influences:

> One of the little girls begged the teacher: 'Could I come to live with you? I'd watch television and you could take me to the zoo.'[36]

Even these clearly selective reports do not manage to present any convincing picture of children struggling to follow communist ideology.

Accounts of teenagers are often more direct and give atheists cause for even greater concern. Tanya Chugunova from Baku wrote to her Aunt Nadya:

> 'I turned to the Lord on 26 November, and if it pleases him I shall be baptized.'

It did please the Lord (in the person of Pyotr Serebrennikov) and Tanya was 'received in communion' into the dark and ignorant world of the fanatics.[37]

This is by no means an isolated example:

> According to the evidence of the witnesses, the schismatics baptized about 40 young men and women in the river Don on 2 May, among

whom were Vera Prokopenko, a student at the Taganrog Medical Academy, aged seventeen, and Vera Shaverina, a student at the Rostov Institute of Civil Engineering, who is a member of the Komsomol.[38]

While school-children are taught the Baptist faith principally in the Sunday schools which operate in private houses, great attention is paid to the religious needs of teenagers at services:

Each sermon was prepared in advance and was full not only of religious themes, but also of instructions to young people that they should fight for the interest of the church and of the 'people chosen by God' against the 'followers of Satan'.[39]

All this information on the zeal of young people for their faith expands our knowledge of the number of young people associated with the reform movement gleaned from Appendix II of the Kryuchkov–Shalashov document, where the ages of prisoners are given.[40]

One atheist commentator suggests that the reformers' activities increased and took on a more political character when the schism was formalized and the name 'CCECB' was adopted:

Such provocative tactics by the Organizing Committee became most apparent in August and September 1965, when in Kiev, Lvov, Zaporozhie, Karaganda, Ryazan and other cities mass meetings and processions were organized which did not have any religious character whatsoever.[41]

There is no corroborating evidence for this, however, and the Kiev document suggests it is untrue.

Some commentators state that the increase in evangelism occurred as a reaction to a general fall in the number of believers:

It is not difficult to understand the reason why the zealous supporters of religion would like to bring children down on their knees and make them pray and sing hymns. Religious faith is dying out in our country and this is an indisputable fact. This, of course, worries the ministers of the cult, but they are even more worried about the future of the church.[42]

It need hardly be pointed out that this is a direct contradiction of most of the evidence about young people from atheist sources presented earlier in the chapter. Even if Baptists were acting decisively because they fear the extinction of the faith, what they are doing is impressive and is having considerable success, as some commentators are forced to admit. While not referring specifically to the reformers, this quotation gives testimony on the general climate:

> Meanwhile, in the village of Ivanisovo itself, besides the Orthodox church, a prayer house for Evangelical Christians and Baptists has appeared. It is true that the local sectarians can so far be counted on the fingers of one hand, while the majority are newcomers. But the Evangelical Christians have already begun to spread their network in the village.[43]

One result of the state's refusal to provide premises on which reform Baptists can meet is that much of their evangelistic effort is taking place in the open air and both the Soviet press and the reformers' own writings refer to this. The major demonstration which took place on a public holiday in Rostov-on-Don in 1966 has already been mentioned in this chapter,[44] but here is a fuller account of it:

> During the May-day celebrations (on 1 and 2 of the month) a great meeting was held at Rostov-on-Don, at which about 1,500 believers were present. Naturally they could not all fit into the small private house and so the meeting took place on the road beside it. A great many non-believers, in fact a whole crowd of them, watched the meeting and listened to the word of God. People were even sitting on the roofs of neighbouring houses and in trees. The Lord wonderfully blessed this meeting. About 80 souls repented (of whom, moreover, the majority were young people); amongst them were, apparently, 23 members of the Komsomol. The authorities were not prepared for such a meeting and could do nothing with such an enormous crowd. Many people expressed the desire to be baptized and entered the church. The next morning all the believers set off across the town to the river Don where the baptism was conducted. The police and special squads surrounded the believers on the river-bank (cars had been driven up). They wanted to arrest those brothers who had organized the meeting. All the believers knelt down and reverently prayed that God would protect his people and enable the meeting to

continue that day. Then the brothers and sisters formed a tight cordon round the church officers and gave the authorities no chance to seize them. The situation was of course very tense. A little later they all re-assembled by the house where they had first met. To the representatives of the local authorities who had appeared the brethren said that, if they would not allow the meeting to continue there, 'we'll walk round the whole town singing.' The authorities were eventually forced to agree and the meeting continued to the end without further interruption.[45]

Lest this account by a Soviet Baptist should seem exaggerated, here is another report of the type of evangelism which was being conducted at Rostov-on-Don, from no less a source than *Pravda*, the Party newspaper, itself :

Recently sectarians in our country have been exceeding all bounds. They have not only been arranging meetings in houses, but also have openly been holding forth in public places. For example, in July last year there was a group of sectarians on the suburban Azov–Rostov train who sang religious music to the accompaniment of a guitar and balalaikas. The passengers were indignant and demanded that this lawlessness should stop. But the leader of the sectarian group, a certain Kolbantsev, started to object, maintaining that the Baptist-*Initsiativniki* sect acknowledges no Soviet laws because it has its own.

Another such group under the leadership of 'God's slave' Prikhodko sang hymns on the Rostov river embankment. Yet others travelled around by boat to the towns of Azov and Volgodonsk and into the Semikarakovskaya,[46] Tsimlyanskaya and Aksaiskaya districts. There they proselytized among the local people, recruiting new supporters into their ranks.[47]

Very similar scenes have been occurring in Moldavia:

I happened to be travelling in a train from Reni to Kishinyov when I suddenly heard the sound of singing in a compartment. It was loud and harmonious and was accompanied by a guitar. It aroused my interest, and other passengers gathered to listen. It turned out that the singers (three boys and four girls, the youngest of whom was about seventeen or eighteen) were singing religious verses to the tunes of Soviet songs and romances. In one of them was repeated the refrain:

'Let us consecrate our youth to God.'

One of the passengers remarked that the singers were schismatic Baptists.

I should add that before this occasion I had twice witnessed such scenes on a train. Previously and again now I noted that these 'holy' people with guitars were behaving in a provocative manner and were singing with the obvious intent of demonstrating. The puzzled passengers shrugged their shoulders. Some moved away expressing indignation, but no-one decided to tell them off, not even the conductor. . . .

In order to kindle fanaticism among the section of believers whom they (the reformers) have deceived, they even organize demonstrations outside in the open air and in public places — on the streets, at stations, in trains and buses and even in state institutions. . . .

On the 1 May this year (1966), when the workers were celebrating their revolutionary festival, a group of schismatic Baptists from the village of Kopchak (Chadyr-Lung district) held a service as a demonstration in a clearing in a wood. A similar affair took place in the village of Zakharovka in the Orgeyev district. Many supporters of the 'Action Group' gathered at the sectarian Maria Donika's house. Wishing, as the saying goes, to preserve their innocence and at the same time to acquire capital, the organizers of this illegal gathering explained that 'the brothers and sisters had come to celebrate the name-day of Maria's little son.' But the real purpose of the name-day was to stage a meeting of sectarians to rival the workers meetings on the Great October revolutionary festival . . .

More than once you have broken the law by organizing trips on service buses through the districts of Moldavia for the Kishinyov 'Action Group' supporters, including both members of the congregation and preachers.[48]

Other republics witnessed public Baptist demonstrations of no less enthusiasm:

On the 7 and 8 November 1965 Harvest Festival (or the Day of Thanksgiving) was celebrated at Sukhumi. There was a great and blessed open-air gathering. Believers from other towns had also come. 47 young people were converted after an evangelical sermon and many other people also expressed the wish to be baptized. After being put to the test they were baptized in the Black Sea. The police arrived when all was already over and caused no special harm. . . .

K

Many thanksgiving services were also held in various places during the Victory Holiday (8 and 9 May). The meeting at Narva (Estonia) was notable. It should be mentioned that the local authorities in Estonia do not behave so barbarically towards Christians. Some ministers and preachers of the registered churches in Estonia are sincere believers. Thus the presbyter of the church in Narva does not keep entirely within the limits imposed by the atheists. He even allows schismatic brethren to preach in his church. A meeting at Narva was held on the premises of the church belonging to the registered Russian and Estonian community. The long morning service and the evening one were led by brothers Baturin and Bondarenko of the CCECB. This young, energetic brother, Iosif Bondarenko, a native of Odessa, is highly disapproved of by the authorities. He was not allowed to take his diploma at the end of his institute course. After his evangelical sermon Iosif Bondarenko turned to his listeners and asked whether any would like to receive the joy of salvation and turn to the Lord. Eighteen people, one after the other, went up to the pulpit: amongst them were two women of about forty, but the rest were very young people.[49]

Another kind of public demonstration occurred near Kiev:

About two years ago the inhabitants of Grebenka in the Vasilkov district (Kiev region) were literally shaken by the incidents which broke out at the burial of the ten year old schoolboy, Tolya V., who had been killed in an accident.

The funeral procession was moving towards the cemetery and the school orchestra was playing funeral music. In front of the coffin boys were carrying Tolya's Pioneer neckerchief[50] on a small cushion. Meanwhile, Prokofiev's supporters, on hearing that a child in the Baptist V.'s family had died, hurried from Kiev to the place where this had happened. They met the procession in the roadway. These fanatics rushed at the boys, pushed them aside, grabbed the coffin, carried it themselves as far as the cemetery, singing psalms.[51]

Congregations are kept in touch with each other by itinerant evangelists:

One of the most active leaders of the illegal Baptist group was P. D. Belenki, an engineer of the *Promventilyatsia* organization. As it came out at the trial, by the nature of his job he travelled all over the Northern Caucasus and the Donets Basin. 'Did you preach there?'

the judge asked Belenki. 'Perhaps; I gave readings,' he concurred. This zealous preacher of the Baptist faith everywhere 'combined' his work in the manufacturing industry with anti-social activity.[52]

Congregations maintain close contact with each other through personal visits in which both adults and children participate. This happened at Cheboksary:

Nonna returned home near midnight. She explained that 'guests' had come from Kazan, so the service had gone on a long time. . . . Leaders of the congregation secretly took children to Gorky, Kazan, Yoshkar-Ola and Zelenodolsk to take part in united services with the local Baptists.[53]

The close contact that these congregations keep with each other is an expression of personal concern and sympathy for others which may ultimately be a more effective tool of evangelism than the public demonstrations which we have described. This man-to-man approach is exactly what atheists have been insisting on for some time in their own efforts to wean believers away from the faith. A presbyter is speaking:

So you want to enter the kingdom of heaven? So be it. But on one condition: each believer must recruit one non-believer into our ranks.[54]

Baptists hold 'love feasts'[55] and show concern for 'those who have been unsuccessful in life and those who are lonely'.[56] They reach the outcasts of society:

They carefully follow the lives of the villagers and try to entice into their toils those who have shown weakness, got into trouble, or made a false step in their personal lives.[57]

Those who are infirm also have a special place:

They managed to play on the spot that hurt her most — Anastasia has had a limp since she was born. Her personal life was not going well and one need hardly say that this young woman found it hard to live with her disability. They gradually lured this nervous woman, who longed for affection, into the sect with their honeyed promises of 'spiritual peace' and 'blessings from above'. Finally they succeeded.[58]

The congregations belonging to the CCECB not only kept in touch with other groups in the same area; they also held 'illegal inter-provincial conferences of their supporters under the guise of prayer meetings'.[59] The Temporary Council of Prisoners' Relatives, whose activities we reviewed in Chapter 4, was only a small part of this:

> A congress of believing women and conferences of ministers of our persecuted, free church have been held in underground conditions.[60]

Undoubtedly the biggest unifying force which has continually communicated to reform Baptists in scattered areas a sense of purpose and solidarity with each other is the unbroken publishing activity which their leaders have organized ever since 1961. The initial appeal of Prokofiev and Kryuchkov for convening an AUCECB congress seems to have been widely circulated among the churches. It has certainly been frequently quoted in Soviet sources.[61] The impression received on reading the articles attacking the reformers is that since then they have released a whole flood of illegal publications which have been circulating widely among Baptist congregations. *Bratsky Listok* appeared with some regularity in 1965 at monthly or bi-monthly intervals, and the texts of several issues which have become available are quoted in this book. There have been a number of references to it in the Soviet press,[62] but they do not give any idea of its contents. We shall have occasion to refer to it again later in this chapter.[63]

There are several articles which give some idea of the amount of publishing activity undertaken by the CCECB.

> Baptists circulate illegal leaflets, the so-called *Fraternal Leaflet*; they mimeograph the draft of a new constitution for the sect and the verses of sectarian poets.[64]

This new draft constitution was circulated in December 1965, following the formal break from the AUCECB, according to *Lyudina i Svit*, the Ukrainian atheist journal,[65] but it is probably a revised version of the Prokofiev–Kryuchkov draft which we print later.[66] Some of the articles which appeared shortly after this suggest that the scale of publishing was stepped up at this time:

> In an underground printing works on the outskirts of the city the 'brothers and sisters in Christ' zealously produced hundreds of copies

of the Baptist magazines, the *Messenger of Salvation, Rules of Conduct for Children* and the *Fraternal Leaflet*.

M. F. Podyachev, a teacher at one of the Rostov institutes of higher education, familiarized himself with this literature and presented the court with his findings. He writes: 'Young people are exhorted actively to propagate religious views.' Indeed, how else can one define these words addressed to young people: 'Take hold of the sword of the spirit which is the word of God'?[67]

The fullest account of these publications is found in an article published recently in Tashkent. The authors, Yu. Kruzhilin and N. Shalamova, devote a great deal of space to quotations and commentaries from some of them and then go on to summarize the situation:

> They set up underground printing presses, a black-market undertaking with Matyukhina in charge. They print and circulate all kinds of *Messengers of Salvation, Rules of Behaviour, Bulletins for Young People, Manuscripts, Sisters' Tales,* and other writings, about the contents of which the reader will have probably gained some idea from this article.[68]

Several other publications are known by quotations from them which have appeared in the Soviet press, or simply by their titles. Those which have reached the West and form a large part of this book are undoubtedly a very small proportion of the total volume of material which has been circulating, but they are almost certainly representative enough to give us a good idea of the direction of these writings. In view of the interpretation of them made by Soviet writers, it would be useful at this point to string together a few quotations from them as they appear in official Soviet publications, while omitting as much as possible of the commentaries which have been added. Here first is the one from which we have the longest extract in an official published source, though it is only a very small proportion of the whole, which consists of 32 manuscript pages.

> The sun is 149 million kilometres from the earth, according to the calculations of astronomers. Yet it gives us light and heat. . . . If nature has created exactly what we need, then she surely knew what

we needed; therefore she thought, and is consequently a thinking being ... it follows that she is an Individual. ...

In order to water the earth the sun's rays lift up many millions of tons of water every 24 hours. The sun takes up from the earth exactly the necessary amount (neither more nor less), for if it raised too much there might be a deluge and if too little, a drought. ...

Atheism is the root of all evil and misfortune. ... It causes nothing but harm: it destroys the moral principles of the family, society and the state. ... When a man no longer sees any justice in people he becomes disillusioned with them and starts to hate them. ...[69]

Here are the quotations from Baptist writings as reported by Kruzhilin and Shalamova in the article we mentioned above:

One of these 'magazines' asks the question: 'What is the use of all this modern technical and scientific knowledge and of other cultural achievements if ... we are merely left wandering and erring at random by ourselves, only to end by coming to the horror of emptiness and purposelessness?' ...

Their *Messenger of Salvation* proclaims : 'Every wise man is powerless and before his creator is as insignificant as a worm.' ...

Now the *Messenger of Salvation* says succinctly: 'The Risen Lord wants to save us all from the captivity of dependence on the world.' Another publication echoes this: 'Every friendship with the world is spiritual depravity.' ...

'A state which gives ... unchristian commands cannot, in the eyes of a Christian, be acknowledged as a power recognized by God.' ...

These lines are composed by Khrapov : 'The Bible must squeeze out of our lives and out of our every-day surroundings all that competes with it.'[70]

The *Address to all Believing Mothers of the Evangelical and Baptist Faith in the Registered and Unregistered Congregations of the USSR* contains the words:

Let us unite in our efforts to pray that God will consecrate to his service the lives of our children from the cradle up.[71]

These latter are words which are supposed to have inspired a woman to commit ritual murder.[72]

All these quotations are most valuable. They presumably collect what is considered to be the most 'incendiary' material written by the reform Baptists, so they show that even the strongest criticism of the Soviet atheism which is expressed is not accompanied by a call to anti-Soviet activity.

As one would expect, there is very little reflection in the Soviet press of the true nature of the relations between the AUCECB and the CCECB. One article, however, gives an official version of how discontent was fomented against a presbyter who was not sufficiently zealous for the tastes of the reformers:

> The Baptists began to be displeased with A. G. Fefelov. The presbyter had become old and had begun to mutter his sermons incomprehensibly, 'without a tear'; there were fewer donations. Serebrennikov fanned the flames of this dissatisfaction as best he could. The work of a presbyter always has its temptations: the position he holds in the sect, the finances of the congregation. . . . Serebrennikov whistled up his godly supporters in Sumgait, N. T. Gurov and M. P. Kabanov, and while the unsuspecting Fefelov continued to mumble his psalms the 'coup' became imminent. At a special prayer-meeting, to which 'the right people' had been deliberately invited, Fefelov was battered with accusations: Baptist ranks were becoming thin, there were no young members, the cashbox was becoming empty. . . .[73]

If we remove the overlay of emotive terminology from this, we are left with a clear picture of a congregation simply deciding that the church's job is to spread the gospel. These people were simply obeying Prokofiev's earliest call to be rid of the Laodicean indifference which had been widespread under AUCECB authority.[74]

Several times the leaders of the CCECB are called opportunists or adventurers[75] who were self-appointed[76] and who attacked the AUCECB merely as a pretext for gaining power for themselves and leading a struggle against the state:

> This 'Action Group' as it called itself, first acted against its own spiritual leaders, then began to take part less in arguments within the church than in anti-social activity and by doing this broke Soviet laws.[77]

The state's extreme dissatisfaction with the activities of the CCECB has occasionally forced atheist commentators, however unwillingly, to admit that there are some virtues in the official Evangelical Christian and Baptist Church:

But apart from registered congregations there exist a number of unregistered 'Pure Baptists' and Evangelical Baptist groups who have broken away from the ECB because they refused to accept the latter's loyal attitude to the Soviet government. Active participation in the building of communism, in social life, the striving to acquire culture and knowledge which lead a significant proportion of believers away from religion, are all assessed in different ways in these movements within the sect. Some consider these things to be merely a natural process which cannot be avoided. Others, however, demand that stricter rules be introduced which would, in their view, weaken the influence of Soviet conditions on believers. They demand that no-one should be allowed to go to the cinema or theatre, listen to the radio or watch television, and that they should not read Soviet literature, and so on. . . .

The leaders of the present ECB congregations are coming round more and more to obeying the commands of the time and the conditions of life in our country and are supporting the struggle for peace, calling believers to work for the good of their fatherland; they no longer forbid believers to go to the cinema or theatre, to listen to the radio or watch television.[78]

The official voice of V. A. Kuroyedov, the head of the Council on Religious Affairs, takes up this point:

In speaking of the 'Action Group', one must of course distinguish their leaders from the ordinary Baptists, the overwhelming majority of whom are Soviet citizens of integrity.[79]

This is not, however, a view with which all would concur:

Religious teaching, whether Baptist or any other sort, is uniformly harmful, for it makes a person direct his gaze towards an insubstantial world and prevents him from accepting objective facts. Thus, to tolerate the 'truth' of Baptist teaching (whether the old or that for which the 'reformers', who have recently appeared, are fighting) would mean tolerating religion itself and abandoning the masses, as V. I. Lenin remarked, to the power of 'spiritual alcohol'.[80]

Even this author would seem to prefer a united ECB Church to a disunited one:

> Don't you be so crafty, 'brother' Gavriil! There's a place of worship for the Baptist congregation in Kishinyov, so there is no reason for you to 'seek the things of God' in the woods and ravines.[81]

Despite so much evidence to the contrary, one commentator maintains that those who have come out in support of the CCECB are not holding out and are realizing the error of their ways:

> And even the comparatively small number of believers who came under the influence exerted by the demagogical appeals of the 'Organizing Committee' are beginning to realize how inadmissible are the methods used by the 'Action Group'. Once the illegality and stupidity of the 'Organizing Committee's' demands have been explained to them, they will undoubtedly refuse their further support.[82]

The specific arguments between the AUCECB and the CCECB are hardly brought up at all, though there is at one point a mention of the demand for unrestricted entry into the sect, a clause in the statutes which the reformers sought to modify.[83] Thus the ordinary Soviet reader with no access to the documents of the Organizing Committee would be unable to establish many issues at stake beyond the basic ones of the reformers' dissatisfaction with the AUCECB leadership and their insistence on leading an evangelical revival.

Several of the commentators are at pains to emphasize that the proportion of Baptists and Evangelicals who support the reformers is insignificant. *Nauka i Religia* stated:

> The overwhelming majority of ECB believers not only do not condone all these antisocial and illegal doings of the 'Action Group', but on the contrary they censure them.[84]

The consistency with which the documents of the reformers claim the opposite is most impressive, and in Chapter 1 we found evidence to suggest that as many as three million believers might possibly have joined the reform movement. Yet atheist sources constantly make a great effort to prove numerical insignificance. *Izvestia* twice stated that the total number of Baptists implicated in the reform movement is less than 5 per cent,[85] yet this figure taken in isolation — even if it were true — has very little meaning. Does it signify 5 per cent of registered congregations? If so, the number of unregistered ones in sympathy must be very much greater. We have already mentioned the impossibility of gathering any satisfactory statistical data on the total number of Evangelical Christians and Baptists in the USSR,[86] but we may be sure that *Izvestia*'s statement does not mean 5 per cent of registered and unregistered congregations combined, because there can be no statistics on the number of unregistered congregations, let alone on the total support of the CCECB. As we saw earlier, the one occasion where an atheist source states an absolute number, as opposed to a percentage, we find 280 out of 380 in a congregation supporting the reformers.[87] We know that Prokofiev and Kryuchkov had especial influence among unregistered congregations,[88] which were twice as numerous as registered ones.[89] Thus the fact that during 1966 far more attention was paid in the Soviet press to the reform Baptists than to any other religious group gives the lie to the Soviet claim that they are numerically insignificant, and it suggests that the authorities are much more severely worried than they care to admit — certainly more worried than one would have expected if the movement were truly limited to a minority group in what is in any case a minority church.

It is now time to catalogue those 'sins' of the CCECB which have not already been mentioned, and the list is a long one. Here again we should bear in mind the traditional Soviet methods of attacking defenceless individuals or groups, particularly the practice of 'trial by newspaper', where a person is adjudged guilty before his court case has come up. Such attacks have often been demonstrated to be based on utter falsehood and fabrication of evidence.

The past records of the leaders are often reported to be reprehensible. We have already quoted the background ascribed to

Prokofiev,[90] but he is not alone in being called a criminal who refused to fight for his country. Here is a description of Pyotr Serebrennikov, of Baku:

In 1930 he was in prison for several years for a criminal offence. In 1942 he was captured by Fascists at the front. Oh yes, he 'loved his enemies' all right, fearing for his own skin. And whilst he was in the village of Yekaterinograd (Stavropol region) he diligently grew a beard as he waited for Soviet Army detachments to arrive. In order to avoid further military service after being freed, he cunningly forged a document which added no less than sixteen years to his real age. Instead of 1909 he put his date of birth at 1892. By that time he had managed to grow his beard. In the rush the forgery went unnoticed.[91]

V. Gulyuk of Rostov-on-Don is no better[92] and N. P. Khrapov of Tashkent has a prison record for 'antisocial activity'.[93] N. I. Panin is supposed to have committed bigamy, leaving his sick child to die in the care of its mother, his first wife.[94]

Not only are these leaders guilty of disloyalty to their fatherland in the past; they also foment anti-patriotism in those with whom they come into contact now, an accusation which, as we have already shown, is totally disproved by the reformers' own writings:

To what monstrous baseness must one be brought in order to smother in the hearts of the young all feeling of patriotism, devotion to their homeland and willingness to defend it sacrificially in the heroic mould against the designs of its enemies![95]

No hard and fast line is drawn between this disloyal attitude and the conspiracy to commit all sorts of crimes which are referred to, usually, under the general description of 'anti-social activity'. Every major article refers to this in general terms, but rarely specifies which particular clause of the Penal Code has been transgressed. In default of pinning down those accused to specific legal points (though see the special section on law),[96] their opponents represent Baptists as harbouring a generally negative attitude to society and the world around them, and this is referred to in almost every article on the subject. This is a direct contradiction of the positive attitude to society which the reform

leaders in fact urge.[97] The reported negative effect on young
people is particularly deprecated, and here is a major reference
describing such a group in the Ukraine:

Right next to them knelt their contemporaries, hiding from the
bright rays of the spring sunshine, from the lively, cheerful world.
They had a dull, glazed look in their eyes and an expression of estrange-
ment on their faces as they pronounced the name of God. The air
reverberated with the hysterical cries of the 'brothers' and 'sisters'
who had fallen into ecstatic prayer. Their psalms, sung in a nasal
voice, smelt of graveyard putrefaction. And these children grew up,
bereft of their red Pioneer neckerchiefs, bereft of children's games and
common human joy.

The bustle and interest of life passed them by. They only had to
stretch out their hand to it, but all 'worldly' things were forbidden
them and kept far away. While their school-fellows were enjoying
sport, artistic and technical creative work, and were making absorbing
expeditions through their own country, these others were bowing
endlessly to the ground. They would not go to the cinema or theatre,
nor read 'Soviet' books, newspapers and magazines, neither would
they listen to the radio. After school these young 'slaves of God'
would spend long hours writing out sectarian sermons and exhortations, studying the Bible and praying until very late, unaware that the
sunny joys of childhood existed.

Baptist ministers were daily robbing these children of their youth
and poisoning their immature minds and hearts with the drug of
religion.[98]

With older people this is reported to have the effect of making
them refuse to join trade unions[99] and the enclave against the
world is kept secure by the refuted refusal of the sect's leaders to
authorize marriage with those who do not share the same views.
One of the illegal Baptist writings is quoted as saying:

Such a marriage is sinful and will never remain unpunished.[100]

The leaders' quarrel over what should be the correct attitude
to the secular world is even said to be one of the chief causes of
the schism, though the only way this occurs in the documents
of the reform leaders is in their accusations against the AUCECB
of political compromise with the state:

This polemic, which in the ideological field is reflected in the struggle between modernist and fundamentalist directions, resulted during the 60's in the schism from the Baptist Church of a reactionary right-wing group, known as the 'Action Group'. Judging by its mimeographed publications signed by the Organizing Committee (since the autumn of 1965 by the so-called CCECB) we gather that they wish to dissociate themselves from the modernist attempts to reconcile scientific communism with the Baptist Church. Being more consistent in their approach to this question, they wish to return to the original form of the Baptist faith which is openly opposed to the theory of scientific communism.[101]

The reform Baptists are not always depicted as people who wish to renounce the world, however. They are sometimes portrayed as money-grubbing and only too ready to grasp temporal power:

Khrapov receives monthly sums from believers to live on. He receives presents from them. If he travels from one end of the country to the other on his 'business', these journeys are also paid for by believers. His whole family lives off the money of others. But this is only an average type of flock and it has to feed not only itself and its families, but Khrapov on top of it all![102]

The sense of this and other similar references would seem to be that it is illegal to live and work as a priest or pastor in Soviet society, yet where registered religious groups are involved this is not so. As CCECB congregations are unregistered, then any financial transaction in which they are involved can be represented as illegal, not least the holding of collections among members for the support of the work of the movement.[103] The winning of any popular support, either material or spiritual, is to deceive the 'poor in spirit'.[104]

Such deception can entail both mental and physical consequences. We have already mentioned the psychological effects which can be caused in a child by the philosophical dualism between Christian home background and Soviet education. This is sometimes reported as leading to a complete nervous breakdown:

Lyuda started having headaches through over-tiredness, while Vera was confined for some time in the nerve department of a children's hospital.[105]

Nor are such manifestations confined to children:

Yet even if Rykova suffered a nervous breakdown, is it not perfectly obvious what caused it?[106]

The reform Baptists are criticized for meeting in insanitary conditions:

The worshippers of obscurantism, members of the ECB sect, met in stuffy rooms.[107]

Yet better premises cannot be obtained, because the groups are unregistered. If, however, they take the more healthy course of meeting in the open they are even more severely taken to task. The administration of baptism rites can have especially injurious effects, it is said, and pastors sometimes take the cure upon themselves:

When I was received into the sect at one in the morning near the canal, I stepped into the water, I stood there for an hour, in the cold water, and caught a bad chill. An ambulance collected me. I lay in bed for six days. Priests (sic) from our sect came to see me and said that it was a sin to lie in bed and that God would punish me even more severely. And I decided brazenly to leave the hospital. And our priest got me 131 ampules of morphine. He gave me three injections per day and charged me 238 roubles for the morphine.[108]

An instance is recorded of a Baptist mother refusing medical help to her child who is critically ill — though she relents, and the incident seems to refer to a member of the legal ECB Church.[109]

Reform Baptists sometimes allegedly resort to physical violence against non-believers in their own family in an attempt to persuade them:

The same day Vera Petrovna cruelly and unmercifully beat her daughter. There are rumours that the enraged fanatic chased her with red-hot fire tongs.[110]

But such 'rumours' would not convince many Soviet readers of their veracity.

During 1966 two cases of murder or attempted murder were reported in the Soviet press and connected with obscure religious practices of sectarians. As they appeared in consecutive months they were almost certainly part of a campaign to discredit Protestant minority groups by any possible means. Such accusations have in the past been brought out at the height of a press campaign against the church — and such timing always puts a question-mark against their truth. There are certainly some very peculiar unexplained features about each to which it is worth referring.

The second of the two articles does not specify which particular sect is being attacked. Tamara, the writer of a letter to the editor of the agricultural daily newspaper, *Selskaya Zhizn*,[111] merely talks of the 'brothers' and 'sisters' with whom she was associated in her religious practices. While this may mean that the episode has nothing strictly to do with the subject under review, it should also be remembered that the Soviet reader would have no more precise guide than we have on the interpretation — and the immediate background in his mind would be other articles on sectarians which had recently appeared. The events occurred at Millerovo in the Rostov region, known to be an area where reform activity had been intense. The Baptists were at that moment under widespread attack (for instance in *Izvestia* the previous month[112] and in *Nauka i Religia* the same month[113]). Thus an incident which, even if true, might have nothing whatsoever to do with the Prokofiev sympathizers can be used as a weapon to combat them. The story itself has peculiarities. A young girl was allegedly forced by her sectarian mentors to put her two-year-old illegitimate daughter to death and decided to throw her under a train. At the last second a man appeared on the other side of the line, sprang forward and dragged the girl to safety. But all this happened on 5 December 1962. Why should it be brought up now? Furthermore, Tamara did not supply her surname, and did not come forward even when the editors of *Selskaya Zhizn* appealed for her to do so.[114] Therefore her identity has never been established.

A much more serious episode was recorded in *Izvestia*,[115] the case of the alleged murder of Valerik Mitichkin by Maria Rykova at Mtsensk, about 170 miles south of Moscow.

His mother hurried back. Maria refused to open the door to her and said through the window that she would not give the boy back until she had received a certificate saying that the money had been returned.[116] Nina now ran to her husband, who came to demand his son. Rykova showed him a knife through the window and declared that if they did not bring the certificate Valerik would live only until two o'clock. The house was carefully locked from the inside, and Maria had sent her own children away somewhere.

Valerik's terrified parents ran for the police. In a few minutes the police car arrived on the scene, having seized Rykova's husband on the way. His pleading with his wife came to nothing. Nina looked through the window and became hysterical. Maria was holding the crying child, on to whom she had just put some sort of a pink vest, and was squeezing him between her knees. She had a knife in her hand.

All hurled themselves against the window and doors and broke into the house . . . but it was already too late.

Let us assume that the *Izvestia* reporter has consciously reconstructed these events as he believed them to have occurred, basing his account on the results of his local enquiries and an interview with Rykova in prison. He is prepared to admit the possibility that she 'suffered a nervous breakdown' — which would presumably absolve her (not to mention the Baptists) from legal responsibility for the crime. Even if Rykova were a religious fanatic, does the pink vest of her alleged victim prove that it was a ritual murder she had committed? Rykova's background was not even a Baptist one at all:

Maria Rykova came to her religion in this way. She was brought up by her grandmother who zealously instilled faith in God in her ('I do not teach you evil, but good'). Then there was Aunt Katya who persuaded the girl that 'true faith' was not found in the church and she brought her to the Jehovah's Witnesses. However, there was something or other she did not like about them, and there was a time when she did not attend any sect at all. Unfortunately, no experienced and intelligent person came into contact with her at that time. Instead, there came Aunt Tanya, who enticed her into an ECB congregation. However, the seeds planted by the Jehovah's Witnesses obviously started to germinate.

Therefore one may ask in what sense it is possible to say the following:

> Whatever expert opinion may decide, whatever the court's decision, the murder of Valerik Mitichkin is on your consciences, Gennadi Kryuchkov and Georgi Vins! It was you, hiding in your dens, who inflamed dark passions in the souls of your followers.

The most precise connection established between Rykova and the CCECB leadership was this, which we have already had occasion earlier in this chapter to quote in part:

> The search after the murder found that she had several issues of the illegal *Fraternal Leaflet* (the most recent being the April number) and the notorious *Address to all Believing Mothers of the Evangelical and Baptist Faith in the Registered and Unregistered Congregations of the USSR*. The latter contained the appeal: 'Let us unite in our efforts to pray that God will consecrate to his service the lives of our children from the cradle up', and the call to 'save our children from the influence of the world'.

The singling out of the above quotation from the *Address to all Believing Mothers* would seem to imply that nothing more incendiary could be found in this literature. Although we have reproduced considerable extracts from various numbers of *Bratsky Listok* ('Fraternal Leaflet'), we unfortunately do not have the April 1966 number. Later in the same article, however, the *Izvestia* reporter seems to admit the true nature of this writing:

> You prophets of evil, you sow only evil, although you preach about goodness and love for one's neighbour.

It may be useful at this point to reproduce the whole of the most recent number of *Bratsky Listok* available (July 1965), which has not been published elsewhere and which may well have been one of those found at Rykova's house ten months after its issue. It will be seen that 'goodness and love for one's neighbour' is indeed the theme, and nowhere in the text is there any call to actions which are anti-Soviet, antisocial or criminal. Here is

L

the complete answer to Soviet accusations against the reformers that their campaign is for the renunciation of the goodness to be found in the world, and it shows creative use of the scriptures, absolute fidelity to all that is best in the Baptist tradition, and the most intense pastoral concern for those whose hearts have been touched by the ideals of Prokofiev, Kryuchkov, Vins and the others who have been slandered in the Soviet press.

REJOICE, ALL WHO STAND TRUE IN THE LORD!

'Be glad in the Lord, and rejoice, ye righteous: and shout for joy, all ye that are upright in heart' (Ps. 32. 11).

On 13 August four years will have passed since the moment when the Lord, having heard the voice of the Holy Spirit, openly began to oppose the deviation from the truth which had occurred in the ECB churches.

Four years is a very short time, but how much blessing and help the Lord has vouchsafed during it!

When we reflectively look back on the road we have travelled with the Lord, we want to bow our knees repeatedly to God our Father, thank him and worship him in spirit and in truth.

The Lord himself raised up this movement for the unity, purity and sanctity of his church. This blessed movement does not strive to establish new doctrine or to accomplish a reformation. Its aim is to purify, sanctify and unite all God's people on the basis of gospel teachings.

Being moved by the Holy Spirit, the supporters of this movement are striving to set up an Evangelical order within the church and to establish the Lord Jesus Christ as one master of his people.

The people of God are fighting to make discord and disorder in the church yield to creativity and sanctity, to make degenerate deviation and compromise with the world, shadowing by the false brethren and betrayal give way to selfless brotherly love and holy intercession. They want to make the spirit of misunderstanding and suspicion yield to mutual trust, and in place of indifference, coolness and unconcern to manifest zeal and responsibility for each other, for all of God's work and for the whole church.

Today the results of these sacred efforts have become evident to many — results achieved by prayer, fasting, hard work and struggle. The Lord is vouchsafing his rich blessing. The church is literally being raised up from its bed of sickness and is being healed of its serious ailment.

We shall unanimously strive further for our Evangelical faith, for all has not yet been accomplished by a long way.

... We shall pray that this healing may touch every brother and sister, every local church to the spiritual benefit of the whole people of God and to the glory of God the Father and our Lord Jesus Christ.

Knowing that the true service which God's people fulfil is not achieved without difficulty, that it costs Christians many tears and much sacrifice, we pray that God may send upon you ever new blessings, and we thank him that he gives us 'exceeding abundantly above all that we ask or think' (Eph. 3. 20–21).

In these anniversary days we are glad to greet all churches which are participating in this holy struggle, helping and supporting one another, and we greet all who by fasting and prayer have made the service of God's people possible in all its aspects.

We sincerely greet you, our brother-ministers of the churches of Christ, who are caring unceasingly for the children of God committed to your charge by the Lord and are affecting their consecration.

'Take heed therefore unto yourselves and to all the flock, over the which the Holy Ghost hath made you overseers, to feed the church of God, which he hath purchased with his own blood' (Acts 20. 28).

We rejoice to greet the churches which have kept to the path of purity and holiness and we wish that all brothers and sisters in them may follow in Christ's footsteps, decisively and fearlessly.

'Stand fast therefore in the liberty wherewith Christ hath made us free and be not entangled again with the yoke of bondage' (Gal. 5. 1).

We greet you, our brother- and sister-workers who mimeographed our fraternal letters and appeals and we praise the Lord for your hard and self-sacrificing work which is so important at this time.

'Be ye steadfast, unmoveable, always abounding in the work of the Lord, forasmuch as ye know that your labour is not in vain in the Lord' (I Cor. 15. 58).

We greet all those who have had to stand before a court and have remained unyielding and courageous throughout these trials. Dear friends, you have borne heroic suffering, but the children of this world saw neither confusion, bewilderment nor fear on your faces, for your hearts affirmed:

'I know whom I have believed, and am persuaded that he is able to keep that which I have committed unto him against that day' (2 Tim. 1. 12).

We greet all you who have been released from your chains and are again able to labour in Christ's church, and we greet you, our beloved brothers and sisters who continue to be ambassadors in chains.

Some of these prisoners we will never see again on earth. They have given up their lives for the work of the gospel and are heirs to a special portion, having likewise accepted their lot unflinchingly, knowing that the Lord himself would meet them.

We greet the families of prisoners and especially the Christian mothers who have been deprived of their young ones or left alone with babes in arms to bring up. You have not despaired, but look in hope and consolation to the Lord, maintaining your internal calm and imperturbability.

With these sufferings all the children of God have again been convinced that truly:

'A father of the fatherless and a judge of widows ... God setteth the solitary in families: he bringeth out those which are bound with chains' (Ps. 68. 5-6).

We send our greetings to the All-Union Council of ECB Prisoners' Relatives and we pray the Lord to grant you patience and strength to complete the difficult but essential service which you are rendering.

'Hereby perceive we the love of God, because he laid down his life for us: and we ought to lay down our lives for the brethren' (I John 3. 16).

We greet all you who sincerely collaborate in appending your signatures to petitions for permission to hold a congress, all who receive our ministers and provide your houses where the people of God may worship. We also greet everyone who gives his mite to participate in God's work and to help families in need. We greet all children who have experienced difficulties for the sake of Jesus Christ and are continuing to do so. We greet all those, too, whom the Lord has joined to his church in these years through baptism into the faith.

We praise God who has acted in all of us and through whom every ministry has become possible. The people of God has drawn close together and everyone has felt the beating of his brother's heart, as it is written:

'They drew near and came. They helped every one his neighbour; and every one said to his brother, Be of good courage' (Is. 41. 5–6).

All have become as of one heart . . .

Today everyone whom God's call has reached is fighting that such an organic unity and sanctity should be the property of the whole people of God, as the Lord himself commanded (John 17. 21).

We also address you, brothers and sisters, who are in a situation where people are indignant with and angrily condemn Christ's ministers through whom he is accomplishing purification and sanctification among his people, unjustly calling you 'schismatics'.

Read I Peter 4. 17: 'For the time is come that judgment must begin at the house of God'.

Among God's people today some are being roused and sanctified according to God's command, while the hearts of a few are being hardened 'through the deceitfulness of sin' and are following the path of destruction (Heb. 3. 13).

Therefore be mindful of what God is doing today! Read the word of God, pray and ask the Lord himself what is happening today in the church, for it is written:

'Because they regard not the works of the Lord, nor the operation of his hands, he shall destroy them, and not build them up' (Ps. 28. 5).

May God vouchsafe you understanding in everything!

We will glorify and thank God because with great longsuffering he is rousing and unifying us, and leading us all along this blessed path of labour and struggle, and because he will be with us and will lead us further towards the desired goal, for such is his changeless commandment:

'And, lo, I am with you alway, even unto the end of the world. Amen' (Mat. 28. 20).[117]

7 Church, State and the Future

The last chapter, by implication, mentioned a number of ambiguities which are apparent in the relations between the reform Baptists and the state. We will now list a few more.

Despite the list of 'sins' which we have catalogued, one finds the surprising admission from time to time that Baptists are by nature quiet, hard-working people. The title of one of the articles about them is 'What the "quiet people" want',[1] and it is stated: 'Our notion of them is that they are quiet, elderly people'.[2] Elsewhere it is admitted that 'a considerable number of them are honest working folk'.[3] The Nefedov family lived at Belgorod:

> Ivan's father was the head of an unregistered Baptist sect whose members used to gather in Nefedov's house for their prayer meetings. ... Gradually the father trained his son as a Baptist preacher. ... During all that time Ivan performed his work honestly, was very sure of his responsibility as a combine-operator, and over-fulfilled his production norm.[4]

These references accord perfectly with the image of the Baptists as we see it in their own writings, and thus we are able to refute the charge of 'anti-Soviet activity' not only from such documents as the *Bratsky Listok* which we quoted at the end of the last chapter, but also from atheist sources themselves.

Baptist leaders are attacked for running an 'underground organization like the so-called Council of Churches of the ECB',[5] yet if they come out into the open, holding services or presenting petitions to the highest authorities in the land they are the more reviled:

> They (the CCECB leaders) instruct these messengers to importune for their illegal demands to be satisfied by any means, even by creating a scandal. They tell them that this is 'a struggle for the true religion'.

As a rule, the petitioners themselves have only a poor understanding of the subtle points of the petition.[6]

Great stress is laid on the fact that these activities are carried on by unregistered and therefore illegal Christian groups:

The demagogues from the Organizing Committee, Prokofiev's followers, took it upon themselves to 'protect' these unregistered Baptist groups from the AUCECB and from the 'satanic authorities'. The position of such *de facto* existing groups of believers clearly contradicts the law.[7]

The CCECB leaders have never conducted a campaign against registration, for it should not affect their religious life:

Bondarenko and his associates maintain that they have always supported the registration of 'autonomous congregations', those groups of believers who had split from the ECB. They say: 'Registration does not contradict our religious teaching, although for us it is a secondary factor.'[8]

Here again is an official admission that CCECB leaders have done their utmost to abide by the law. Yet what happens when a Baptist group tries to make its organization legal by registering it?

Fridrikh Gegeniger, their leader, acts cunningly, trying to unite all the 'brothers' and 'sisters' into a congregation and to get it registered. Compare the Bryansk case, p. 115.[9]

As one of the CCECB documents printed in an émigré periodical succinctly puts it:

The authorities refused our requests to register our congregations, and now they are persecuting us on the grounds that we are not registered.[10]

How much the state interferes in church affairs is a question which can be answered only in the light of the total evidence presented in this book. Whatever one's judgment may be on this, the extraordinary claim is constantly made that the state either cannot or does not interfere at all:

> Already the leaders of the 'Organizing Committee', the 'Council of Churches', have been refused recognition of the legality of their movement and have not been granted permission to hold an All-Union ECB Congress. It was explained to them that a decision on the question of leadership of the ECB union and of a church congress was a matter for believers themselves and that any satisfaction of their demands by the government would entail state interference in internal church affairs.[11]

Even a seemingly authoritative statement like this is inconsistent, for it does not explain how a religious movement can be branded as 'illegal' if the state is not going to interfere in it. M. A. Orlov's statement at the inception of the AUCECB[12] is also a direct contradiction of the above claim of separation.

The question of how far the Baptist attempt at reform can justly be called a form of 'political' opposition to the Soviet state (as opposed to an attempt to stand out against certain specific religious policies which the Prokofiev supporters wish to see changed) is another issue which can be decided only with reference to the sum of the evidence brought together in this book. Certainly they are reported as asking:

> 'Why do they write about us in the newspapers and give us lectures? Why do they represent us in a bad light? This shouldn't be.' In a word, they pretend that they were all meek and mild.[13]

Or again:

> 'We are not political people; the cares of the world don't interest us.[14]

The reformers themselves pay a great deal of attention to the letter of Soviet legality (as we saw from the Kryuchkov–Vins document[15]), and one of them, G. G. Songrov, is reported as saying:

> It is written in black and white: 'The church is separated from the state, therefore every citizen may confess any religion or none.' This

is from the decree signed by Lenin in 1918 — clauses 1 and 3, to be exact. . . . [16]

Despite this insistence on legality, Soviet commentators pay little attention to the specific legal reforms which the CCECB supporters wish to see introduced. They are content to generalize, to represent any attempt to change the laws as showing political opposition to the state or indulging in anti-Soviet activity, and any attempt to lead a Christian life unsullied by the world is adjudicated to be flagrantly political conduct:

This is what Khrapov tries to get from his congregation. He wants people who have grown up in a Soviet country and under Soviet rule not to recognize that authority. We have before us an appeal to believers: to refuse to take part in the social life of the country and not to fulfil one's civil obligations or use one's rights.[17]

To further their own political ends the reform Baptists pretend that they are repressed, because 'they now need "victims of persecution" and "martyrs for the faith" ':[18]

They write a great deal about self-sacrifice in the name of Christ, about the necessity of suffering for the faith. Those who suffer in the name of Christ are extolled as 'having received baptism from the Holy Spirit. . . . In trying to create the impression that 'Christians are persecuted' in the USSR, the schismatic Baptists have been breaking the law in order to provoke the use of administrative measures.[19]

Nevertheless, they are said to be unsuccessful in projecting such an image:

These are not innocent 'martyrs for the faith' who face the court (for there are none such in the USSR), but people who break the law.[20]

It is most revealing, however, that even some atheist commentators admit that there have been such illegal 'administrative measures' brought against Baptists:

At the same time, leaders of the 'Organizing Committee' have cunningly exploited to their own advantage the dissatisfaction of believers at the incorrect actions carried out towards them by some local administrators.[21]

Some commentators turn this statement inside out and say that it is the CCECB leaders who have been guilty of persecuting other Soviet citizens. This is a subject which obviously worries the authors of an article in the Central Asian newspaper *Pravda Vostoka*, for they come back to it several times in the course of expounding their theme:

> ... religious views must not be forcibly implanted ... Khrapov and those who will sit with him in the dock lay special emphasis on the fact that everyone has the right publicly to uphold his own opinions. But for some reason the 'Council', while willingly acknowledging such a right for themselves, do not wish to admit it for atheists. ... However, all those are criminals who, like Khrapov, force their religious views on others or have the intention of persecuting atheists for their convictions.[22]

This article does not go on to tell us how Christians can persecute atheists in modern Soviet conditions. Does it mean infiltration into atheist meetings to carry out an organized opposition to them? This is the only recorded example which could conceivably be relevant, though it is really too trivial to mention at all as an example of 'persecution'. Even this reference does not make special mention of the CCECB:

> Sometimes they try to interfere. During lectures and organized evenings they let out malicious cries and ask provocative questions. Sectarians engage especially actively in this.[23]

This does show us, however, that some opposition to the massive atheist campaign is being organized.

NEW LEGISLATION OF 1966

It is not possible to say exactly why it was that new decrees on religion were introduced in 1966, but it is our task here to compare them with the legislation previously in force in order to establish whether they represented a tightening up or an easing of the situation.

Let us first give the full text of the new decrees:

DECREE OF THE PRESIDIUM OF THE SUPREME SOVIET OF THE RSFSR

On administrative responsibility for infringing the laws on religious cults

The Presidium of the Supreme Soviet of the RSFSR decrees that:

Infringement of the laws on religious cults through the following acts:

refusal by the leaders of religious societies to register the said groups with the state authorities;

breaking the rules which have been legally laid down for the organization and conduct of religious meetings, processions and other religious observances;

organizing and conducting of special children's and young people's meetings by ministers and members of religious societies, and also their organizing working, literary or other circles and groups which are not connected with the performance of worship —

carries a fine of up to 50 roubles imposed by the administrative commissions of the executive committees of the district and town *soviets* of Working People's Deputies.

Chairman of the Presidium of the Supreme Soviet of the RSFSR,
N. Ignatov.

Secretary of the Presidium of the Supreme Soviet of the RSFSR,
S. Orlov.

Moscow, 18 March 1966.

DECREE OF THE PRESIDIUM OF THE SUPREME SOVIET OF THE RSFSR

On the introduction of supplementary clauses into Article 142 of the Penal Code of the RSFSR

The Presidium of the Supreme Soviet of the RSFSR decrees that:

Article 142 of the Penal Code of the RSFSR is to be supplemented by a second part with the following contents:

'The same acts committed by a person who has previously been sentenced for infringing the laws on the separation of church from state and of school from church, and similarly the organizing of activity directed towards the implementation of these acts —

is punished by up to three years deprivation of liberty.'

Chairman of the Presidium of the Supreme Soviet of the RSFSR,
N. Ignatov.

Secretary of the Presidium of the Supreme Soviet of the RSFSR,
S. Orlov.

Moscow, 18 March 1966.

DECREE OF THE PRESIDIUM OF THE SUPREME SOVIET OF THE RSFSR

On the application of Article 142 of the Penal Code of the RSFSR

In connection with the questions which are raised by the practical application of Article 142 of the Penal Code of the RSFSR, the Presidium of the Supreme Soviet of the RSFSR decrees, on the basis of Clause 3 of § 33 of the Constitution of the RSFSR, that:

What is understood by infringement of the laws on the separation of church from state and of school from church, incurring criminal responsibility under Article 142 of the Penal Code of the RSFSR, should be elucidated as follows:

compulsory collections and levy of taxes for the benefit of religious organizations and ministers of religion;

the preparation for the purpose of mass distribution or the mass distribution itself of petitions, letters, leaflets and other documents which call for the infringement of the laws on religious cults;

the performance of deceitful acts with the aim of arousing religious superstitions among the public;

the organization and staging of religious meetings, processions and other religious ceremonies which are prejudicial to social order;

the organization and systematic holding of religious instruction courses for minors which infringe the rules legally laid down;

the refusal to accept citizens at work or into an educational institution, their dismissal from work or exclusion from an educational institution, depriving them of privileges or advantages guaranteed by the law, and similarly any material restrictions on the rights of citizens in respect to their religious adherence.

Chairman of the Presidium of the Supreme Soviet of the RSFSR,
N. Ignatov.

Secretary of the Presidium of the Supreme Soviet of the RSFSR,
S. Orlov.

Moscow, 18 March 1966.[24]

A careful reading of this text suggests that these decrees could well have been introduced with the Baptists specifically in mind, though they certainly have a wider application as well. Refusing to register religious groups, breaking the rules on conduct of services and processions, organizing special religious gatherings for children, printing and distributing of petitions and religious literature: these are all activities which, while they do not of necessity apply to Baptists and no-one else, are undoubtedly those activities for which the CCECB had principally incurred the displeasure of the authorities and against which popular and nation-wide anger is said to be aroused. We have given details of how Baptists were accused in 1965–66 of just such offences, and it can be categorically stated that during these two years the Soviet press carried no such systematic campaign against any other religious group.

There does, therefore, seem to be a connection between the Soviet desire to suppress the CCECB within a certain framework of legality and the introduction of these laws.

Does a comparison of the amended version of Article 142 of the Penal Code and the old form bear out this assertion?[25]

Registration was not mentioned in the version of Article 142 which had been valid up to March 1966, though it did appear in the 1929 decree 'On Religious Congregations'.[26] The ban on the preparation and distribution of letters and documents appealing to people to break the law on religious cults is new, but the prohibition on the organization and conduct of gatherings and processions which disturb public order was already contained in Article 143. The rewording of the clause on the religious education of minors seems to be significant. According to an earlier code in force up to 1958 this had not been allowed 'in state or private educational institutions and schools',[27] but now any systematic conduct of courses infringing 'the rules legally laid down' is banned. These 'rules' are almost certainly unpublished instructions and we have no means of knowing what they are, but it seems that the teaching of religion is now made even more specifically illegal than it was earlier in Article 227.[28]

No. 219 above in fact removes the old alternative of one year's corrective labour to a 50-rouble fine for a simple violation of the laws under Article 142, but No. 220 gives a new increased penalty of three years imprisonment for recividists (who were not singled out in the earlier version, where one year's corrective labour was the maximum for the offence).

The banning of 'obligatory collections' is not new, while the clause on deceitful acts which arouse religious superstition, though new, would not seem to have any special relevance to Baptists. Discrimination against citizens for religious reasons was not specifically banned in the previous version of Article 142.

To summarize this discussion, there are two points — the rewording of the prohibition on religious education for children and the clause on the circulating of petitions — which would seem to tie in specifically with the 1966 press reports on the reform Baptists which we have reviewed.

The first of these in particular is a key issue. It does seem as though previously there may have been some difficulty in demonstrating the illegality of holding Sunday school classes in private houses and we earlier showed just how avidly many Baptists have been doing this.[29] As we shall see shortly,[30] this question of organizing religious education for children came up in every single trial of reform Baptists in 1966 of which we have any record.

The promulgation of these decrees caused a great deal of comment in the West. It would not be necessary to mention these reactions but for the fact that they were referred to in the Soviet press by V. A. Kuroyedov:

However, several Western press organs from time to time make slanderous accusations and all kinds of insinuations about the position of religion in the USSR. Thus the newspaper *Parisien Libéré* (4 April 1966) made a sensation out of announcing to its readers the new legislation on the church in the RSFSR, and in doing so it drew the categorical conclusion that 'a new attack against Christian sects' was being organized in our country . . .

These decrees and resolutions were passed in order to regulate current legislation on the cults. This regulation affected principally the question of the separation of church from state and school from church, and it took the following directions. First and foremost, the new legislative acts have now concretely defined for which contraventions of the stated law one can be the subject of criminal proceedings. Previously Article 142 of the Penal Code of the RSFSR did not have such concrete definitions. Moreover, it should be especially emphasized that the range of offences resulting in judicial punishment has been significantly reduced. For individual types of infringement administrative responsibility has been introduced instead of criminal.

Essentially it is a question of the easing of punishment in relation to first offenders against the law on separation of church and state. However, increased penalties are established for those citizens who have already been sentenced for such offences and similarly if they have expanded any activities planned to secure such contravention.

Such an influential church publication as the *Bulletin of the World Council of Churches* (No. 17, 26 May 1966) wrote:

'At the beginning of April various press agencies published communications from Moscow, according to which restrictions on religious freedom had been introduced by a decree of the Supreme Soviet in Russia (RSFSR). A study of the text, which in fact contains three decrees, demonstrated that these decrees basically confirm, define and in some instances introduce greater flexibility into the laws which already exist. In contradiction to what was published in the newspapers, not one of these decrees prohibits free collections designed to meet the needs of churches, nor is it recognized that discrimination against people in connection with their religious adherence can be legal.

In order to illustrate the easing of conditions which previously existed, it may be noted that some violations of the law which were previously punished by imprisonment now merely carry a fine of up to 50 roubles . . .'[31]

It is perhaps significant that the Ukrainian anti-religious journal, *Lyudina i Svit*,[32] did not refer to any 'easing' of the situation in its interpretation of the identical new decree to the one under discussion approved in the Ukraine on 26 March 1966.

Before trying to assess the real effect of this new legislation we must mention an addition to Article 190 of the Penal Code of the RSFSR made on 16 September 1966:

Organization of or active participation in group actions that violate public order.

The organization of, as well as participation in, group actions that grossly violate public order, involve clear disobedience to the lawful demands of representatives of authority or entail disruption of the operation of transport, state and public enterprises or institutions —

is punishable by deprivation of freedom for a period not exceeding three years, by corrective labour for a period not exceeding one year or by a fine not exceeding 100 roubles.

> A. Khakhalov, Vice-Chairman of the Presidium,
>   Supreme Soviet of the RSFSR.
>
> S. Orlov, Secretary of the Presidium.

Moscow, 16 September 1966.[33]

This does not apply specifically to religion, but could certainly refer to Baptist activities, according to our analysis of them from the Soviet press.

After March 1966, holding a service in a public place could be punished by a maximum of a 50-rouble fine for a first offender, which provision was interpreted by Kuroyedov and others as an 'easing' of the situation. From September 1966, however, this activity could be covered by Article 190 of the Penal Code, and is now punishable by up to three years deprivation of liberty for a first offence. This represents greatly increased severity.

ADMINISTRATIVE MEASURES

We need not further labour the point of whether the March and September laws in fact meant an 'easing' of the situation.[34] The Western view on this is of quite secondary importance compared with that of the reform Baptists themselves, and there is no doubt about what they felt:

And then there came March. In the sect the propaganda to resist Soviet laws increased.[35]

One of the documents written by a Baptist and published in the West also states:

After the 23rd Party Congress the repressions against our church were intensified.[36]

This congress took place in March–April 1966, immediately after the promulgation of the new decrees, and the Kiev document provides an even more emphatic statement that the situation took a sharp turn for the worse at this time,[37] while some representatives of Western public opinion were making premature statements that the new legislation would guarantee increased freedom for the Russian Christians.

Kryuchkov and Vins, in their appeal to Mr. Brezhnev, also made a point which is of extreme relevance here: that changes in the law in the past had invariably preceded renewed persecutions.[38] The most convincing evidence that this was to be so yet again comes not from any document written by the reformers, but from the Soviet press in 1966. As an absolute minimum, 21 of their leaders were officially reported as being arrested and brought to trial for religious crimes in 1966. This figure is arrived at through a collation of six newspaper articles listing the names of those imprisoned and in some cases their sentences.[39] It should be emphasized that this list does not claim to be complete, and very certainly is not. It is taken solely from the Russian language press (while much reform activity has been conducted in areas where such languages as Ukrainian, Moldavian, Estonian and Uzbek are principally spoken); also these articles have been difficult to trace systematically, as they have not been listed in the religious or legal section of the monthly reference publication, *Letopis Gazetnykh Statei* ('Index of Newspaper Articles'), which claims to catalogue all material of importance appearing in the Soviet press.

M

Unfortunately the tendentious style of these articles makes it difficult to separate the exact legal charges brought against the defendants from the journalist's own opinions, and in half of the instances not even the article of the Penal Code under which the charges were brought is cited.

The trial of Maria Braun and Yelena Chernetskaya was reported on 18 March 1966 (the same day as the new decrees), as having taken place 'recently' and therefore predated them. On the legal side it was stated:

The state authorities cannot allow the law to be transgressed under the guise of practising religion. In particular, special prayer meetings for children and young people have been organized; similarly, circles and 'schools' for the study of religion have been formed. This has been demonstrated with full clarity at the trial in the Sokuluk district.

The court found Yelena Chernetskaya and Maria Braun guilty of the crimes they had committed and it sentenced each of them to five years deprivation of liberty. The court's verdict was unanimously approved by the numerous representatives of the public present at the trial.[40]

Although the article of the Penal Code which had been transgressed is not stated, it would probably have been 227 or its equivalent in the Kirgiz SSR.

V. Golub, N. Butkov and A. Balatsky, three young men of 36 and under, were imprisoned at Lugansk in July 1966.[41] They too were found guilty of organizing religious education for young people. Their sentences were not stated, but they could have been charged under the new laws.

Much more is known about the Rostov-on-Don case in August. P. D. Belenki had recently been attacked in *Pravda*[42] for being an 'authority' on the religious education of children. Now he and three associates (their surnames are given as Zhovmiruk, Bolgova and Yerisov) were accused as follows:

Under the pretext of freedom of conscience and without the knowledge of the local authorities, the defendants organized a street procession by their co-religionists in the city and a baptism in the Don on 2 May 1966. These violated public order and aroused the legitimate indignation of the local residents. The defendants set up their own printing press, where they illegally mimeographed literature steeped in a spirit of hostility towards Soviet conditions and sometimes containing open exhortations to believers not to submit to Soviet legislation.

The defendants also have it on their conscience that they organized a Baptist Sunday school for children, where ignorant and fanatical 'teachers' taught 'the word of God' to children of between eight and eleven, persistently and systematically inculcating upon them a religious outlook on life.

The six defendants, on the basis of Article 142 (clause 2) of the Penal Code of the RSFSR, have been sentenced by the Court of the Criminal Affairs Collegium of the Rostov region to various terms of imprisonment. The local public warmly approved the just sentences.[43]

These four people were imprisoned for organizing a street procession, mimeographing literature and running a Sunday school, all of which had been specifically made illegal by the March decree. It was this case which attracted the attention of the West to the plight of the Baptists, and in London *The Times* carried a correspondence on the subject initiated by Professor Leonard Schapiro, which lasted from September to December 1966, under the title, 'Persecution of Baptists'.[44]

Yuri Alexandrov, the Moscow lawyer whose article on religious legislation we quoted in Chapter 1,[45] contributed to the correspondence, revealing extraordinary Soviet sensitivity on this subject. He disclosed the length of the sentences, a piece of information which had not been included in the original report:

Sir,
Though I am not an 'apologist of the ways of dictatorship' still I make so bold as to contend with Professor Leonard Schapiro (1 September), and reintroduce the truth, with which, as it seems to me, he is not on good relations.

Let me begin by saying that the court decision in the case of the Rostov Baptists levels no accusation of 'anti-social activities' or of 'poisoning children's minds', as Professor Schapiro claims. The Rostov Baptists were convicted for violating the law on the separation of the church from the state, concretely expressed in their arrangement of worship and meetings of prayer in streets and parks and on beaches whereby they violated order and traffic safety in public places, which in Britain so far as I know is penalized, too.

Further, the people sentenced organized underground schools for the religious instruction of children, which is forbidden by law in the USSR, as only parents may engage in that. Young men desirous of taking the vows are trained at the theological seminaries and academies maintained by the appropriate religious centres. As if that was not enough, the Rostov Baptists illicitly circulated leaflets urging Soviet citizens to disobey the law on the separation of the church from the state.

These people were prosecuted under Article 142 of the Criminal Code of the Russian Federation, which deals with violation of laws concerning the separation of the church from the state and of the school from the church and not at all under the mythical charges Professor Schapiro ascribed to the court. Incidentally the Rostov Baptists were given sentences from a suspended term of one year to three years of detention in a corrective labour camp.

To put everything in its place and enable the British public to view without bias the point Professor Schapiro has raised, I think it necessary to add that Article 143 of the Criminal Code of the Russian Federation and the analogous articles in the Criminal Codes of the other Soviet constituent republics, make it a crime to obstruct religious worship conducted in accordance with the law. Furthermore, last March the Presidium of the Supreme Soviet of the Russian Federation passed a ruling on the application of Article 142 of the Criminal Code of the Russian Federation considerably restricting prosecution for violation of laws on the separation of the church from the state.

Sincerely,

Yuri Alexandrov, Jurist.

12 Fourth Tverskaya Yamskaya, Flat 39,
Moscow.[46]

A few weeks later a Kiev newspaper reported:

A few days ago the Kiev regional court passed sentence after criminal proceedings against I. D. Bondarenko, N. K. Velichko, P. S. Overchuk, A. T. Kechik and V. N. Zhurilo. They had been accused under Article 138 (clause 2) of the Penal Code of the Ukrainian SSR.

In the past it had more than once been explained to the accused that their conduct was illegal, but they took no notice of the warnings and continued organizing a campaign against Soviet legislation on the cults. By exploiting the ignorance of ordinary Baptists, they dragged them into this illegal activity. They systematically organized gatherings of believers in places of recreation outside Kiev, in which discussion of religious questions was replaced by coarse attacks on our system and our standards of conduct in public places were flouted. They distributed literature, about the aims of which we have already written. They tried to corrupt the minds of children, deterring them from school and setting them against society . . .

The regional court, with Yu. I. Matsko presiding, sentenced I. D. Bondarenko to three years deprivation of liberty, the term to be spent in strict-regime corrective labour colonies. N. K. Velichko was given three years, P. S. Overchuk two and a half years, V. N. Zhurilo and A. T. Kechik two years each.

In our country people are not sentenced for their religious convictions, but no-one is allowed to transgress Soviet law![47]

This case may have resulted partly from the incident in Kiev described in detail in Chapter 5[48] and it saw the end for the time being of I. D. Bondarenko's activities as one of the most influential leaders of the CCECB. He had already been imprisoned at least twice before, as the Temporary Council of Prisoners' Relatives had recorded his name and sentence,[49] and this would explain why he received the maximum penalty prescribed by the new laws. Presumably the others were also recidivists.

We have already quoted extensively from the article in October 1966 indicting four citizens from Tashkent, but in this case the article about them appeared before the trial itself:

The Tashkent citizens, N. P. Khrapov, G. G. Gortfeld, N. P. Matyukhina and M. I. Belan, are to appear before the people's court, accused of breaking the Soviet law on the religious cults.[50]

It appears that Fadyukhin's claim two years earlier that the schism in his congregation had been healed was premature.[51] The above article is not specific about the exact nature of the legal charges, but takes great pains to point out that 'You are not being tried for your faith, Khrapov' (the title) and describes at some length the activities of the group in publishing and instructing children in the faith. No news of the sentences imposed has subsequently become available.

A month later a further case was reported:

Using various methods, even open blackmail, they have been enticing our children into a religious circle, forbidding them to wear a Pioneer neckerchief, to take part in expeditions, read Gaidar[52] and go to the cinema . . .

At the trial which lasted almost a whole week, there was revealed a complete picture of the activities of these corrupters of children's minds — Bykova, Nikolaeva, Mayorova, the active member of the sect, Vasiliev, and the so-called presbyter, Ignatiev . . .

The final words of the sentence resound:

'We find V. S. Mayorova, N. P. Bykova and N. P. Nikolaeva guilty under the second clause of Article 142 of the Penal Code of the RSFSR. They are each sentenced to three years deprivation of liberty, to be served in a corrective labour colony.'[53]

Assuming that the letter of the law was adhered to, these must also have been recividists, like the Kiev group, for they received the maximum sentence. It is interesting that the trial lasted as long as a week. The record of it which we have must recount only the tiniest fraction of what went on there.

The reactions of the Baptists to the campaign against them have been extremely brave. They are fully prepared to 'suffer for their faith'[54] and to say as much in front of the court:

No, they did not at all repent of what they had done. Golub proclaimed: 'I am glad that I am not being sentenced as a thief . . .'[55]

Some would not even speak in their own self-defence, presumably considering that the whole matter had been pre-judged before the opening of the trial:

Although the accused categorically refused to give evidence, the court gradually uncovered all the cynicism of their 'instructive' activities.[56]

There were even sympathy demonstrations for the accused at the trials, in spite of the repeated assurance that the activity of these Baptists had aroused popular ire throughout the length and breadth of the land.[57] This incident refers back to a slightly earlier period than we have just been discussing:

In 1964 at Kishinyov B. Gladkevich was sentenced for breaking Soviet laws. He was a schismatic Baptist, so a whole mob of his sympathizers turned up at his trial. Believe it or not, the fanatic, G. P. Madan, who got this crowd together, struck up a Christian hymn with them in the court waiting room.[58]

There were such expressions of sympathy in 1966, too:

During the trial certain young women were present who gazed in admiration at the defendants and stared at the atheistically minded public in a hostile manner.[59]

Despite the 1966 campaign which silenced at least 21 active CCECB supporters in eight months, the claim is sometimes ruefully made that the real ringleaders stay free. The names of Kryuchkov and Vins were mentioned in this way in June that year,[60] and on 22 November it was reported:

It is a pity that only the executives were put in the dock. The direct instigators of the Cheboksary sectarians remained in the background — the notorious leaders of the self-constituted CCECB, G. Kryuchkov, G. Vins, N. Baturin and some others, including V. Kozlov, their emissary from Yoshkar-Ola. It is they who have been giving the direct orders for the organization of religious instruction for children which directly infringes our laws.[61]

Earlier in the year it had been reported in a Baptist document (possibly written in late May, after the series of demonstrations in Moscow):

Many members of the Council of Churches are in prison (G. Kryuchkov, G. Vins, Baturin, Kozlov, Bondarenko, etc.).[62]

There is, therefore, some uncertainty about whether these leaders are in fact free men at present or not. The imprisonment referred to by the Baptists may have been only for 10–15 days, as it is a common Soviet practice to put citizens away for a short period of time as a warning gesture. Neither do we know exactly how many still remain in prison from the 1961–64 series of arrests.

The Soviet authorities have obviously had a problem over whether or not to bring Kryuchkov, Vins, Baturin and Kozlov to trial, because the reform movement has gained in public esteem through the example of its martyr-figures like Prokofiev and I. D. Bondarenko. They may have been secretly tried, and it seems very unlikely that they were free for the important events of October 1966.

THE AUCECB CONGRESS, 4–8 OCTOBER 1966

The holding of another Baptist congress in 1966 may reflect the intense pressure which the CCECB had put on the AUCECB and on Soviet society since the previous such gathering in 1963, but it also had to take place because the revised constitution stipulated an assembly every three years.[63] It is still difficult to assess the significance of the 1966 congress, because we do not have adequate information on it at the time of writing. *Bratsky Vestnik* No. 6, 1966, devoted its whole space to the congress, but it did not become available until May 1967, when this book was already at the printers. It has not therefore been possible to include any detailed consideration of it. Even more seriously, we do not yet have any document from the reformers which sets out their attitude to the congress. At the point where vital information on this might have been recorded by *Bratsky Vestnik*, we are told merely:

> The leader of the session announced that there were two representatives of the 'Council of Churches' in the hall, brothers Ye. T. Kovalenko and G. I. Maiboroda, who had been entrusted with the mission of reading an address to the delegates at the congress and a statement to it from the 'Council of Churches'.[64]

Two *Novosti* press releases contain a summary of the events:

I

The 39th All-Union Congress of the Evangelical Christians and Baptists has opened at the prayer house of the Moscow community of this religious organization. It is attended by 705 delegates elected at

63 republic, area and regional conferences of representatives of these religious communities.

Before the opening of the congress a divine service was conducted in the same prayer house. Opening the congress with a brief speech, Yakov Zhidkov, the aged president of the AUCECB, declared that he had not seen so representative a congress before. Messages of greetings were read from the Moscow community of the Seventh-Day Adventists, the Moscow ECB community and from foreign Baptist organizations — the Baptist World Alliance, the European Baptist Federation and the Russian–Ukrainian Baptist Union in the United States.

A report on the activities of the AUCECB was delivered by its general secretary, Alexander Karev, who dwelt on the history of religious trends represented at the congress. Next year these trends will mark the centenary of their emergence. Karev pointed to the multi-national and multi-lingual character of the ECB organization in the USSR which does not recognize any national discrimination or racial segregation, like that in the United States. The council, he said, is a body of the organization which rallies people of many religious trends; they are united by a number of main dogmas and reject the 'modernistic' attempts of some groups of Evangelical Christians and Baptists in the West to replace the faith in Jesus Christ as God by worshipping him as a divine man.

Saying that the council does not keep exact statistics of its members, the speaker noted at the same time that the membership of the organization, together with those affiliated with it, approaches 500,000.[65]

Alexander Karev dealt with the question of senior and local presbyters, the organization of choirs and musical accompaniment, and the publishing activity of the council. He made known that the council was about to start the publication of the Bible and collected religious songs in three languages and was going to increase the edition of its magazine *Bratsky Vestnik*.

The report told of the broad ties of the council with Evangelicals and Baptists abroad. The need to maintain these ties was explained by the fact that they, first, help in the struggle against the modernization of teaching in some foreign organizations and, second, promote the international struggle of Evangelical Christians and Baptists against the threat of a new war.

'Mankind must rally in the struggle for peace,' Karev declared. 'It must organize fire brigades to put out the seats of war, one of which is burning in Vietnam and represents a grave threat to world peace.'

The speaker dwelt on the council's attitude toward the ecumenical movement. He announced that the council had joined the movement for founding a world church, believing that it envisages the rapprochement, not a merger, of churches.

He devoted much attention to the tasks of consolidating ECB unity. At present the different trends — Evangelical Christians, Baptists and Pentecostals — are united in one organization. The previous national congress raised the question of merging with the Mennonites. Discussions are still continuing within communities among ECB believers who hold different views, and elements of intolerance are manifested during these discussions. This brings harm to unity. The year 1961 saw the emergence of the 'Action Group' whose work has also been detrimental to unity. Later on it changed its name to the 'Organizing Committee' and then to the 'Council of Churches'. The leaders of this movement were not elected by anyone and were not authorized by the fraternity. Nevertheless, they claimed the right to solve important questions, to excommunicate members, depose presbyters. The 'Action Group' declared that the present congress was not valid. They violate the laws of the church and the state. The 'Action Group' had been joined by an insignificant number of ECB believers and many of those who had diverged again returned to the ECB fold.

'There are observers from the "Action Group" at this congress,' Karev said, 'and we hope that its work will clear up the misunderstandings and that unity will be restored.'

'We would be happy to see restoration of unity and our re-unification by the centenary of our fraternity.'

Discussion began after the reports of the general secretary, the treasurer of the presidium of the council, the book-keepers of the office and the Auditing Commission. Among those who contributed to the discussion were senior presbyters of the Ukraine, the Far East, Eastern and Western Siberia, Kazakstan, the Central Asian republics, the Caucasus and Transcaucasia.

The convention will last till 7 October inclusive. Its agenda includes the following questions: the ECB faith, the approval of changes and amendments to the constitution adopted in 1963, the question of unity, papers on unity and the ministry of presbyters, and the election of leading bodies.

II

The All-Union ECB Congress, which was held in Moscow over four days, closed on Saturday, 8 October, with a special church service. Participating in the congress were more than 700 delegates. The report of the AUCECB was submitted by Alexander Karev, its secretary general. The congress considered and adopted a new charter in accordance with which Evangelical Christians, Pentecostals, Baptists and Mennonites are included in the union as equal churches. Changes have been introduced in the former charter. In particular, it has been established that senior presbyters and their assistants are to be elected at regional, interregional and republican meetings of presbyters. Another new principle is that councils of presbyters are to be elected to assist senior presbyters and that church affairs are to be decided in a collective manner.

One of the questions of the congress agenda was the adoption of the religious doctrine of the Evangelical Christians and Baptists, i.e. the basic dogmas and symbols of faith of this religious organization. The religious doctrine which was proclaimed in 1913 and drawn up by Ivan Kargel, a prominent religious leader who enjoyed equal authority among Baptists and Evangelical Christians, was adopted without any changes and amendments.

The question of unity occupied a prominent place in the congress proceedings. Representatives of all churches which in earlier years had signed agreements on the organization of a single union addressed the congress. These included Evangelical Christians, Pentecostals, Baptists, Apostolic Christians and Mennonites.

The congress was also addressed by representatives of what is known as the 'Action Group' (otherwise the 'Organizing Committee' or 'Council of Churches'). This movement which started in 1961 led to the withdrawal from the union of part of its members, an insignificant number to be sure (approximately 5 per cent). Some of the speakers pointed out that as a result of the wishes of their like-minded brethren in the schism and being impressed by the congress and its conciliatory trend, they were breaking with the Organizing Committee and would return to the united organization. Only two of the 'Action Group' read out statements in which they sharply condemned the activities of the AUCECB and the congress itself and refuted the possibility of unity through reconciliation. The congress adopted a decision on the need to strengthen unity between all churches included in the union.

The congress turned down as unfounded the accusations against the AUCECB and the congress made by the leaders of the 'Action Group'. The congress elected a commission of neutral persons which was charged with drawing up measures for a rapprochement with the 'Action Group' which had broken away.[66]

Further details of the congress are supplied by Josef Nordenhaug, General Secretary of the Baptist World Alliance, who was in the USSR on an official visit to the AUCECB later in the month in which the congress took place:

Representatives of these dissenting groups were invited to participate in the All-Union Congress, 4–6 October 1966, and to speak out freely and openly on every point of disagreement. Most of them accepted the invitation, and at least two of their representatives were elected to the AUCECB. The spirit of reconciliation was evident on both sides. Some groups rejoined the union.

Many of the leaders in the dissenting groups are Christians of deep convictions. But there are others who major on separatism. Some of these travel among the affiliated Baptist churches to turn them against the union. They send abusive circulars among the brotherhood. A few have a craving for being martyrs on a limited scale and deliberately seek to be arrested.

The number of 'dissenters' was estimated at about 15,000. The Baptist Union has an estimated membership of 550,000 in about 4,500 congregations. These dissenting groups within the local congregations are of great concern to the union leaders, who have pleaded with the authorities for 'leniency for their brethren in Christ' who are in prison. The result is not yet known. The congress in October named a committee to explore the possibilities of reconciliation with the remaining 'Action Group' supporters.

Perhaps the most significant step taken by the congress was the reorganization of the council into a more representative structure. During the last twenty years the leadership has been concentrated in the hands of a few 'elder leaders'.

The congress held 4–6 October 1966 had been under thorough preparation all over the Soviet Union since early spring. No less than 64 regional conferences were held for electing delegates to the congress. A total of 1,026 representatives attended. Of these 711 were delegates.

The need for defining more clearly the Baptist faith received thorough attention. With people of the diverse background of Baptists, Evangelical Christians, Pentecostals, and Mennonites it was felt that this was one of the primary needs. Many 'confessions' were used in the past as guides by the congress, but there was general acceptance of the doctrinal guide lines written by I. G. Kargel in 1913, which express the main teachings largely held by Baptists.

A new constitution was adopted in which the administrative set-up was revised. The Central Council (Executive Committee) was expanded to 25 with eight additional 'candidates' (standing proxies who will become regular members as vacancies occur). The council in turn elects nine of its members as the 'Presidium' (Administrative Committee).

Ilya Ivanov was elected president of the council to succeed Yakov Ivanovich Zhidkov; Alexander Karev was re-elected general secretary, and Ivan Motorin secretary-treasurer.

The congress meets every three years. The council meets when called. The president and the secretary of the congress are elected by the voting delegates of the congress to serve for that particular assembly.

Each geographic section has an area superintendent who oversees the work in his region and acts as the connecting link with the council of which he is a member. Delegates to the regional meetings are named directly by the churches on the basis of one representative for every 50 members.

The congress decided to place regional administration in the hands of local ministers' councils in each district. There are at present 47 regional superintendents and 17 'deputies'.[67]

Other sources add little extra to these accounts. A Czech Protestant newspaper published an account of the congress in November. On the opposition to the AUCECB it stated:

There remained numerous 'unregistered' little groups which were not connected with the AUCECB. A sober estimate speaks of about 25,000 believers. Moreover, in recent years a certain number of believers split from the AUCECB and followed their local leaders who did not agree with the central leadership of the church. This division cut across the congregations. A report by the European Baptist Press Service states that about 8 per cent of members have seceded from the AUCECB ... Numerous groups joined (or rejoined) the union of the entire church. Yet there still remain a very considerable number of those whose leaders 'do not wish to have any connection with the central leadership of the church.'[68]

This report summarizes the concessions thus:

Practically, this means a return to decentralization and church democracy which have proved themselves so well in our churches and which will surely profit our fraternal Baptist Council in the Soviet Union.[69]

On the retirement of the chairman, we are told:

The title of Honorary President was bestowed by the conference on Ya. I. Zhidkov. Alas, he could not enjoy this title for long. As early as the end of October God recalled him to the heavenly dwellings to which he himself showed the way to so many people.[70]

Our final source, a Soviet publication designed for distribution in Germany, adds nothing to our knowledge of the congress, but it does mention that Ya. I. Zhidkov, A. Kiryukhantsev and I. Motorin had been elected to the Executive Committee of the Baptist World Alliance.[71] However, by the time this article appeared, not only Zhidkov, but Kiryukhantsev too, was dead, the latter at an early age.[72]

1966 was an exceptionally unfortunate year for the AUCECB, for two of its leaders who had taken a most prominent part in the 1963 congress also died during the year: Nikolai Levindanto on 10 January and Alexei Andreyev on 16 April.[73]

These reports raise many more questions than they answer, and the *Bratsky Vestnik* account by no means clears them all up. One cardinal issue is whether or not CCECB opinion was adequately represented at the congress. Apart from Maiboroda and Kovalenko, it seems that no-one participated in the discussions from the point of view of the CCECB leadership, and Alexander Karev states that 'the "Council of Churches" not only itself refused to participate in the congress, but even called on its supporters not to do so.'[74] In other words, a boycott was in operation, almost certainly because the reformers did not consider that the elections to representation on it had been democratically carried out, or that no solution was possible while the state was terrorizing the reformers. The 1,026 representatives who attended were twice as many as those present in 1963,[75] but there is no indication of what proportion of these had ever supported the reform movement. Some ex-Prokofiev supporters addressed the congress and stated that they would return to the AUCECB, but — even making the likely assumption that they were genuine and not infiltrated for the purpose — they cannot have represented anyone but themselves. Despite this, some of what they say is impressive and it is more than a little surprising to find *Bratsky Vestnik* recording it. N. I. Vysotsky from Odessa stated:

The zealous supporters of the AUCECB are the first obstacle. They are more Catholic than the Pope, for they are ready to call all the schismatics 'servants of the devil'. . . . The work of unity is hindered by some ministers who firmly maintain a position of being too sure of their sinlessness.[76]

I. P. Bondar (from the Vinnitsa region) said:

Some senior presbyters are to blame for the schism, for they have been acting administratively, without considering the opinion of the church. People unjustly excluded from their congregations joined the 'Organizing Committee' because they had nowhere else to go.[77]

Even more notable were the words of M. I. Azarov (Belgorod), who declared that he was still not able to make a final decision whether or not to return to the AUCECB:

Here at the congress many have been blaming the 'Organizing Committee' for the schism. But in fact some of the regional senior presbyters appointed by the AUCECB are to blame for it — they were not senior (*starshimi*) but terrible (*strashnymi*). The senior presbyter of the Belgorod region has caused much pain, and until such men are removed we cannot be reunited.[78]

Azarov then turned to Alexander Karev and put three questions to him, the last of which was:

On the question of those who are undergoing terrible ordeals'[79] will they be helped and prayed for? Brother A. V. Karev replied that he himself had undergone terrible ordeals, so he had never forgotten and never would forget to pray for such people. This was a personal matter. Each believer could give material help out of his personal budget.[80]

In assessing the full significance of these words it should be remembered that the prominent Kiev newspaper, *Pravda Ukrainy*, had published its account of the imprisonment of I. D. Bondarenko, one of the most highly regarded members of the CCECB, on the very day on which the congress opened.[81] The news of his sentence to three years hard labour must have been weighing heavily indeed upon the congress (and the state authorities must have intended it to be so). The question therefore arises of how far this seriously prejudiced any chances of a true reconciliation from the outset. Certainly those non-repentant supporters of the CCECB present were under severe pressure, which makes Azarov's words the more remarkable.

As in 1963, the main business of the congress was to adopt an entirely new constitution, and this was done on the second day,[82] again it seems without any discussion of the points at issue. It is a more positive document than the 1963 version had been, with §§ 1 and 3 now clearly setting out what the aims of the ECB Church should be.[83] There are two most significant concessions in the direction of the demands of the reformers.

Firstly, there was the introduction of a new and more democratic way of appointing senior presbyters. §7 of the 1963 constitution had stated that 'the AUCECB appoints senior presbyters for each district, region and republic.'[84] §14 of the new constitution states:

(a) The AUCECB appoints senior presbyters and their helpers with the approval of the churches of which they are members and through their election at regional, inter-regional and republican meetings of presbyters;

(b) in order to help senior presbyters, these meetings elect councils of experienced ministers of the church. . . .[85]

It must be said, however, that the exact mechanism for the appointment of senior presbyters is left rather vague by the wording of this clause.

Secondly, greater independence certainly seems to have been

granted to local churches in the handling of their own affairs. §§ 19, 20 and 26 taken together are a much more positive statement of the aims and position of the local church than anything in the 1963 constitution. §26 now reads:

Each church which enters the ECB Union maintains its independence and autonomy; in its general meeting it decides the most important internal church questions, such as: the election and re-election of church officials, the reception and excommunication of members and other important questions presented by the church council for the church's decision.[86]

Previously the word 'excommunication' had been found only in the Prokofiev version of the statutes.[87]

Further apparent concessions to the demands of the reformers are to be found under §6, which introduces Prokofiev's demand that the members of the AUCECB must be 'worthy'.[88] §9 (e) contains a specific concession in stating that there will now be courses and seminars for ministers, preachers and choir trainers.[89] The AUCECB must now represent the interests of its member churches before the state (§9 (h)),[90] and there can no longer be any question of government representatives working in the AUCECB headquarters, for 'only members of the church may work in the office' (§ 13).[91] Places of worship can now be officially provided on the premises of private houses (§23)[92] — another specific concession to Prokofiev. The decisive factor in judging these changes is whether they will make any practical difference to the life of the church, and it is far too early yet to make any pronouncement on this.

In our preliminary assessment of the work of the congress we should finally mention the new composition of the AUCECB. There were changes in it because its plenum expanded to 25 members.[93] Josef Nordenhaug states that two former Prokofiev supporters were elected to it,[94] and we can identify one as V. F. Vasilenko.[95] However, this body can never be democratic while the congress does not represent all ECB communities (registered and unregistered) who wish to enter the union. Even with this proviso, it seems unlikely that the AUCECB plenum is designed

N

to exercise effective control over the ECB Church, because, as before, it need not meet more than once a year,[96] so the practical day-to-day running of affairs is not its responsibility. This devolves upon the presidium, now as before. Before the end of the congress the AUCECB plenum elected the following as members of the presidium: Ya. I. Zhidkov (honorary chairman), I. G. Ivanov (chairman), N. N. Melnikov and S. T. Timchenko (vice-chairmen), A. V. Karev (general secretary), A. I. Mitskevich (assistant general secretary), I. I. Motorin (treasurer), I. Ya. Tatarchenko, A. N. Kiryukhantsev and M. Ya. Zhidkov.[97] All these names are well-known as old AUCECB supporters, so it does not seem that there has been any substantial change in effective leadership. Owing to the deaths of Ya. I. Zhidkov and Kiryukhantsev so soon after the congress, this statement cannot be regarded as final, however.

One's tentative conclusions about the 1966 congress are that because of its composition it could not represent the true strength of the reformers, but it did allow some airing of basic issues and introduced concessions which suggest a real desire to be conciliatory on the part of the compilers of the new constitution. This could be of real significance in the future. The overriding issue of whether the AUCECB, which has been excommunicated by the CCECB, can represent the Evangelical Christians and Baptists of the Soviet Union in any democratic and spiritual way has not been solved. The issues at stake are of immense importance in the spiritual history of the 20th century and they are basic to the question of the struggle for human rights in the Soviet Union. Therefore it would hardly be conceivable that a short congress which made a few constitutional concessions should resolve the situation or suppress future discussion of the path the Protestant Christian must take under an atheist government.

In 1967 it became known that the CCECB leaders of Central Asia and Kazakhstan had not accepted the results of the congress[98] and there was news of further arrests.[99] A woman supporter of Prokofiev in Belorussia was executed for allegedly murdering her daughter, who had refused to join the sect.[100]

Epilogue

Although the CCECB has failed to gain the thoroughgoing reform of the AUCECB which it set out to achieve, and many of its most active supporters are now in prison for a second or third term, it would be a mistake to call the movement a failure. It is even doubtful whether the urge for reform has been suppressed or significantly conciliated. While the desire to disturb the *status quo* was confined to a minority church, the state was confronted with a problem which was irritating, but which it could hope to control. What it obviously feared was any possible spread of this disaffection into the Orthodox Church, a body not only receiving a certain degree of sympathy among intellectuals, but also of much greater numerical strength. 1965 saw the beginnings of a movement in the Russian Orthodox Church remarkably similar to the Baptist attempt at reform.

The first hint that something was afoot came from *Zhurnal Moskovskoi Patriarkhii*:

It was decided: 1. to release His Grace Archbishop Yermogen of Kaluga and Borovsk from his authority over the Kaluga diocese at his own request. In view of the fact that at present there is no suitable vacant see, he may retire. The Monastery of the Dormition at Zhirovitsy is designated as his residence.[1]

It was immediately apparent that there was something of more than usual importance behind these words, but it was hardly possible to guess its magnitude.

Full details soon became available, however, By April 1966 a series of letters reached the West which explained what lay behind the Archbishop's dismissal. The Eshliman–Yakunin documents[2] are undoubtedly the most significant texts on church–state relations to come out of the Soviet Union since the Revolution, and they take the subject of this book — the struggle for the church's right to govern its own affairs without state interference — into a much wider context.

The three documents were written and signed by two priests of the Moscow Diocese, Nikolai Eshliman and Gleb Yakunin, and they were dated November and December 1965. They were in the form of open letters, copies of which were sent to all bishops of the Moscow Jurisdiction of the Russian Orthodox Church.

The third document is the shortest and is merely a covering letter to the other two for the benefit of the bishops. It shows that in the summer of 1965 Archbishop Yermogen took the initiative in gathering together a delegation of eight bishops who went to the Patriarchate in order to present a petition criticizing the decision of a Council of Bishops which had taken place in 1961.[3] When the Archbishop of Kaluga presented his petition, he came under pressure from Archbishop Alexis of Tallin, an official of the Patriarchate. As a result, Archbishop Yermogen requested a transfer, but instead he was forced to retire, according to Eshliman and Yakunin, 'to please atheist bureaucrats'.[4]

The first document is an appeal to Mr. Podgorny, Chairman of the Presidium of the Supreme Soviet. Its main theme is this:

During the period 1957–64, under personal pressure from Khrushchev ... the Council for Russian Orthodox Church Affairs radically changed its function, becoming instead of a department for arbitration an organ of unofficial and illegal control over the Moscow Patriarchate.[5]

The authors go on to list eight specific categories of interference, with full legal references to show exactly in what way Soviet law has been contravened. They demand that the illegal control of the church by the Council for Russian Orthodox Church Affairs should cease, so that Christians should have the chance of again becoming loyal Soviet citizens; also that the many monasteries, seminaries and churches forcibly closed under Khrushchev should be reopened.

The second and longest document is addressed to the Patriarch. Expressing the deepest grief, yet preserving a spirit of loyal humility, Fathers Eshliman and Yakunin accuse the Moscow Patriarchate of complicity in the degeneration of church life which they had outlined in the first document. The essence of what they are saying is contained in these words:

> The submission of the Moscow Patriarchate to the secret oral dictates of atheist officials and the affirmation (by the 1961 Council of Bishops) of the Synodal decree, which placed the pastor in a position of a hireling, was an assault on the life of the Russian Church.[6]

Eshliman and Yakunin claim, in other words, that the introduction of the Council of Twenty had done more than anything else to undermine the life of the church.

We find here, as in the Baptist reform movement, the suggestion that the church authorities have been too supple in their relations with the state. The authors deliberately avoid making rash accusations, confining themselves to a documentation of objective facts in strict legal terminology. Always, however, they show that they wish to base themselves entirely on established Christian doctrines and in no way to break away from tradition as it is enshrined in the Orthodox Church. They call for an end to state interference in church affairs, they beg the Patriarch to be more rigorous in preventing this, but they underline that there must be no schism from the official church.

Was there a cross-fertilization of ideas from the smaller ECB Church into the massive Russian Orthodox Church? There are several pieces of evidence to suggest that this was so.

The timing is of great significance. The Kryuchkov–Vins document[7] was dated 14 April 1965, and seems to have been a direct ancestor of those written by Eshliman and Yakunin eight months later. Both reflect a broad intellectual approach to the problem of church–state relations and show that Russian Christians are now masters of a logical exposition of their rights. They are prepared to speak out in a new way, disregarding the fear of reprisal. The legal grasp of both Baptist and Orthodox documents is most impressive. The respective authors are at pains to avoid the charge of anti-Soviet activity, putting their demands firmly within the framework of the Constitution. In both documents the charge is brought that the state has forced the church to accept legislation which cannot be reconciled with basic guarantees of freedom contained in the Constitution. This has led to the exacerbation of the feelings of believers and could tempt them into rebellion against the regime. The Baptists do not at any point leave room for argument about their loyalty to the basic tenets of the faith of their church and no doctrinal issues are under discussion in the Organizing Committee's activities; the Orthodox, with a more hierarchical church order, emphasize their absolute loyalty to the Bible, canon law and the specific beliefs of their church.

Despite their moderation, Fathers Eshliman and Yakunin were asked by the Patriarch to retract what they had said. When they refused, the Patriarch took this action against the priests on 13 May 1966:

With the aim of shielding the Mother-Church from this disruption of its internal peace, we consider it essential to relieve them from their duties and ban them from priestly activities until their full repentance; moreover we warn them that if they continue their sinful activity we will be compelled to resort to sterner measures against them, in accordance with the demands of canon law.[8]

On 27 July Paul Anderson, editor of *Religion in Communist Dominated Areas* published by the National Council of Churches in New York, wrote to Metropolitan Nikodim, expressing his concern at what had been happening and requesting authoritative confirmation of it. This was forthcoming, and indeed Dr. Anderson was given specific permission to publish a circular letter from the Patriarch to all Bishops of the Russian Orthodox Church, dated 6 July.[9] Here the Patriarch forbids the Bishops to allow anyone in their dioceses to follow the initiative of Eshliman and Yakunin, for such activity gives the enemies of the Russian Church abroad ammunition for slandering it and could lead to schism.

Despite the Patriarch's warning, evidence is accumulating that support for Eshliman and Yakunin is increasing and spreading well beyond their own diocese of Moscow. There is now a very real danger of schism in the Orthodox Church similar to that among the Baptists, but if this should occur, it may well be asked

who is to blame. Is it the reformers (who as far as is known have
not disobeyed the Patriarch's ban on their continuing to serve as
priests)? Has the Patriarch shown lack of pastoral insight in
dealing with a difficult situation? (One should remember that
he is now ninety years old and is almost certainly incapable of
dealing with a major crisis.) Or has the state here directly inter-
fered in church affairs again and forced the Patriarch to take the
action he did?

The most outspoken supporter of Fathers Eshliman and
Yakunin is Anatoli Levitin, who writes under the pseudonym of
A. Krasnov. He had been ordained deacon in the 'Living
Church', a body which had tried to introduce certain reforms into
the Orthodox Church in the 1920's and had for a time enjoyed
state support. Later, however, he joined the Orthodox Church
as a layman and spent seven years in concentration camps. After
being amnestied in 1956 he became a frequent contributor to
Zhurnal Moskovskoi Patriarkhii.[10] He was the most outspoken
opponent of the campaign against the church during the later
Khrushchev period,[11] and he has now returned to the lists with
renewed vigour.

Two major letters by Levitin were published during 1966, but
they appeared in the Russian émigré press only and attracted very
little attention. In the first, entitled 'With Love and Anger',[12]
Levitin repudiates a fulsome encomium which he wrote on the
Patriarch's eightieth birthday in 1957 and which was published
in *Zhurnal Moskovskoi Patriarkhii*.[13] In words less moderate than
those of Fathers Eshliman and Yakunin, Levitin accuses the
Patriarch of a disastrous failure at the most critical point of his
ministry and demands that he should rescind his decision on the
suspension of the two priests.

The second letter, 'Listening to the Radio',[14] came soon after.
The title was occasioned by a B.B.C. broadcast from London —
a symposium of Western press reactions to the Eshliman-
Yakunin affair. In his article Levitin gives detailed information
of how the church has acquiesced in allowing the state to control
parochial and episcopal appointments. He cites several examples
of this, among which is the case of Bishop Antoni Vikarik, who

was appointed to the see of Smolensk in 1965. On arrival there he found the diocese in a chaotic and disgraceful state, so he set about restoring it and seemed destined for success when he bravely dismissed A. P. Zhirov, whom Levitin calls a notoriously ill-living archdeacon. However, Bishop Antoni was summoned to the Moscow Patriarchate and forced to reinstate Zhirov. After this the Bishop totally lost all the authority which he had had in his diocese.

During the first part of 1966 the Soviet press maintained silence about the situation in the Orthodox Church, while saying a great deal about the punitive measures which were being taken against the Baptist reformers. This silence was broken dramatically in October, and perhaps in the way one would least have expected. *Nauka i Religia* decided to publish a severe attack on Levitin, thus dispelling any doubts which may have lingered on in the West about the genuineness of his letters and drawing much greater attention to his writings than had previously been manifested.[15]

The article does not refer directly to the Levitin documents discussed above, but it gives lengthy quotations from a third, 'The Ailing Church'. By eliminating the commentary one is left with a catena of quotations from this letter. When they are strung together they show Levitin's argument quite clearly, and here is *Nauka i Religia*'s version of what he wrote:

Many bishops of the Russian Orthodox Church, maintains the author, 'are branches of a dead, sterile and useless fig tree. . . . There are many gangrened church members who are playing a pernicious role in its life; they are infecting it with their putrid exhalations and injecting poison into its most secret depths. Therefore the Russian Church is ill — seriously ill. . . . The most serious ailment is the age-old one of Caesaro-Papism (subjugation of the church to the narrow nationalistic interests of the secular state). . . . Is it not reprehensible that these lines are being written not by one of the hierarchy or by a member of the Holy Synod, but by me, a simple layman and school-master? . . . I am writing because you are silent; I am defending the church because you are failing in your duty. You should be ashamed! . . . ' If leaders do not oppose the state, he proclaims:

'They should still remember that the patience of Orthodox believers is not unlimited, and that their unworthy conduct can easily lead to schism.'

The article ends with a warning that there are laws which defend the interests of all Soviet citizens and they apply as much to Levitin as to anyone else. The author does not state whether or not it is the March 1966 law forbidding the circulation of religious manuscripts which he has in mind.[16] Levitin's offence, in fact, seems to be that

'he is trying to provoke the hierarchy of the Russian Orthodox Church to protest against repressions which are a figment of their own imagination.'[17]

This article may well be the herald of a change of policy by the Soviet Government towards the Orthodox Church. The authorities may have decided that their campaign to suppress the reform Baptists has been successful and has done so little harm to the image of the Soviet Union abroad that now a similar policy can be adopted towards the Orthodox Church. Certainly this is the type of article which has usually preceded an arrest in the past.

Yet the Soviet government may well be mistaken if it thinks that it can suppress this movement in the Orthodox Church by force. Although it is far too early to assess what will be the total reaction of the Orthodox Church to the Eshliman–Yakunin initiative, it would be unwise to underestimate the support which the Orthodox movement for reform already seems to command. Recently a document has become available which suggests that the diocese of Kirov is behind the Orthodox reformers almost *en masse*.[18]

Whether or not the attempt of Prokofiev and his supporters to purify and revitalize the ECB Church is ultimately successful, they may have triggered off an urge for reform which will sweep through all the Christian churches of the Soviet Union. If this should happen everywhere with such determination as has been shown in the ECB Church, Christianity may yet prove itself to be one of the most dynamic forces in the future evolution of Soviet society.

Appendix I   Constitution of the ECB Church in the USSR

The statutes of 1944 and 1948 were never published and are not known. Those of 1960 are known only from the Prokofiev–Kryuchkov document, while the 1963 constitution was published in *Bratsky Vestnik*.

The words in column I which the reformers wanted omitted are printed within square brackets,[ ]. The new words in column II which the reformers wanted included are printed within angular brackets, ⟨ ⟩, which are also used in column III to indicate those places where concessions seem to have been made. New words in column III are within half-brackets, ⌐ ⌐.

1960 Statutes	*Revision suggested by Prokofiev and Kryuchkov, 1961*	*1963 Constitution*[1]
	I GENERAL	
1. The ECB Union in the USSR is an association of believers of the Evangelical and Baptist faith.	1. The ECB Union in the USSR is a ⟨voluntary⟩ association of believers of the Evangelical and Baptist faith.	1. The ECB Union in the USSR is a ⟨voluntary⟩ association of churches of the Evangelical and Baptist faith. ⌐It embraces the former association of Evangelical Christians, Baptists, Christians of the Evangelical Faith,[2] and Mennonites.⌐

2. No change.[3]

2. No change.

2. The Holy Scriptures (the canonical books of the Old and New Testaments) form the doctrinal foundation of the Evangelical Christian and Baptist movement.

II STATUTES OF THE AUCECB IN THE USSR

THE AUCECB

3. In order to carry out the business of the ECB Church in the USSR, a central supervising body [has been created] — the AUCECB.

3. ⌐The supreme governing body of the ECB Union is the assembly of representatives of the ECB churches.

The assembly of church representatives is convened as necessary, but at least every 3 years.

The assembly of church representatives :

  (a) meets to examine questions affecting the internal life of the ECB Church ;⌐[7]

⟨(b) hears and ratifies reports from the AUCECB and its Auditing Commission ;

  (c) reviews, changes and confirms the statutes of the ECB Union.⟩

4. The AUCECB consists of 10 members, the most experienced [active members] of the ECB Church.

4. The AUCECB consists of 10 members, experienced ⟨ministers⟩ of the ECB Church, ⟨who are full of the Holy Ghost and wisdom (Acts 6. 3)⟩.

1960 Statutes	Revision suggested by Prokofiev and Kryuchkov, 1961	1963 Constitution
		⌐(d) To put into action the decisions of the assemblies of church representatives⌐ and to carry out the business of the ECB Union ⌐between assemblies⌐, ⟨the assembly of church representatives elects⟩ ⌐from among its participants⌐, by a simple majority vote, a central supervising body, the AUCECB, consisting of 10 members, ⌐5 candidate members and an Auditing Commission composed of 3 people⌐.4
		4. The AUCECB elects a Presidium from among its members consisting of ⌐five⌐ people :5 a chairman, ⌐two vice-chairmen⌐, a general secretary and a treasurer.
5. The AUCECB elects a working Presidium from among its members, located in Moscow and consisting of three people : a chairman, a general secretary and a treasurer.	5. No change.	

6. The AUCECB plenum meets as necessary.	6. The AUCECB plenum meets as necessary, ⟨but at least once every six months⟩.	5. The AUCECB plenum meets as necessary, ⟨but at least once a year⟩.[6]
7. The AUCECB has a seal and a stamp.	7. No change.	11. The AUCECB has a seal and a stamp.
8. The AUCECB has an office under the Presidium.	8. No change.	12. The AUCECB has an office under the Presidium.
9. The AUCECB keeps in a current account with a savings bank or the State Bank the voluntary contributions which come in from communities and individual believers.	9. No change.	13. The AUCECB keeps its material resources in a current account with the State Bank.
10. The AUCECB unites all [registered] ECB communities active on the territory of the USSR.	10. The AUCECB unites all ECB communities ⟨and groups⟩ active on the territory of the USSR ⟨according to the principle of voluntariness⟩. ⟨NB. Communities and groups have the right of withdrawing freely from the AUCECB. The latter may maintain contact with those who	(See 6(b) below)

1960 Statutes	*Revision suggested by Prokofiev and Kryuchkov, 1961*	*1963 Constitution*
	have left it and consider them to be brothers only when the withdrawal did not take place for reasons of heretical teaching or deviation from the word of God (2 John v.10, Tit. 3. 10).⟩	
		7. ⌐To keep in touch with⌐ ECB Churches and ⌐to give them spiritual and organizational help⌐, the AUCECB appoints senior presbyters for each district, region and republic. Senior presbyters are appointed from among experienced active members of the ECB brotherhood, ⟨with the agreement of the churches of which they are members⟩.⁷
11. The AUCECB [appoints and replaces] senior presbyters and examines their activities, both general and financial.	11. The AUCECB ⟨confirms the election and removal⟩ of senior presbyters and examines their activities, both general and financial.	
		8. The AUCECB ⌐periodically⌐ examines the activities of senior

presbyters, both general and financial.

6. Duties of the members of the AUCECB are :

   (a) ⌐to put into effect the decisions of the assembly of church representatives.⌐

   (b) to keep in touch with the ECB churches, both by correspondence and by visits ;

   (c) ⌐to give spiritual and organizational help to the ECB churches, both through the senior presbyters and directly.⌐

12. The AUCECB adheres to this principle of worship : ⟨both⟩ the members of the AUCECB ⟨and⟩ the senior presbyters ⟨accountable to it are considered to be⟩ only senior spiritual religious observers who see that ⟨God's word is observed (I Peter 5. 1–3).⟩

⟨NB. All instructions, decisions and documents of higher-ranking ministers, including those of the AUCECB, are accepted by the church only in so far as they do not contradict the Holy Scriptures (Gal. 1. 8–9).⟩

13. The AUCECB maintains contacts with communities ⟨and groups⟩, both by correspondence and by visits of its repre-

12. The AUCECB adheres to this principle of worship : [neither] the members of the AUCECB [nor its appointed] senior presbyters [take part in the performance of religious services], but are only senior spiritual observers who see that [the required discipline is maintained in the communities, in accordance with the decisions of the AUCECB and the Soviet laws on religious cults].

13. The AUCECB maintains contacts [only] with [registered] communities, both by correspondence and by visits of its

1960 Statutes	Revision suggested by Prokofiev and Kryuchkov, 1961	1963 Constitution
representatives [who do not take part in the performance of religious services by local ministers and do not replace the latter, but only observe and give instructions on complying with the required discipline in the communities and do not permit any violations of the present statutes].	sentatives. ⟨(Acts 15. 22–36 and 41; 16. 4–5, etc.)⟩	
14. The AUCECB keeps an [accurate] record of the communities, of senior presbyters, ministers and the number of members in the communities.	14. The AUCECB keeps a record of the communities, senior presbyters, ministers and the number of members in the communities.	(Cancelled)
15. The AUCECB [helps with] the training of [its] ministers [through practical advice and instructions].	15. The AUCECB ⟨organizes⟩ the training of ⟨ECB⟩ ministers through ⟨seminars and Bible courses⟩.	(Cancelled)

16. The AUCECB publishes the necessary religious literature.

17. The AUCECB maintains contact with related religious associations in foreign countries, corresponds with them, and when the need arises sends its representatives to their congresses and conferences.

18. Members of the AUCECB are elected [at special conferences of responsible representatives] by a simple majority of votes.

19. The accounts of the AUCECB are examined [during the plenary sessions of the

o

16. The AUCECB publishes the necessary religious literature ⟨and supplies it to the communities⟩.

17. The AUCECB maintains contact with related religious associations in foreign countries, corresponds with them, and when the need arises sends its representatives to their congresses and conferences ⟨and invites foreign spiritual leaders to visit it⟩.

18. Members of the AUCECB are elected ⟨at an All-Union Congress⟩ by a simple majority of votes.

19. The accounts of the AUCECB ⟨and of the Auditing Commission are examined by the All-

9. The AUCECB publishes the necessary religious literature ⟨for the ECB churches⟩.

10. The AUCECB maintains contact ⌐with other churches and associations close to it in faith⌐, and also with other Christian churches and organizations in foreign countries ; it conducts correspondence with them and, when the need arises, sends representatives to their congresses and conferences ; ⟨it also invites foreign spiritual leaders to the USSR⟩.

(See 3(d) above)

14. The auditing of finances, documents and financial reports is the concern of the Auditing

1960 Statutes	*Revision suggested by Prokofiev and Kryuchkov, 1961*	*1963 Constitution*
AUCECB by the Auditing Commission. The latter is made up of responsible active members of the Union elected in the same way as members of the AUCECB and consists of a chairman, a secretary and one additional member].	Union Congress of the ECB Church⟩.	Commission of the AUCECB. ⌐The Auditing Commission reports the results of its audits¬ ⟨to the assembly of church representatives⟩, and at plenary sessions of the AUCECB.
20. Changes in the statutes of the ECB Union are to be made by [decision of two-thirds of the votes of a plenum of the AUCECB].	20. Changes in the statutes of the ECB Union are to be made by ⟨the All-Union Congress of the ECB Church⟩.	(See 3(c) above)

III   REGULATIONS ON SENIOR PRESBYTERS

		ECB SENIOR PRESBYTERS
21. In order to [ensure that] ECB religious activities [are properly carried out in the regions and republics of] the USSR, [the AUCECB appoints] senior presbyters [wherever this may be necessary].	21. In order to ⟨watch over⟩ the religious activities of ECB ⟨communities⟩ in the USSR, ⟨individual communities elect⟩ senior presbyters ⟨(see also 11 above).⟩	(See 7 above)

[NB. Senior presbyters are appointed from the most worthy and experienced active members of the ECB Union].

15. It is the duty of the senior presbyters of the republics and regions :

(a) ⌜to help⌝ the churches situated in their territories, ⌜both spiritually (taking part in services, giving spiritual instruction, and explaining to believers the correct attitude to their Christian and civil obligations) and also from the organizational standpoint⌝ ;

⟨⟨Cancelled⟩⟩

(b) ⌜to share when possible in the administration of the church and in the ordinances of the church and in the choosing of the church's ministers⌝ and to ordain them ;

22. A senior presbyter has the following duties :

(a) to watch over the religious activities of each community situated in his territory ;

⟨⟨Cancelled⟩⟩

(b) to see that new ministers are ⟨properly elected⟩ and to ordain them ;

22. A senior presbyter has the following duties :

(a) to watch over the religious activities of each [registered] community situated in his territory, [especially with regard to the admission of new members and the character of religious services and meetings] ;

(b) [to ensure compliance with strict church discipline] ;

(c) to see that new [worthy] ministers are [made available] and to ordain them ;

1960 Statutes	*Revision suggested by Prokofiev and Kryuchkov, 1961*	*1963 Constitution*
(d) to keep an [accurate] list of ministers, [registered] communities and church members in his territory.	(c) to keep a list of ministers, communities, and church members in his territory.	(c) to keep a list of the churches and numbers of church members in their territories.
		(d) ⌜Senior presbyters of republics, in addition to this, direct the work of regional senior presbyters and keep a list of churches and church members in the whole republic.⌝ [8]
23. Senior presbyters are appointed, removed or transferred [by the AUCECB only].	23. Senior presbyters are appointed and removed ⟨by regional ECB conferences with the approval of the AUCECB⟩. NB. The transfer of senior presbyters is made by the AUCECB ⟨with the approval of the communities concerned⟩.	(Cancelled) [9]

24. Senior presbyters [have to] report to the AUCECB :

   (a) on their activities — [in quarterly religious reports] ;

   (b) [concerning financial matters, in monthly financial reports] ;

   (c) regional senior presbyters [in republics of the USSR] report on their activities [and on financial matters not only to the AUCECB, but also] to the senior presbyters of the republic ;

   (d) [the activities and financial reports of senior presbyters are periodically examined by representatives of the AUCECB].

24. Senior presbyters report on their activities to :

   (a) ⟨the regional conferences⟩ ;

   (b) the senior presbyters of the republic ;

   (c) the AUCECB.

10. (a) Regional senior presbyters report on their activities and finances to the senior presbyter of the republic.

   (b) Senior presbyters of republics periodically report to the AUCECB on their activities and finances.

IV REGULATIONS ON ECB CHURCHES AND THEIR MINISTERS

IV REGULATIONS ON ECB CHURCHES AND THEIR MINISTERS

ECB CHURCHES AND THEIR MINISTERS

25. The ECB churches are associations of believers who have

25. The ECB churches are associations of believers who have

17. The ECB churches are an association of believers of the

1960 Statutes	Revision suggested by Prokofiev and Kryuchkov, 1961	1963 Constitution
received water baptism [as adults].	received water baptism ⟨for their faith⟩.	Evangelical and Baptist faith who are of age and have received water baptism ⟨for their faith⟩.
26. Only persons who [are of age and who have gone through a trial period of not less than 2–3 years] may be members of the ECB churches.	26. Only persons who ⟨have received water baptism on profession of their faith and have been accepted by the church⟩ may be members of the ECB churches ⟨(Acts 8. 12)⟩.	
27. Any person desiring to receive baptism for his faith [makes the necessary application] to the minister of the church.	27. Any person desiring to receive ⟨water⟩ baptism for his faith ⟨declares this verbally or in writing⟩ to the minister of the church ⟨depending on the established order of the church⟩.	18. Each person wishing to receive water baptism for his faith makes a written request to the minister of the church, ⌜and undergoes the corresponding examination⌝.
28. Water baptism is performed by immersion of the person being baptized [and, as a rule, during the summer].	28. Baptism is performed by immersion of the person being baptized ⟨(Acts 8. 38)⟩.	(Cancelled)

29. The ECB churches conduct their services [only in places of worship] provided by the state, [or in suitable rented quarters].

30. The ECB churches [usually] meet for worship on Sundays and [on a week-day which is convenient under local conditions] ; in addition, worship is held at festivals [such as Christmas, New Year, Epiphany, the Circumcision, Annunciation, Easter, Ascension, Trinity, the Transfiguration, Harvest Festival and the Day of Unity].
[NB. No kind of worship meetings should be held in a private dwelling, with the exception of funerals.]

31. The breaking of bread in ECB churches is [usually] observed once a month, [on the first Sunday of each month].

29. The ECB churches conduct their services ⟨either⟩ in ⟨premises⟩ provided by the state ⟨or by private persons⟩.

30. The ECB churches meet for worship on Sundays, on ⟨Christian⟩ festivals, and on ⟨any week-days at the discretion of the church⟩.

31. The breaking of bread in ECB churches is observed ⟨at the discretion of the church, but at least⟩ once a month ⟨(Acts 2. 46 ; 20. 7)⟩.

19. The ECB churches conduct their services in houses provided by the state or on rented premises.

20. The ECB churches meet for worship on Sundays and also ⟨on week-days⟩ at the discretion of the church and on ⟨Christian⟩ festivals : Christmas, New Year, Epiphany, the Circumcision, Annunciation, Easter, Ascension, Trinity, the Transfiguration, Harvest Festival and the Day of Unity.

21. The breaking of bread in ECB churches is observed ⟨at the discretion of the church⟩, usually on the first Sunday of each month.

1960 Statutes	*Revision suggested by Prokofiev and Kryuchkov, 1961*	*1963 Constitution*
32. (a) The minister of the church is the person principally responsible for services ;	32. No change.	22. (a) The minister of the church is the person principally responsible for services ⌈and the spiritual education of church members⌉.
(b) [the executive body of the church consists of three members elected according to the established principles ; it supervises all the affairs of the church] ;	⟨(Cancelled)⟩	(b) The minister is elected by the church.
		(c) ⌈A church council of three persons is elected by the church.⌉ 10
(c) as each church has a financial account into which the voluntary offerings of believers are paid, an Auditing Commission of three persons is elected, which periodically audits the accounts of the church and compiles the corresponding statement of accounts.	No change.	(d) As each church has a financial account into which the voluntary offerings of believers are paid, an Auditing Commission of three persons is elected ⌈by the church⌉, which periodically audits the accounts ⌈and the material effects of the church⌉, and compiles the corresponding statement of accounts.

23. The minister performs all the ordinances of the church.
    NB. In the case of the illness or absence of the minister, ⌐members of the church council or preachers of the church perform the ordinances, on the instructions of the minister and the church council⌐.

24. Besides the minister, ⟨other church members may take part in the preaching at services⟩, ⌐on the instructions of the minister and church council⌐.

33. The minister ⟨and persons appointed for this purpose by the church⟩ perform all the ordinances of the church, such as baptism, breaking of bread, marriage and funeral services, prayers for the sick ⟨and for children⟩.

34. ⟨Members of the church at the descretion of the community⟩ take part in the sermon at services.

⟨⟨Cancelled⟩⟩

33. The minister performs all the ordinances of the church, such as baptism, breaking of bread, marriage and funeral services and prayers for the sick.
    [NB. In case of the illness or absence of the minister, these ordinances are performed by one of the members of the executive body of the community.]

34. [Only persons belonging to the executive body] take part in the sermon at services. [No other person, either from the church or guests from other places, may participate in the sermon.]
    [NB. In case of the absence of the minister and of members of the executive body from the meeting (through illness or reasons of work), members of the community who belong to the Auditing Commission may

1960 Statutes	*Revision suggested by Prokofiev and Kryuchkov, 1961*	*1963 Constitution*
be permitted to take part in the sermon.]		
35. The minister is elected by the church.	35. No change.	(See 22(b) above)
36. (a) All matters of the church are decided [by its executive body] ;	36. (a) All matters of the church are decided ⟨by its church council⟩ ;	25. (a) ⌜Spiritual questions⌝ are decided ⌜by the minister⌝, together ⟨with the church council⟩ and ⌜the preachers of the church⌝ ;
(b) [more complicated problems] are referred, [if necessary], to the church for its decision. [Such matters may include] : the election of church officers, [their replacement, the repair of church premises, the election of members of the executive body of the church and of members of the Auditing Commission].	(b) the election of ministers, ⟨admission to church membership, penalties, excommunications and other important problems⟩ are submitted to the community for their decision.	(b) all other matters are decided by the church council with the participation of the minister and members of the Auditing Commission ;
		(c) the most important questions (such as the election of church officers or their replacement, the election of members to the church council

and the Auditing Commission and other major questions are referred by the church council to the church for its decision.

⟨(Cancelled)⟩

26. (a) In ECB churches, in addition to preaching and prayer, congregational and choral singing (⟨with musical accompaniment⟩) is an intrinsic part of worship.

(b) Singers in the choir, their trainers and accompanists are, ⌜as a rule⌝, believers of the Evangelical and Baptist faith.

[NB. Minutes are kept of all meetings of the executive body and of the community, which are signed by the executive body of the community.]

⟨(Cancelled)⟩

37. (a) No change. ⟨(Ps. 150. 3–6)⟩

(b) ⟨Choir members, choir trainers and organists have to be members of the church.⟩

---

37. (a) In ECB churches in addition to preaching and prayer, congregational and choral singing is an intrinsic part of worship ;

(b) [the choir consists only of persons who are members of the church ; they receive no kind of remuneration for taking part in choral singing and the choir performs only in its own church] ;

1960 Statutes	*Revision suggested by Prokofiev and Kryuchkov, 1961*	*1963 Constitution*
(c) [choir trainers and organists are also members of the church and may be paid by the church] ;	⟨(Cancelled)⟩	
(d) [choral singing is carried out on a limited scale, without transforming the service into a religious concert].	⟨(Cancelled)⟩	
[NB. No other instruments except a harmonium or organ — and in exceptional cases an upright piano — may be used at church services.]		
38. (a) Each church has its own financial account, into which the voluntary offerings of believers are paid ;	38. No change.	27. (a) Each church has its own financial account, into which the voluntary offerings of believers are paid ;
(b) the church's funds are spent : on the upkeep of church premises, on the main-		(b) the church's funds are spent : on the upkeep of church premises, on the maintenance of

church officers and for other church purposes ; ⌜such as quotas to AUCECB funds and also to the funds of the senior presbyters of the regions and the republic⌝ ;

(c) a book for recording income and expenditure is kept in each church ; this is examined periodically by the church's Auditing Commission, which prepares statements of accounts ;

(d) each church has an inventory book, in which the property of the church is entered — both what is received from the state ⌜by contract⌝ and what is bought and donated.

---

tenance of church officers and for other church purposes ;

(c) a book for recording income and expenditure is kept in each church ; this is examined periodically by the church's Auditing Commission, which prepares statements of accounts ;

39. Each church has an inventory book, in which the property of the church is entered — both what is received from the state and what is bought and donated ;

39. No change.

The changes and additions to the text of statutes of the ECB Union in the USSR which are now in effect have been made by the Action Group for the

1960 Statutes	Revision suggested by Prokofiev and Kryuchkov, 1961	1963 Constitution
	Convening of an Extra-ordinary All-Union ECB Congress in the USSR. By authorization of the Action Group for the Convening of the Congress, Presbyters : A. F. Prokofiev G. K. Kryuchkov.	

Appendix II   List of Prisoners

This list is provided as a tentative guide to those members of the Baptist reform movement imprisoned since 1961. Conflicting information appears in different sources. While the most likely variant has been included, several names and details should be regarded as provisional only. The principal sources are *Communist Exploitation of Religion* (U.S. Government Information Office, Washington, D.C., 1966) and the unpublished Appendix II to the Kryuchkov–Shalashov document. A further list of people imprisoned in 1967 appears on p. 247 (see p. 63).[1]

Name	First names or initials	Date of birth	Place of residence/trial*	Date of arrest	Length of sentence†	Press ref.‡	Remarks
Aglicheva	L. D.		Smela, Ukraine.	1964	5p		
Akhmetvaleyeva	Lidia		Kazan, Tatar ASSR.	1963	5p		
Alexandrov	P. V.		Dedovsk, Moscow region.	1961	5d	SKu 3/2/62	
Altrekhov	M. T.		Tula region.	1961	5d		
Altukhov	I. I.		Semipalatinsk, Kazakhstan.	1962	5sr		
Antonenko	Vladimir I.		Minsk, Belorussia.	1962	5p		
Arent	Yu. V.	1888	Semipalatinsk, Kazakhstan.	1962	1p	KzP 12/12/62	Released by 1964.

* RSFSR unless otherwise stated.   † p=prison ; d=deportation ; sr=strict regime. ‡ see pp. 231–2 for abbreviations.

Name	First names or initials	Date of birth	Place of residence/ trial*	Date of arrest	Length of sentence†	Press ref.‡	Remarks
Arilkin	P. P.		Kursk.	1961	5d		
Artyushenko	B. T.		Kursk.	1961	5d		
Avetisov	V.		Yangi-Yul, Uzbekistan.	22/3/61			
Azarov	M. I.		Belgorod.	1963	5d		
Babich	Trofim Trofimovich	1933	Tselinograd, Kazakhstan.	March 1962			
Balatsky	A.	1930 or later	Lugansk, Ukraine.	July 1966		KZn 16/7/66	
Ballikh	Ya. I.		Kant, Kirgizia	Between 1961 and Feb. 1964			
Bannikov	G.		Pikhtovka, Novosibirsk region.	1962	5d		
Barishev	Vasili Yakovlevich		Tselinograd, Kazakhstan.	March 1962			
Bartolomei	I. N.		Slavuta, Ukraine.	1962	3½p	Pos 25/11/66	Second term?
Baturin	N. B.		Shakhty, Rostov region.	1962	5d	SRo 22/11/66	— reported free.

Name	Initials	Born	Place	Date	Sentence	Source	Notes
Bazilyuk	P.		Tselinograd, Kazakhstan.	March 1962			
Belan	M. I.		Tashkent, Uzbekistan.	1966		*PrV* 22/10/66	
Belenki	P. D.		Rostov-on-Don.	August 1966	3p(?)	*Pr* 19/2/66 *UGa* 23/8/66 *Times* 22/9/66	
Belotserkovsky	L. A.		Ponomarevka, Novosibirsk region.	1962	5d		
Benishchuk	K. F.		Vovkivchiki, Ukraine.	1962	3p		
Bezmatny			Cherkassk, North Caucasus region.	1962	5d		
Boiko	L.		Tselinograd, Kazakhstan.	March 1962			
Bolegov Bolgova	A. E.		Perm. Rostov-on-Don.	1962 1966	5d 3p(?)	*UGa* 23/8/66 *Times* 22/9/66	
Bondarenko	Iosif Danilovich	1936	Odessa, Ukraine.	1962	5p and 3d	*PrU* 4/10/66	Released early.
			Kiev, Ukraine.	1966	3sr	*Pos* 25/11/66	

* RSFSR unless otherwise stated. † p=prison ; d=deportation ; sr=strict regime. ‡ see pp. 231–2 for abbreviations.

Name	First names or initials	Date of birth	Place of residence/trial*	Date of arrest	Length of sentence†	Press ref.‡	Remarks
Bondarenko	Vasili Danilovich	1929	Kirovograd, Ukraine.	1962	5p and 5d		
Bortyuk	D. I.		Presluzh, Ukraine.	1961	5d		
Braun	Maria		Sokuluk, Kirgizia.	March 1966	5p	SKi 18/3/66 SKi 15/6/67	
Brykov	M. I.		Ordzhonikidze, North Ossetia ASSR.	1961	5d		Released 1964.
Budemir	I. M.		Barnaul, Altai region.	1962	2p		
Butkov	N.	1930 or later	Lugansk, Ukraine	July 1966		KZn 16/7/66	
Bykov	M.		Kursk region.	1963	5d		
Bykova	N. P.		Cheboksary, Chuvash ASSR.	1966	3p	SRo 22/11/66	
Chernetskaya	Yelena		Sokuluk, Kirgizia.	1966	5p	SKi 18/3/66 SKi 15/6/67	
Chernikov	I. K.		Ossetinsk region.				Released.

Name	Initials	Birth year	Place	Date	Sentence	Source
Chesenko	B.		Cherkassy, Ukraine.	1964		
Disenko	I. Yu.		Tevriz, Omsk region.	1963	5d	
Dyumin	N. B.		Kursk.	1963	4d	
Esau	Yakov		Issyk, Kazakhstan.	1962		
Fedin	N. P.		Kopeisk, Chelyabinsk region.	1963	5d	
Fedorchuk	Ye. N.		Brest, Belorussia.	1963	3p	*SBe* 12/5/63
Fenin	I. I.		Krasnodar, North Caucasus region.	1962	5d	
Garmashov	Boris I.	1933	Tashkent, Uzbekistan.	1963	5p	*PrV* 29/2/64
Gernikov	N. K.		North Ossetia ASSR.	Between 1951–64		
Gladkevich	B.		Kishinyov, Moldavia.	1964	4p and 5d	*SMo* 15/9/66
Glukhoi	Leonid A.	1938	Kirovograd, Ukraine.	21/12/62	5p and 5d	
Golub	V.	1930	Lugansk, Ukraine.	July 1966		*KZn* 16/7/66

* RSFSR unless otherwise stated.   † p=prison ; d=deportation ; sr=strict regime. ‡ see pp. 231–2 for abbreviations.

Name	First names or initials	Date of birth	Place of residence/ trial*	Date of arrest	Length of sentence†	Press ref.‡	Remarks
Gortfeld	German G.	1942	Semipalatinsk, Kazakhstan.	1962	5sr		Released early.
			Tashkent, Uzbekistan.	October 1966		PrV 22/10/66	
Graboshchuk	A. M.		Vovkivchiki, Ukraine.	1962	3p		
Grosheva	Nadezhda	1938			1p		
Grubich	Nikolai Iosifovich		Poltava, Ukraine.				
Grunvald	I. E.		Alma-Ata region, Kazakhstan.	1962	3p	KzP 19/12/62	
Gubarev	V.		Gasmishchevo, Belgorod region.	1963	5d		
Inina	A. F.		Novocherkassk, Rostov region.	1964	5d		
Kasler	D. I.		Tevriz, Omsk region.	1963	5d		
Kavchuk	F. N.		Shepetovka, Ukraine.	1962	3p		
Kayukov	A. L.		Dedovsk, Moscow region.	1961	5d	SKu 3/2/62	
Kechik	A. T.		Kiev, Ukraine.	1966	2p	PrU 4/10/66	

Surname	Name	Born	Place	Date	Sentence†	Source	Notes
Keyatungen	V.		Mezhdurechensk, Kemerovo region.	1963	5d		
Khlopina	Yevgenia		Nikitovka, Ukraine.	1964	4p		Released 1964.
Khmara	Nikolai Kuzmich		Kulunda, Altai region.	1963	3p	SYu 9, 1964	Died in Barnaul prison on 9/1/64.
Khmara	Vasili Kuzmich	1916	Kulunda, Altai region.	1963	3p	SYu 9, 1964	
Khoroshenko	M. K.		Ust-Ishim, Omsk region.	1963	5d		
Khrapov	Nikolai Petrovich	1913	Tashkent, Uzbekistan.	March 1961	7p		Released 1964.
			Tashkent, Uzbekistan.	October 1966		PrV 22/10/66	
Kirilov	I. G.		Krasnodar, North Caucasus region.	1962	5d		
Klassen	A. P.		Issyk, Alma-Ata region.	1964	4p	KzP 18/8/67	Fresh sentence at Alma-Ata 1967.
Klassen	David Ivanovich		Karaganda, Kazakhstan.	Between 1961 and Feb. 64		KzP 18/8/67	Length and initials not stated.

* RSFSR unless otherwise stated.   † p=prison ; d=deportation ; sr=strict regime.   ‡ see pp. 231–2 for abbreviations.

Name	First names or initials	Date of birth	Place of residence/ trial*	Date of arrest	Length of sentence†	Press ref.‡	Remarks
Kobzar	I. S.		Krasnodar, North Caucasus region.	1962	5d		
Korobka	Anna P.		Dergachi, Ukraine.	1963	3p		
Kotovich	I. A.		Brest, Belorussia.	1963	4p	SBe 12/5/63	
Kovalchuk	A. I.		Rovno, Ukraine.	1962		Church Times 15/9/67	Tortured 1963; re-investigated 1966; wrote account.
Kovalev	P. G.		Omekh, Omsk region.	1961	2d		
Kozlov	V. I		Yoshkar-Ola, Mari ASSR.	1961 1966	5d	Pos 25/11/66 SRo 22/11/66 KzP 18/8/67	
Krivko	M.		Merefa, Ukraine.	1961	1½p		Released.
Krivosheyev	Nikolai Konstantinovich	1931	Semipalatinsk, Kazakhstan.	1962	5sr	KzP 12/12/62	1963 released.
Kroker	K. K.		Mezhdurechensk, Kemerovo region.	1962	5d		

Kryuchkov	Gennadi Konstantinivich				Pos 25/11/66 —reported in prison. SRo 22/11/66 —reported free.
Kucherenko	Nikolai Samoilovich	Nikolaev, Ukraine.			22/1/62 died during police investigation.
Kuksenko	Yu. F.	Kazan, Tatar ASSR. Kokchetav region.	1961	5d	
Kun⎱ Kun⎰			Between 1961 and Feb. 1964		Father and son of this surname arrested.
Kuzmicheva	N.	Kazan, Tatar ASSR.	1963	5p	
Lapaev	M. F.	Tselinograd, Kazakhstan.	March 1962		1963 died in prison.
Latyshev	A.	Novorossiisk region.	Between 1961 and Feb. 1964		
Lavrinov	V. S.	Spassky district, Primorsky region.	1961	5d	Released 1964.

* RSFSR unless otherwise stated.   † p=prison ; d=deportation ; sr=strict regime.   ‡ see pp. 231–2 for abbreviations.

Name	First names or initials	Date of birth	Place of residence/ trial*	Date of arrest	Length of sentence†	Press ref.‡	Remarks
Lebedev	G. D.		Barnaul, Altai region.	1962	4sr		
Legostaev		1913	Arkhangelsk.	1963			
Leshchenko	Anna Mikhailovna	1938	Kirovograd, Ukraine.	21/12/62	4p		
Levchuk	A. N.		Khmelnitsky, Ukraine.	1962	5p and 5d		
Levchuk	T. N.		Khmelnitsky, Ukraine.		4p and 4d		
Lozovaya	Marta		Kharkov, Ukraine.	1961	3d		
Lozovoi	A. D.		Kharkov, Ukraine.	1961	5d		
Lozovoi	V. A.		Kharkov, Ukraine.	1961	1½p		1963 released.
Lvova	Nadezhda		Novosibirsk.	1962	5d		
Makarenko	Grigori M.		Minsk, Belorussia.	1962	2p		
Maks	Fyodor		Tselinograd, Kazakhstan.	Between 1961–63			1963 died in prison.
Matveyuk	S. A.		Brest, Belorussia.	1963	5p	SBe 12/5/63	

				PrV 22/10/66	SRo 22/11/66
Matyukhina	N. P.	Tashkent, Uzbekistan.	1966		
Mayorova	V. S.	Cheboksary Chuvash ASSR.	1966		3p
Merkulov	V. V.	Kazan, Tatar ASSR.	1963		5p
Mikhalkov	Yu. I.	Barnaul, Altai region.	1962		3p
Minaev	N. I.	Kursk.	1963		5d
Minipov	D. V.	Barnaul, Altai region.	1962		5sr
Minyakov	Dmitri B.				
Miroshnichenko	I. M.	Kozharka, Novosibirsk region.	1962		5d
Morozovsky	V. I.	Khmelnitsky, Ukraine.	1962		3p
Mosha	V. K.	Kharkov, Ukraine.	1961		3p
Movchan	V.	Kharkov, Ukraine.	1963		3p
Nalivaiko	Ya. M.	Sumy region, Ukraine.	1961		4d
Nefedov	A. P.	Bokhovets, Belgorod region.	1963		5d

* RSFSR unless otherwise stated.   † p=prison; d=deportation; sr=strict regime.   ‡ see pp. 231–2 for abbreviations.

Name	First names or initials	Date of birth	Place of residence/ trial*	Date of arrest	Length of sentence†	Press ref.‡	Remarks
Nesredov	F. F.		Tselinograd, Kazakhstan.	March 1962			
Neverov	Alexei I.		Tashkent region, Uzbekistan.	1964	5p	*PrV* 29/2/64	
Neverov	Leonid	1933	Tashkent, Uzbekistan.				
Nikolaeva	N. P.		Cheboksary, Chuvash ASSR.	1966	3p	*SRo* 22/11/66	
Novozhilov	L. S.		Perm.	1963	5d		
Obusova	Yevdokia		Perm.	1962	5d		
Ogorodnikov			Tashkent, Uzbekistan.				Released 1964.
Olkhov	S. F.		Krasnodar, North Caucasus region.	1962	5d		
Ovchinnikov	L. D.		Kiev, Ukraine.	1961	3d		
Overchuk	P. S.		Tselinograd, Kazakhstan.	1966	2½p	*PrU* 4/10/66	
Parishev	V. Ya.			March 1962			
Peters	D. D.		Kortitsa, Orenburg region.	1964	5d		
Peters	Yekaterina		Kortitsa, Orenburg region.	1964	5d		

Pigareva	A. T.		Nikitovka, Ukraine.			Released 1964.
Pilipenko	Alexei P.		Minsk, Belorussia.	1962	3p	
Plit	Asaf G.	1943	Semipalatinsk region, Kazakhstan.	1962	1p	Released 1963.
Plit	Erna	1936			1p	
Popov	A. Ya.		Nikitovka, Ukraine.	1964	5p	Released 1964.
Prokhorenko	F. Ya.		Vitebsk, Belorussia.		5p and 5d	
Prokofiev	Alexei Fyodorovich	1913	Volnovaya, Ukraine.	August 1962	5sr and 5d	*SMo* 27/1/63
Pugaryova	Taissa		Nikitovka Ukraine.	1964	4p	
Pusanov	I. I.		Kursk.	1961	5d	
Pusanov	P. I.		Kursk.	1963	5d	
Putinin			Tashkent, Uzbekistan.			Released 1964.
Radyonov	P. T.		Demidov, Smolensk region.	1963	3p	
Renina	Yelena		Tatar ASSR.	Between 1961 and Feb. 1964		

* RSFSR unless otherwise stated.   † p=prison ; d=deportation ; sr=strict regime.   ‡ see pp. 231–2 for abbreviations.

Name	First names or initials	Date of birth	Place of residence/ trial*	Date of arrest	Length of sentence†	Press ref.‡	Remarks
Rogozhin	Ya. S.		Rostov-on-Don.	1963	4d		
Rudnev	Viktor Trofimovich	1926	Semipalatinsk, Kazakhstan.	1962	5sr	*KzP* 12/12/62	
Rumachek	P. V.		Dedovsk, Moscow region.	1961	5d	*SKu* 3/2/62	
Rumyantsev	Trifon Petrovich	1893 or earlier	Tashkent, Uzbekistan.				Released 1964.
Rybalka	V.		Nikitovka, Ukraine.	1964	5p		Released 1964.
Rykova	Maria		Mtsensk.	1966		*Izv* 5/6/66	Under investigation at Mtsenk.
Ryzhenko			Cherkassk, North Caucasus region.	1962	5d		1963 died at place of deportation.
Ryzhuk	V. F.		Nakhabino, Moscow region.	1961	5d	*SKu* 3/2/62	
Sadonikov	S. A.		Ust-Ishim, Omsk region.	1963	5d		
Samokhvalov	I. S.		Perm.	1962	3d		Released 1964.

Name	Christian name	Place	Date of birth	Date	Sentence†	Source	Remarks
Samsonenko	F. I.	Novorossiisk, North Caucasus region.	1903	1963	5d		Released 1963.
Saveliev	Stepan I.	Baku, Azerbaijan.		Between 1961 and Feb. 1964		BkR 7/4/63	
Savin	I. V.	Kazan, Tatar ASSR.		1963	5p		
Semeryuk		Tashkent, Uzbekistan.					Released 1964.
Shalypin	D. A.	Demidov, Smolensk region.		1963	5sr and 5d		
Sharanov	M.	Tselinograd, Kazakhstan.		March 1962			
Shatunov	L. F.	Kursk.		1962	5d		
Shepel	N.	Cherkassy, Ukraine.		1964			
Shepetunko	G. N.	Brest, Belorussia.		1963	5p	SBe 12/5/63	
Shevchenko	Nikolai Pavlovich	Odessa, Ukraine.	1913	1962	4p and 3d		
Shevchuk	Maria N.	Namangan, Uzbekistan.		1963	2p	PrV 15/11/63	
Shevchuk	P. D.	Pechersky, Ukraine.		1963	2p		

* RSFSR unless otherwise stated.   † p= prison ; d=deportation ; sr=strict regime.   ‡ see pp. 231–2 for abbreviations.

Name	First names or initials	Date of birth	Place of residence/ trial*	Date of arrest	Length of sentence†	Press ref.‡	Remarks
Shiva	P. G.		Tashtagol, Kemerovo region.	1962	5d		
Shokha	N. M.		Smela, Ukraine.	1964	5p and 5d		
Shornik	Agrippina		Protopopovka, Ukraine.	1963	3p		
Shornik	P. S.		Protopopovka, Ukraine.	1963	2p		
Shostenko	G. F.		Rostov-on-Don.	1963	2d		
Shoza	P. M.		Crimea region.	Between 1961 and Feb. 1964			
Shtefin	T. P.		Issyk, Kazakhstan.	1964	5sr		
Shvertser	A. A.		Barnaul, Altai region.	1962	5sr		
Sirokhin	Ye. M.		Sokolovo, Ukraine.	1962	3p		
Smirnov	V. Ya.		Dedovsk, Moscow region.	1961	5d	SKu 3/2/62	
Sogachev	Ye. Ye.		Kursk.	1961	5d		
Sokolov	I. V.		Kursk.	1963	4d		

Name	Initials	Place	Date	Sentence†	Notes
Soloshenko	Ia. Ia.	Lebedinsky district, Ukraine.	1962	5d	
Solovyov	Pyotr Pavlovich	Tselinograd, Kazakhstan.	March 1962		
Starkov	M. G.	Perm.	1962	5d	
Streltsov	A.	Kharkov, Ukraine.	1961	$1\tfrac{1}{2}$p	Released 1963.
Subbotin	F. I.	Kulunda, Altai region.	1963	5p	*SYu* 9, 1964
Suchkov	V. S.	Kazan, Tatar ASSR.	1964	3p	
Sulin	M. A.	Kaliningrad.	1962	5d	Released 1964.
Syromyatnikov	D. G.	Laptevka, Belgorod region.	1963	5d	
Terentiev	A.	Kazan, Tatar ASSR.	1963	5p	
Tkachenko	Taisia D.	Namangan, Uzbekistan.	1963	2p	*PrV* 15/11/63
Troyan	B. G.	Ust-Ishim, Omsk region.	1963	5d	
Trufanov	Ya. G.	Kursk.	1961	5d	Released 1964.
Tymoshchuk	S. K.	Pashchuki, Ukraine.	1962	5p	

* RSFSR unless otherwise stated. † p= prison ; d= deportation ; sr=strict regime. ‡ see pp. 231–2 for abbreviations.

Name	First names or initials	Date of birth	Place of residence/ trial*	Date of arrest	Length of sentence†	Press ref.‡	Remarks
Vedel	I. I.		Yurga, Kemerovo region.	1962	5d		
Vekazin	Georgi		Namangan, Uzbekistan.		8p	PrV 15/11/63	Alleged rape.
Vekazina	Yekaterina K.		Namangan, Uzbekistan.	1963	2p	PrV 15/11/63	
Velichko	N. K.		Kiev, Ukraine.	1966	3P	PrU 4/10/66	
Vibe	Otto P.		Karaganda region.	Between 1961 and 1963			Died in prison on 30/1/64.
Vinokurov	N. M.		Volzhsk, Mari ASSR.	1962	5d		
Vins	Georgi P.		Moscow.	19/5/66		Pos 25/11/66 SRo 22/11/66	— reported him in prison. — reported him as free.
Volf	P. I.		Issyk, Kazakhstan.	1962			
Voronenko	P. A.		Staraya Yurko-biga, Ukraine.	1964	2½d		
Yakimenko	P. A.	1925	Uzlovaya, Tula region.	1961	5d		

Name	Initials	Date	Location	Year	Sentence	Source	Notes
Yants	N. Ya.		Slavgorod, Altai region.	1963	3d		
Q Yastrebov	V. S.		Dergachi, Ukraine.	1963	5p and 5d		
Yerisov	D. P.		Rostov-on-Don.	1964	5d		Released early.
Zakharov			Rostov-on-Don.	1966	3p	UGa 23/8/66 Times 22/9/66	
	P. F.		Prokopievsk, Kemerovo region.	1964	3p and 5d	PrV 29/2/64	
Zdorovets	Boris M.	1933 or before	Olshany, Ukraine.	1961	5sr and 3d		
Zel	L. B.		Pikhtovka, Novosibirsk region.	1962	5d		
Zhovmiruk	V. V.		Rostov-on-Don.	1964	2p		
			Rostov-on-Don.	1966	3p	UGa 23/8/66 Times 22/9/66	
Zhuchenko	K. P.		Cherkassy, Ukraine.	1964	5p		
Zhurilo	V. N.		Kiev, Ukraine.	1966	2p	PrU 4/10/66	
Zikunov	I. Ye.		Sumy region, Ukraine.	1961	3d		
Zubov	Aksyon F.		Tashkent, Uzbekistan.	1964	5p	PrV 29/2/64	

Notes

ABBREVIATIONS

Ag	*Agitator* (Moscow)
BaW	*The Baptist World* (Washington, D.C.)
BkR	*Bakinsky Rabochi* (Baku)
Bul	*Bulletin* (Institute for the Study of the USSR, Munich)
BV	*Bratsky Vestnik* (Moscow)
CER	*Communist Exploitation of Religion* (U.S. Government Printing Office, Washington, D.C., 1966)
Izv	*Izvestia* (Moscow)
JMP	*Zhurnal Moskovskoi Patriarkhii* (Moscow)
KBe	*Kommunist Belorussii* (Minsk)
KmP	*Komsomolskaya Pravda* (Moscow)
Kom	*Kommunist* (Moscow)
KTa	*Kommunist Tatarii* (Kazan)
KUz	*Komsomolets Uzbekistana* (Tashkent)
KZn	*Komsomolskoye Znamya* (Kiev)
KzP	*Kazakhstanskaya Pravda* (Alma-Ata)
LiS	*Lyudina i Svit* (Kiev)
LPr	*Leningradskaya Pravda* (Leningrad)
LtG	*Literaturnaya Gazeta* (Moscow)
NDFN	*Nauchnye Doklady Vysshei Shkoly: Filosofskiye Nauki* (Moscow)
NiR	*Nauka i Religia* (Moscow)
Nov	*Novosti* (Soviet News Agency)
Pos	*Posev* (Frankfurt am Main)
Pr	*Pravda* (Moscow)
PrU	*Pravda Ukrainy* (Kiev)
PrV	*Pravda Vostoka* (Tashkent)
PZh	*Partiinaya Zhizn* (Moscow)
RCDA	*Religion in Communist Dominated Areas* (National Council of Churches, New York)
SBe	*Sovetskaya Belorussia* (Minsk)
SGP	*Sovetskoye Gosudarstvo i Pravo* (Moscow)
SKi	*Sovetskaya Kirgizia* (Frunze)
SKu	*Sovetskaya Kultura* (Moscow)
SLi	*Sovetskaya Litva* (Vilnius)

SMo	Sovetskaya Moldavia (Kishinyov)
SRo	Sovetskaya Rossia (Moscow)
SVS	St. Vladimir's Seminary Quarterly (New York)
SYu	Sovetskaya Yustitsia (Moscow)
SZh	Selskaya Zhizn (Moscow)
TIs	Turkmenskaya Iskra (Ashkhabad)
UGa	Uchitelskaya Gazeta (Moscow)
VVS	Vedomosti Verkhovnovo Soveta RSFSR (Moscow)
WGO	WGO: Die wichtigsten Gesetzgebungsakte in den Ländern Ost-, Südosteuropas und in den ostasiatischen Volksdemokratien (Hamburg)

CHAPTER ONE

1. F. Fedorenko, *Sekty, ikh vera i dela*, Moscow, 1965.
2. *NiR* 6, 1966, p. 88.
3. *NiR* 1, 1966, p. 95
4. *NiR* 9, 1966, p. 21.
5. See pp. 97 and 154.
6. *Religion & the Search for New Ideals in the USSR* (ed. William C. Fletcher & Anthony J. Strover), New York, 1967.
7. *BV* 3–4, 1954, p. 91.
8. See p. 131.
9. Fedorenko, *Sekty, ikh vera i dela*, p. 166.
10. *BaW*, February 1967, p. 8. Correspondingly, *Nov* on the 1966 congress (*RCDA* Vol. V, 21, p. 167) quotes the half-million membership figure, but says that this includes sympathizers with the movement as well as baptized members.
11. Fedorenko, *Sekty, ikh vera i dela*, p. 166.
12. *BV* 6, 1966, p. 17.
13. See p. 26.
14. See p. 48.
15. On religion and the law in the USSR, see *WGO* 5, 1966, pp. 258–77.
16. See the discussion of the 1966 legislation, pp. 158–64.
17. Decree, 'On Religious Societies', issued by the All-Union Central Executive Committee and the *Soviet* of People's Commissars, 8 April 1929. See *WGO* 5, 1966, pp. 265 & 273.
18. *BV* 6, 1963, p. 51. The AUCECB has, however, been criticized for recognizing only registered communities — see p. 29.
19. *Ag* 13, 1966, p. 58.

20. *WGO* 5, 1966, pp. 259–61.
21. See pp. 53–62.
22. Document quoted by G. Bailey, *The Reporter* (New York), 16 July 1964, p. 28.
23. See p. 155.
24. See p. 36; cf. *Pos* 25 November 1966, p. 4.
25. *WGO* 5, 1966, p. 265.
26. For a more detailed discussion, see pp. 47–49.
27. W. Kolarz, *Religion in the Soviet Union*, London, 1961, p. 304.
28. *NiR* 9, 1966, p. 22.
29. *Izv*, 30 August 1966, p. 4.
30. *BV* 1, 1945, p. 21.
31. *BV* 2, 1946, p. 42.
32. Kolarz, *Religion in the Soviet Union*, p. 304.
33. Cf. the Baptist reformers' version of these years in the Kryuchkov–Shalashov document, pp. 53–62.
34. *RCDA*, Vol. VI, 4, pp. 29–31.
35. *BV* 6, 1963, p. 35.
36. *Ibid.*, p. 21.
37. *NiR* 9, 1966, pp. 22–23.
38. *Izv*, 6 October 1960, p. 5.
39. *BV* 6, 1963, p. 35.
40. *Ibid.*, pp. 35–36.
41. *BkR*, 7 April 1963, p. 3.
42. *Ibid.*
43. *BV* 6, 1963, p. 36.
44. *NiR* 9, 1966, p. 24.
45. *PrU*, 4 October 1966, p. 4.
46. Fedorenko, *Sekty, ikh vera i dela*, p. 167.
47. *Pr*, 27 January 1960, pp. 1–2.
48. *SMo*, 29 January 1960, p. 4; *SBe* 18 February 1960, p. 6.
49. *Pr*, 18 October 1961, p. 11.
50. *BkR*, 19 June 1963, p. 4.
51. *PZh* 2, 1964, pp. 22–26.
52. Well-documented accounts of these events are to be found in the following articles: I. Swan, 'The disappearance of Metropolitan Nikolai', *Bul* 5, 1961, pp. 46–47; T. E. Bird, 'Party, the Patriarch and the World Council', *Commonweal* (New York), 13 April 1963, p. 56; N. Teodorovich, 'Increasing Pressure on the Moscow Patriarchate', *Bul* 10, 1962, pp. 46–47.

53. *JMP* 8, 1961, p. 6.
54. *Ugolovny kodeks RSFSR*, Moscow, 1964, p. 91. See a discussion of this in *NiR* 3, 1963, pp. 35–48.
55. *Uspekhi sovremennoi nauki i religii*, Moscow, 1961, pp. 20–21; *SRo*, 21 June 1960, p. 4; cf. *LtG*, 10 April 1962, p. 2.
56. Nikita Struve, *Christians in Contemporary Russia*, London, 1967, pp. 304–10.
57. *Ibid.*, p. 296f.
58. *KmP*, 14 June 1961.
59. *SVS* Vol. 10, Nos. 1–2, 1966, p. 70.
60. Struve, *Christians in Contemporary Russia*, p. 310.
61. Compare, for example, *JMP* 4, 1960, p. 41 with *JMP* 5, 1961, p. 38.
62. *Russkaya Pravoslavnaya Tserkov*, Moscow, 1958, pp. 109–10.
63. *JMP* 4, 1965, p. 47.
64. *SVS* Vol. 10, Nos. 1–2, 1966, p. 70.
65. B.B.C. Central Research Unit, London, *Background Note* No. 4, 24 February 1967, p. 3.
66. *Ibid.*, pp. 1–3.
67. *Izv*, 6 October 1960, p. 5.
68. *The Times*, London, 4 January 1963, p. 8.
69. *Nov*, 9 January 1963.
70. J. C. Pollock, *The Christians from Siberia*, London, 1964, pp. 172–186.
71. *Nov*, 9 January 1963.
72. Moscow Radio in English to North America, 14 February 1963, quoted by Pollock, *The Christians from Siberia*, p. 184.
73. *The Times*, 4 January 1963, p. 8.
74. Unpublished document.
75. *The Times*, 4 January 1963, p. 8.
76. Pollock, *The Christians from Siberia*, p. 174.
77. *KBe* 2, 1966, p. 68.
78. Pollock, *The Christians from Siberia*, p. 175.
79. *Newsweek*, Dayton, Ohio, 28 January 1963, p. 45.
80. *Nov*, 9 January 1963.

CHAPTER TWO

1. pp. 191–210.
2. This text is partially quoted in *Pos*, 15 July 1966, p. 3.

3. *The Reporter*, New York, 16 July 1964, p. 28. A longer version than either quoted here has just been published in *Gospel Call,* Pasadena, California, March 1967, pp. 3–4 and April 1967, p. 4. This seems to be based on the complete text and confirms what is quoted here.

4. See p. 33.

5. *Ibid.*

6. *LiS* 11, 1966, p. 33.

7. I. D. Bondarenko, for example. See also 'youth and religion' in index.

8. *SMo*, 27 January 1963, p. 4.

9. '4th century — the time when Christianity became a state religion' (note by F. Garkavenko, the author of the article). He is certainly wrong. The reference is to Rev. 2. 13, where Pergamum is represented as being one of the Seven Churches 'where Satan's throne is'.

10. *NiR* 9, 1966, p. 19; cf. Kryuchkov–Shalashov document, pp. 55–56.

11. Fedorenko, *Sekty, ikh vera i dela*, p. 167. The first two sentences are also quoted verbatim in *NiR* 9, 1966, p. 23.

12. Date confirmed in *BV* 6, 1963, pp. 21–22. Cf. p. 65.

13. *NiR* 9, 1966, pp. 24–25.

14. *Ibid.*, p. 25.

15. This passage printed here for the first time, but cf. *Le Monde*, Paris, 25 November 1966, p. 2.

16. See pp. 47–49.

17. *Pos*, 25 November 1966, p. 4.

18. *The Watchman Examiner*, Somerset, N. J., 26 January 1967, p. 43.

19. *PrV*, 29 February 1964, p. 3.

20. *Izv*, 23 January 1962, p. 4.

21. See pp. 191–210.

22. *BaW*, February 1967, p. 7.

23. *BV* 6, 1963, p. 13.

24. This document is here published for the first time.

CHAPTER THREE

1. *BV* 6, 1963, p. 2.

2. *Ibid.*, p. 36.

3. *Ibid.*, p. 52.

4. See p. 37.

5. See pp. 192 and 195.
6. Document published here for the first time.
7. Cf. p. 125.
8. See pp. 22–23, 49–50.
9. i.e. the 1960 *Letter of Instructions.*
10. At this point in the original document follows the statistical information on the Ukraine and Latvia which we quoted on p. 26.
11. Quoted in part in *Pos* 15 July 1966, p. 3.
12. *Izv*, 30 August 1966, p. 4.
13. *Kostnické Jiskry*, Prague, 30 November 1966, p. 2.
14. *BaW*, February 1967, p. 8. For a fuller discussion of the most recent estimates of the strength of the reform movement, see pp. 141–2.
15. See p. 36 and *Pos*, 25 November 1966, p. 4.
16. *Lis* 11, 1966, p. 33. For support among registered communities, see p. 65.
17. *SBe*, 12 May 1963, p. 3.
18. *Ag* 13, 1966, p. 58.
19. *SBe*, 12 May 1963, p. 3.
20. *Ibid.*
21. *SMo*, 27 January 1963, p. 4.
22. See p. 223.
23. *SMo*, 27 January 1963, p. 4.
24. *Izv*, 23 January 1962, p. 4.
25. *Ibid.*
26. *SMo*, 27 January 1963, p. 4.
27. *CER*, pp. 34–42.
28. *SKu*, 3 February 1962, p. 4.
29. *CER*, p. 34.
30. *SKi*, 8 December 1962, p. 4.
31. *KzP*, 12 December 1962, p. 2.
32. *CER*, p. 37.
33. *KzP*, 19 December 1962, p. 4.
34. *SBe*, 12 May 1963, p. 3.
35. *CER*, p. 37 (prisoners 88–91).
36. *PrV*, 15 November 1963, p. 4.
37. *NiR* 1, 1962, pp. 81–82; *PrU*, 19 June 1962, p. 4; *Pr*, 21 June 1962, p. 4; *KmP*, 5 July 1962, p. 4; *NiR* 7, 1962, pp. 55–57; *BkR*, 9 August 1962, p. 4; *TIs*, 8 September 1962, p. 3; *KmP*, 25 September 1962, p. 2; *TIs*, 7 October 1962, p. 2; *SRo*, 22 December 1962, p. 4; *SLi*, 5 March 1964, p. 4.

38. 'Committee of State Security', the most recent name for the secret police.
39. Earlier names for the secret police.
40. Text quoted p. 13.
41. As far as is known, there are no press references for many of these, which suggests that we are by no means in possession of all the facts on this wave of arrests.
42. Cf. *SKu*, 3 February 1962, p. 4.
43. See p. 62.
44. Identical with Article 227 of the Penal Code of the RSFSR.
45. Unpublished document.
46. Unpublished document.

CHAPTER FOUR

1. *NiR* 9, 1966, p. 24; cf. *LiS* 11, 1966, p. 33.
2. *BV* 6, 1963, pp. 6–55.
3. *Ibid.*, p. 7.
4. *Ibid.*, p. 47.
5. *Ibid.*, pp. 33 42.
6. e.g. *LiS* 11, 1966 p. 33.
7. *SBe*, 12 May 1963, p. 3.
8. See p. 92, where 197 is given as the total, of whom five had died and 22 were not imprisoned until 1964. It is not known how many of those imprisoned in 1963 lost their freedom after the October congress.
9. See p. 75.
10. *Pos*, 25 November 1966, p. 4.
11. See p. 75
12. *BV* 6, 1963, p. 39.
13. *Ibid.*, p. 36.
14. *Ibid.*, p. 40.
15. *BV* 4, 1964, p. 71.
16. *BV* 6, 1963, p. 49.
17. *Ibid.*, p. 11,
18. *BV* 3, 1961, pp. 64–67.
19. *BV* 6, 1963, p. 37.
20. *Ibid.*, p. 42. See pp. 75–77 for the Organizing Committee's discussion of this.
21. See pp. 191–210. A somewhat different interpretation of these

changes will be found in *Religion & the Search for New Ideals in the USSR* (ed. William C. Fletcher & Anthony J. Strover), p. 71.

22. *BV* 6, 1963, p. 50.
23. *Ibid.*, pp. 51–53.
24. *Ibid.*, p. 42.
25. *Ibid.*, p. 51.
26. *Ibid.*, p. 42.
27. *BV* 4, 1964, p. 79.
28. See pp. 77–83.
29. *BV* 4, 1964, pp. 71–75.
30. *BV* 2, 1963, pp. 74–75.
31. *BV* 3, 1965, pp. 77–78.
32. *KUz*, 2 February 1964; *PrV*, 29 February 1964, p. 3.
33. *BV* 2, 1964, p. 1.
34. *BV* 6, 1964, pp. 41–43.
35. *Ibid.*, p. 48.
36. *Ibid.*, pp. 3–4.
37. *Ibid.*, p. 3.
38. *BV* 6, 1963, p. 42.
39. These passages are published here for the first time.
40. *SYu* 9, 1964, p. 27.
41. *RCDA*, Vol. III, 16, pp, 122–5.
42. *KzP*, 18 August 1967, p. 4.   For a reference in July 1965, see p. 152.
43. *CER*, pp. 30–42.
44. e.g. *PrV*, 15 November 1963, p. 4.
45. *Kom* 1, 1964, p. 38.

CHAPTER FIVE

1. See pp. 122–3
2. *SGP* 1, 1965, pp. 39–45.
3. See p. 119.
4. *Pr*, 12 January 1967, p. 2.,
5. *KmP*, 15 August 1965, pp. 3–4; cf. *Ag* 4, 1966, pp. 45–47; V. A. Kuroyedov concurs — *Izv*, 30 August 1966, p. 4.
6. *NiR* 6, 1966, pp. 7–8.
7. *Ag* 5, 1965, p. 36.
8. See, among many examples, *KBe* 3, 1966, p. 80; *KBe* 6, 1966, pp. 29–32; *NiR* 7, 1966, p. 11; *KTa* 8–9, 1966, pp. 70–74;

      KzP, 20 July 1966, p. 4; *NiR* 8, 1966, pp. 34–36; *LPr*, 27 August 1966, p. 3; *SZh*, 13 January 1967, p. 4; *SZh*, 7 February 1967, p. 4.

9. *KzP*, 15 December 1966, p. 2.
10. At this point in the original document there follows a discussion of the 1963 congress, as quoted on pp. 74–77.
11. See pp. 42–46.
12. Not available.
13. Zhidkov.
14. Karev.
15. Extracts taken from a complete copy of *Bratsky Listok* 2–3, 1965. Quoted in part *Pos*, 15 July 1966, p. 3.
16. Full text in *Pos*, 5 August 1966, pp. 4–5.
17. *LiS* 11, 1966, p. 33. Cf. *NDFN* 5, 1966, p. 123.
18. *Izv*, 5 June 1966, p. 6.
19. *Pos*, 15 July 1966, p. 4.
20. *Pos*, 25 November 1966, p. 4.
21. *NiR* 7, 1966, p. 25.
22. *The Times*, London, 23 May 1966, p. 8 (early editions).
23. *NiR* 7, 1966, p. 25.
24. *Pos*, 25 November 1966, pp. 4–5. Cf. unpublished appeal of 20 May 1966.
25. See pp. 159–61.
26. The reference is to Khrushchev.
27. *SGP* 1, 1965, pp. 39–45.
28. Quoted in full in *Nashi Dni*, Bryte, California, 24 December 1966, pp. 2–4.

CHAPTER SIX

1. *SKi*, 18 March 1966, p. 4.
2. *LiS* 11, 1966, p. 33.
3. *PrV*, 22 October 1966, p. 4.
4. *SKi*, 18 March 1966, p. 4.
5. *Izv*, 6 March 1965, p. 4.
6. *PrU*, 4 October 1966, p. 4.
7. *LiS* 11, 1966, p. 33.
8. *Ibid.*
9. *KZn*, 16 July 1966, p. 3.
10. *BkR*, 27 April 1966, p. 4.

11. *Pos*, 25 November 1966, p. 4.
12. *Ibid.*
13. *SMo*, 15 September 1966, p. 4.
14. *SRo*, 22 November 1966, p. 2.
15. *LiS* 11, 1966, p. 33.
16. *Izv*, 5 June 1966, p. 6.
17. *Izv*, 6 March 1965, p. 4.
18. *Pr*, 19 February 1966, p. 2.
19. See p. 160.
20. *KmP*, 8 December 1966, p. 4.
21. *SKi*, 18 March 1966, p. 4.
22. *SRo*, 22 November 1966, p. 2.
23. *BkR*, 27 April 1966, p. 4.
24. *Pr*, 19 February 1966, p. 2.
25. *PrV*, 22 October 1966, p. 4.
26. *Ibid.*
27. *SKi*, 18 March 1966, p. 4.
28. *KZn*, 16 July 1966, p. 3.
29. *UGa*, 23 August 1966, p. 4.
30. See p. 19.
31. *Izv*, 5 June 1966, p. 6.
32. *UGa*, 23 August 1966, p. 4. The Pioneers are the most junior branch of the Communist youth organization, and their insignia is a red neckerchief.
33. *PrV*, 22 October 1966, p. 4.
34. V. Tendryakov, *Chudotvornaya*, Moscow 1958,
35. *Izv*, 5 June 1966, p. 6.
36. *UGa*, 23 August 1966, p. 4; see also *PrV*, 22 October 1966, p. 4.
37. *BkR*, 27 April 1966, p. 4.
38. *UGa*, 23 August 1966, p. 4.
39. *LiS* 11, 1966, p. 34.
40. See pp. 211–29.
41. *LiS* 11, 1966, p. 33.
42. *LiS* 9, 1966, p. 4; cf. *NiR* 9, 1966, p. 24.
43. *SZh*, 7 February 1967, p. 4.
44. See pp. 129–30.
45. *Pos*, 25 November 1966, p. 4.
46. There seems to be a misprint in *Pravda* here. It writes 'Semikara-korskaya', whereas the best atlases give 'Semikarakovskaya'.
47. *Pr*, 19 February 1966, p. 2.

48. *SMo*, 15 September 1966, p. 4.
49. *Pos*, 25 November 1966, p. 4.
50. See note 32 of this chapter.
51. *PrU*, 4 October 1966, p. 4.
52. *UGa*, 23 August 1966, p. 4.
53. *SRo*, 22 November 1966, p. 2.
54. *BkR*, 27 April 1966, p. 4.
55. *LiS* 11, 1966, p. 32.
56. *PrV*, 22 October 1966, p. 4.
57. *KzP*, 18 March 1966, p. 4.
58. *BkR*, 27 April 1966, p. 4.
59. *NiR* 7, 1966, p. 25.
60. *Pos*, 25 November 1966, p. 4.
61. See, for example, *NiR* 9, 1966, p. 19; Fedorenko, *Sekty, ikh vera i dela*, p. 167; *LiS* 10, 1966, p. 35; *PrU*, 4 October 1966, p. 4.
62. *Pr*, 19 February 1966, p. 2; *UGa*, 23 August 1966, p. 4; *Izv* 5 June 1966, p. 6.
63. See pp. 150–3.
64. *Pr*, 19 February 1966, p. 2. Cf. *SMo*, 15 September 1966, p. 4; *Izv*, 30 August 1966, p. 4.
65. *LiS* 11, 1966, p. 33.
66. See pp. 191–210.
67. *UGa*, 23 August 1966, p. 4.
68. *PrV*, 22 October 1966, p. 4. A much more comprehensive account still, with lengthy quotations and mentioning eight children's publications by name, has just appeared in *NiR* 3, 1967, pp. 62–65. These quotations confirm that these publications do not contain any incitement to anti-Soviet activity.
69. *NiR* 7, 1966, pp. 14–17.
70. *PrV*, 22 October 1966, p. 4.
71. *Izv*, 5 June 1966, p. 6.
72. See pp. 147–9.
73. *BkR*, 27 April 1966, p. 4.
74. See pp. 24–25.
75. *Izv*, 30 August 1966, p. 4; *SRo*, 22 November 1966, p. 2.
76. *PrV*, 22 October 1966, p. 4.
77. *NiR* 7, 1966, p. 24; cf. *UGa* 23, August 1966, p. 4.
78. Fedorenko, *Sekty, ikh vera i dela*, p. 167.
79. *Izv*, 30 August 1966, p. 4.

80. *SMo*, 15 September 1966, p. 4.
81. *Ibid.*
82. *NiR* 7, 1966, p. 25.
83. *LiS* 11, 1966, p. 33.
84. *NiR* 7, 1966, p. 25.
85. *Izv*, 5 June 1966, p. 6 and 30 August 1966, p. 4.
86. See pp. 2–3
87. See p. 48.
88. See p. 48.
89. See p. 36.
90. See pp. 22–23.
91. *BkR*, 27 April 1966, p. 4.
92. *Pr*, 19 February 1966, p. 2.
93. *PrV*, 22 October 1966, p. 4.
94. *BkR*, 27 April 1966, p. 4.
95. *KZn*, 16 July 1966, p. 3; cf. *SKi*, 18 March 1966, p. 4 and *PrU*, 4 October 1966, p. 4.
96. See pp. 158–64.
97. See p. 28.
98. *KZn*, 16 July 1966, p. 3.
99. *Izv*, 6 March 1965, p. 4.
100. *PrV*, 22 October 1966, p. 4.
101. *NDFN* 5, 1966, p. 123.
102. *PrV*, 22 October 1966, p. 4; cf. *BkR*, 27 April 1966, p. 4; *KZn*, 16 July 1966, p. 3. and *Izv*, 5 June 1966, p. 6.
103. *SMo*, 15 September 1966, p. 4; *NiR* 7, 1966, p. 25.
104. *PrV*, 22 October 1966, p. 4.
105. *KZn*, 16 July 1966, p. 3.
106. *Izv*, 5 June 1966, p. 6.
107. *Pr*, 19 February 1966, p. 2.
108. *Izv*, 6 March 1965, p. 4; cf. *PrV*, 22 October 1966, p. 4.
109. *KzP*, 16 September 1966, p. 2.
110. *BkR*, 27 April 1966, p. 4; cf. *Pr*, 19 February 1966, p. 2.
111. *SZh*, 17 July 1966, p. 4.
112. *Izv*, 5 June 1966, p. 6.
113. *NiR* 7, 1966, pp. 24–25.
114. *SZh*, 1 October 1966, p. 6.
115. *Izv*, 5 June 1966, p. 6; cf. *SBe*, 15 August 1967, p. 4, and *Izv*, 18 August 1967, p. 4.
116. A loan Rykova had given to Valerik's parents.

117. *Bratsky Listok* 7, July 1965. The original 3-page text is hecto-graphed and part of it is difficult to read. This translation has reconstructed illegible words in one or two places.

CHAPTER SEVEN

1. *SMo*, 15 September 1966, p. 4.
2. *UGa*, 23 August 1966, p. 4.
3. *PrV*, 22 October 1966, p. 4.
4. *Ag* 5, 1965, p. 34.
5. *Izv*, 30 August 1966, p. 4.
6. *Izv*, 5 June 1966, p. 6.
7. *LiS* 11, 1966, p. 33.
8. *Ibid.* p. 32.
9. *KzP*, 18 March 1966, p. 4.
10. *Pos*, 25 November 1966, p. 4.
11. *NiR* 7, 1966, p. 25; cf. *SKi*, 18 March 1966, p. 4.; *Izv*, 30 August 1966, p. 4; *SMo*, 15 September 1966, p. 4; *PrU*, 4 October 1966, p. 4.
12. See p. 7.
13. *SMo*, 15 September 1966, p. 4.
14. *PrV*, 22 October 1966, p. 4.
15. See pp. 105–13.
16. *SMo*, 15 September 1966, p. 4.
17. *PrV*, 22 October 1966, p. 4.
18. *Izv*, 5 June 1966, p. 6.
19. *NiR* 9, 1966, p. 24.
20. *PrV*, 22 October 1966, p. 4.
21. *NiR* 7, 1966, p. 24.
22. *PrV*, 22 October 1966, p. 4.
23. *Ag* 14, 1966, p. 41.
24. *VVS* 12, 1966, pp. 219–20.
25. See *RCDA*, Vol. V, 13–14, 1966, pp. 115–16 for a version of the law prior to amendment. The most recent editions of *Ugolovny Kodeks RSFSR* omit the explanatory clauses printed here.
26. See p. 109.
27. *Ugolovny kodeks RSFSR*, Moscow 1957, p. 65.
28. See p. 13.
29. See pp. 126–9.
30. See pp. 166–71.

31. *Izv*, 30 August 1966, p. 4.   Kuroyedov means *Ecumenical Press Service*.   The Russian version (given here) is not completely faithful, but its main points stand.

32. *LiS* 6, 1966, p. 32.

33. *VVS* 38, 1966, p. 819.

34. *Izv*, 30 August 1966, p. 4.

35. *Izv*, 5 June 1966, p. 6.

36. *Pos*, 25 November 1966, p. 4.

37. See pp. 119–24.

38. See p. 110.

39. *SKi*, 18 March 1966, p. 4; *KZn*, 16 July 1966, p. 3; *UGa*, 23 August 1966, p. 4; *PrU*, 4 October 1966, p. 4; *PrV*, 22 October 1966, p. 4; *SRo*, 22 November 1966, p. 2.   See also *KzP*, 18 August 1967, p. 4.

40. *SKi*, 18 March 1966, p. 4.   Cf. *SKi*, 15 June 1967, pp. 3–4.

41. *KZn*, 16 July 1966, p. 3.

42. *Pr*, 19 February 1966, p. 2.

43. *UGa*, 23 August 1966, p. 4.

44. *The Times*, London, 1, 3, 5, 8, 16, 22, 27 September and 2 December 1966.

45. See pp. 4–5.

46. *The Times*, 22 September 1966, p. 11.

47. *PrU*, 4 October 1966, p. 4.

48. See pp. 119–24.

49. *CER*, p. 36, Prisoner 67.

50. *PrV*, 22 October 1966, p. 4.

51. See p. 67.

52. An orthodox Soviet novelist.

53. *SRo*, 22 November 1966, p. 2.

54. *NiR* 9, 1966, p. 24; cf. *PrV*, 22 October 1966, p. 4.

55. *KZn*, 16 July 1966, p. 3.

56. *SKi*, 18 March 1966, p. 4.

57. *Izv*, 6 March 1965, p. 4; *Pr*, 19 February 1966, p. 2; *Izv*, 5 June 1966, p. 6; *SMo*, 15 September 1966, p. 4.

58. *SMo*, 15 September 1966, p. 4.

59. *UGa*, 23 August 1966, p. 4.   Cf., very remarkably, *KzP*, 18 August 1967, p. 4.

60. *Izv*, 5 June 1966, p. 6.

61. *SRo*, 22 November 1966, p. 2.   Kozlov is now in prison (*KzP*, 18 August 1967, p. 4).

62. *Pos*, 25 November 1966, p. 5.
63. See p. 192.
64. *BV* 6, 1966, p. 60.
65. This phrase in fact conceals a crucial drop in membership. See p. 3.
66. Full text in *RCDA*, Vol. V, 21, 1966, pp. 166–9. As no Russian text is available, this translation has been used here with adaptation to fit the terminology of this book.
67. *BaW*, February 1967, pp. 8–9 (very slightly adapted to fit the terminology used here).
68. *Kostnické Jiskry*, 30 November 1966, p. 2.
69. *Ibid.*
70. *Ibid.*
71. *Die Sowjetunion Heute*, 23–24, Cologne, 1966.
72. *Baptist Times*, London, 29 December 1966, p. 4.
73. *BaW*, February 1967, p. 6.
74. *BV* 6, 1966, p. 32.
75. *BV* 6, 1963, p. 7.
76. *BV* 6, 1966, p. 68.
77. *Ibid.*, p. 69.
78. *Ibid.*, p. 70.
79. i.e. imprisonment.
80. *BV* 6, 1966, p. 71.
81. *PrV*, 4 October 1966, p. 4.
82. *BV* 6, 1966, pp. 48–53. The text could not be included in Appendix I.
83. *Ibid.*, p. 50.
84. See p. 194.
85. *BV* 6, 1966, p. 51.
86. *Ibid.*, p. 53.
87. See p. 206.
88. *BV* 6, 1966, p. 50; cf. Prokofiev's statutes, p. 192.
89. *BV* 6, 1966, p. 51; cf. p. 196.
90. *BV* 6, 1966, p. 51.
91. *Ibid.*
92. *Ibid.*, p. 52.
93. *Ibid.*, pp. 78–79.
94. *BaW*, February 1967, p. 8.
95. *BV* 6, 1966, p. 79.
96. *Ibid.*, p. 51.

R

97. *Ibid.*, p. 79.
98. *SKi*, 15 June 1967, pp. 3–4.
99. *KzP*, 18 August 1967, p. 4.
100. *SBe*, 15 August 1967, p. 4; *IzV*, 18 August 1967, p. 4.

EPILOGUE

1. *JMP* 12, 1965, p. 3.
2. *SVS*, Vol. 10, Nos. 1–2, 1966, pp. 67–111.
3. *Ibid.*, pp. 110–11.
4. *Ibid.*, p. 111.
5. *Ibid.*, p. 68.
6. *Ibid.*, p. 103.
7. See pp. 105–13.
8. *Le Messager Orthodoxe*, Paris, 35, 1966, p. 57.
9. *RCDA*, Vol. V, 15–16, 1966, pp. 126–8.
10. For further biographical details, see *Pos*, 7 January 1967, pp. 5–7.
11. *Zashchita very v SSSR*, Paris, 1966.
12. *Russkaya Mysl*, Paris, 7 July 1966, pp. 4–5.
13. *JMP* 11, 1957, pp. 25–55.
14. *Pos*, 23 September 1966, pp. 3–4, and 1 October 1966, pp. 3–4.
15. *NiR* 10, 1966, pp. 25–26.
16. See p. 160.
17. *NiR* 10, 1966, p. 25.
18. *Vestnik Russkovo Studencheskovo Khristianskovo Dvizhenia*, Paris, 82, 1966, pp. 3–20. Cf. *ibid.*, 83, 1967, pp. 29–64.

APPENDIX I

1. *BV* 6, 1963, pp. 43–47. Order adapted to facilitate comparisons. In cols. I and II some words are illegible in the original document and these have been reconstructed. The 1966 constitution arrived too late for inclusion, but is referred to in these notes.
2. Alternative name for Pentecostals.
3. I. G. Kargel's 'doctrinal guide lines' approved at 1966 congress (see p. 175). Kargel had been quoted by the reformers (see p. 35).
4. Expanded to 25 members and eight candidate members at 1966 congress (see p. 177; *BV* 6, 1966, pp. 78–79).
5. Expanded to nine in 1966 (see p. 177; *BV* 6, 1966, p. 79).

6. Partial concession only.
7. Partial concession (cf. 21 in column II). Fuller concession here in 1966 (see p. 175; *BV* 6, 1966, p. 51).
8. In 1966 it was established that councils of presbyters should be elected to assist senior presbyters in their work (see p. 175; *BV* 6, 1966, p. 51).
9. Full concession made here in 1966 (see p. 175; *BV* 6, 1966, p. 51).
10. A new emphasis on 'collective' decisions was introduced in 1966 (see p. 175; *BV* 6, 1966, p. 53).

APPENDIX II

Additions to list of prisoners in 1967:

SKi 15/6/67 — Frizen, V. I., and Tishchenko, Fyodor S., of Frunze, Kirgizia, under investigation.

SBe 15/8/67 — (see also *Izv* 18/8/67) Abushenko, Yevdokia, born 1904, shot August 1967 for alleged murder of daughter; Vlasenko, S., sentenced to 10 years' imprisonment for complicity. Both of Gomel region, Belorussia. Kopenkov, F., of Ut, Belorussia, directs religious activities from prison.

KzP 18/8/67 — Antonov, of Alma-Ata, and Dubovoi, S. G., of Dzhezkazgan, are on new lists of prisoners which circulate. Bondar and Telegin, of Alma-Ata, tried 1967.

Unpublished communication to the ECB Church, dated 20/5/66, mentions Khorev, M. I., as arrested in Moscow on the previous day.

Index

Index

References to the alphabetical list of prisoners (pp. 211–29) are not included here